IMAGES
of America

AUSTINTOWN

On the cover: **FITCH HIGH SCHOOL, 1926 GIRLS MAHONING COUNTY CHAMPIONS.** Seen here are team members, from left to right, manager Thora Chubb, Evelyn Isch, Helen Young, captain Isabel Bishop, Imogene Young, and Marion Moore. Not pictured are coach Ina Riehl, Dorothy Glenn, and Alice Crum. (Courtesy Austintown Historical Society.)

IMAGES
of America

AUSTINTOWN

Joyce Hunsinger Pogany

ARCADIA
PUBLISHING

ISBN 978-0-7385-5119-7

Published by Arcadia Publishing
Charleston, South Carolina

Printed in the United States of America

Library of Congress Catalog Card Number: 2007920224

For all general information contact Arcadia Publishing at:
Telephone 843-853-2070
Fax 843-853-0044
E-mail sales@arcadiapublishing.com
For customer service and orders:
Toll-Free 1-888-313-2665

Visit us on the Internet at www.arcadiapublishing.com

I dedicate this book to my family and to the past, present, and future residents of Austintown.

Contents

ACKNOWLEDGMENTS

An African proverb says it takes a village to raise a child. For me, it took an entire township to write this book. Many residents and organizations very generously shared information, stories, artifacts, and precious photographs to allow me to complete this book. Due to limited space, I could not include everything. For this, I sincerely apologize. I am extremely grateful to the Austintown Historical Society (AHS), Ron Neff, Mary and Jack Hutchison, Ben Post, Rich Edwards, Dan DeSalvo, St. Anne's Ukrainian Catholic Church, Tom Arne, Nils Johnson Sr., Sam and Karen Stambaugh, Mike Liposchak, John "Rooster" Kohut, Wes and Ted O'Connell, George and Mike Shuba, Patty and Ray Kachurek, Andy Frost, Bob and Pat Boyer, Howard and Lillian Boyer Divelbess, Bernice Fee Boyer, Mike Staffrey, Dorothy Hood, Marty Kalbasi of the Mahoning Valley Sanitary District, Betty Patterson, Bob Gavalier, Ken and John Wilcox, Marjorie Jane Brown Hephner, Marge and Idabelle DeHoff, Larry and Sandy Snell, Bob Lucente, Mike Garcia, Catherine and Warren "Bo" Pritchard, Tom and Carol Stellars, Dan and Charen Fink, Dan Bokesch, Lois Ripple Peterson, Harold and Diane Ripple, Evelyn Ripple Berndt, Ron and Alice Wertz, Bob and Dot Bishop, Gay Bishop Blackann, Bill O'Hara, Ken Zinz, Jean and Harold and Kay Wilson, George Smolko, Linda Newbery, Jim Bartell, Tom Shutrump, Don and Dawn Evans, Emil Bertolini, Bob Senn, Sue Allen, Walter Terlesky, Ann Harris, Roger Templeton, Carole Powers, Dorothy Roth Fizet, Bob Glasser, Bob and Doris Ricker, Joe Pellegrini, Bob Lloyd, Walt and Genevieve Shively, Jan Keich McHenry, Bob and Mary Rose Steiskal, Chick Whitman, Carol Fye, Pat Brothers, Veronica Terzak, Betty Hunsinger Ruane, Gene and Pat Benyo, Lenny Schiavonne, Emil and Yole Schiavonne Conte, John and Dorothy Chlebus, Margaret Peters, Jack Mayo, Arnold Sabo, Ray and Jean Hottinger Ong, Ray Stricklin Jr., Josephine Baker, Myron Yeager, Indiana State Library, West Austintown United Methodist Church, Mahoning Valley Historical Society, Ed Winters at Chessnotes, Steve Love of Hiram College, Ohio Northern University, Steve Hanna of Ashland University, the Photograph Place, and United States Military History Museum. Thank you, too, to Dr. Pam Pogany Gent, my daughter, research assistant, and typist without whom I could not have completed this book.

In my thanks, I must include my late parents, Kenneth and Nora Monroe Hunsinger, who lived in Austintown when I was born; my late husband Paul Louis Pogany, who moved me "back home" to Austintown in 1957; my children, the late Paul Joseph Pogany, Rich and Pam Pogany Gent, Donald and Phyllis Pogany Smail, Perry Pogany and Kay Cook, Mark and Peggy Pogany Gocala; my grandchildren, Stephanie Gent, Heather Smail, Matthew Smail, Josh Smail, Ethan Gent, Maxwell Gocala, Megan Gocala, and Lexie Pogany-Cook; and my great-grandson Jacob Smail.

INTRODUCTION

As president of the Austintown Historical Society, I always thought it would be nice to have a book on the history of Austintown. Because so many past residents are gone and with their passing, their knowledge of the history of Austintown has gone too, I wanted to write the book now before more history was lost.

In many ways, the growth of Austintown Township mirrors the growth of the United States. This book traces the growth of Austintown from its first settler in 1798 to its current status as the eighth-largest urban township in Ohio. Austintown, located between Lake Erie and the Ohio River, near the Pennsylvania border, was originally populated by the Wyandot, Chippewa, Delaware, and Ottowa tribes. Austintown was a pathway for Native Americans who went to the four salt springs spread over two to three acres near the Mahoning River. *Mahoning* is a Native American word meaning "at the salt lick." In 1914, Native American village remains and two burial grounds were found in Austintown; one of these burial grounds was on John Fitch's farm on Mahoning Avenue.

Austintown, and much of northeastern Ohio, was a part of Connecticut. On April 25, 1662, King Charles II of England gave the colony of Connecticut title to all land between the 41st and 42nd parallel from "sea to sea" beginning at Connecticut's eastern seaboard. Over the next century, several other states also claimed these lands. After the Revolutionary War, the federal government asked all states to surrender their claims to these western lands. Connecticut refused. In a compromise reached on September 13, 1786, the federal government assumed all of Connecticut's Revolutionary War debts, and in exchange, Connecticut gave up its western land claims but reserved, until 1800, an area of northeastern Ohio equal in size to Connecticut. This land, the Connecticut Western Reserve, stretched 120 miles along Lake Erie west from Pennsylvania to near present-day Sandusky, Ohio, and extended 71.5 miles south to what, in Mahoning County, is known as Western Reserve Road.

On February 10, 1788, Connecticut sold the Western Reserve's Salt Springs Tract to Gen. Samuel Holden Parsons of Middlebury, Connecticut. The 25,450-acre Salt Springs Tract included all of what are now Weathersfield, Lordstown, Austintown, and Jackson Townships. Because salt was a necessary and precious commodity, Parsons bought the land with the hopes of becoming rich by making salt from the briny water. He never made any money; the water was not salty enough. He died when his canoe overturned on the Beaver River on November 17, 1789. Since he died before he made payment on the land, the land reverted back to Connecticut.

On September 2, 1795, to raise money for a public school system, Connecticut sold 2,841,471 acres east of the Cuyahoga River in the Western Reserve to the Connecticut Land Company for $1.2 million, a cost of roughly 40¢ per acre. The Connecticut Land Company consisted of

45 investors. Readers familiar with northeastern Ohio will recognize the names of these investors as being similar to towns, townships, and streets—Joseph Howland, Nehemiah Hubbard, Elijah Boardman, Samuel P. Lord, Oliver Phelps, Henry Champion II, Jonathan Brace, Daniel Coit, Titus Street, Joshua Stow, Benjamin Kent, Ephraim Root, and Moses Cleaveland. In 1796, the land was partitioned into 218 townships, each five miles square. The townships were formed by parallel horizontal lines; the ranges were formed by the longitudinal meridian lines beginning at the Pennsylvania border. Range 1 was in the extreme southwestern corner of the Western Reserve in present-day Poland. Range 3, Township 2, Meander Township, now known as Austintown Township, contained Great Lots 4 through 10 of the Salt Springs tract. Austintown was in Trumbull County. After 1846, when the state legislature divided Trumbull County, Austintown became part of Mahoning County.

Some settlers walked, with no path or road to lead them, from Connecticut to Pittsburgh where they boarded boats and paddled up the Ohio River to the Mahoning River. Other settlers walked from Connecticut to Ohio, encountering hardwood forests so dense they were overjoyed when they came to a break in the trees through which they could see the sky. Joseph Osborn, who settled in the Cornersburg area in 1809, said the forests were unbroken but the landscape was pleasing. John Lane's 100 acres were described as "virgin forested" land. Clearing trees from the land took much time and energy. The settlers often girdled the trees; that is, they removed a section of bark all around the trunk of the tree so the tree would die. John Ripple, who moved to Austintown after 1820, talked about deadening trees instead of cutting them down, and then letting strong winds knock over the trees. He then planted crops among the dead trees and removed the trees later. The woods were filled with bears and black rattlesnakes; wolves were so plentiful there was a $5 bounty on each wolf scalp.

Wendell Grove, who settled in Austintown in 1801, was five miles away from his nearest neighbor. James, Benjamin, and William Sisco, whom the census describes as "free colored men," settled on the southeast corner of South Turner and Kirk Roads before 1801. Archibald Ewing, who arrived in Austintown in 1802 with his wife Sarah Pauley Ewing; his widowed mother, Ann; his brother John; and his sisters Catherine and Eleanor, reported seeing Native Americans on his 160 acres located near Turner and New Roads. The family slept under a walnut tree their first night in Austintown. Robert Russell came to Austintown in 1806 and slept in a hollowed-out tree until he built a log hut. Then he walked back to Pennsylvania, and together with his parents, Robert and Eve Russell, returned to Austintown, built a log cabin, and later a bigger log house. The Cotton brothers—Theophilus, Jacob, and John, accompanied by their families and their parents, Theophilus and Lucy Little Tyler Cotton—built a pole shanty on their land east of Austintown Center near the present-day Kimberley Acres. John and Nancy Casey Duncan walked from Washington County, Pennsylvania, settling in the Cornersburg area of Austintown in 1803. Their son Thomas later described their cabin as "a poor one, a child could have crawled through the cracks in the walls." Jacob Parkhurst came to Austintown in 1802 with his pregnant wife, Anna Daisy, and their six children, the youngest who was not yet a year old. On their 1,000 acres, he erected a log cabin with window openings cut out of the sides of the house and a door opening covered by a quilt in bad weather. The floor was a few loose boards, there was no ceiling, and the fireplace had no hearth. He made all the furniture. Two years later, he sold the cabin and several hundred acres to Joseph Osborn and built a newer, bigger house for his family.

Pioneers made their own soap and candles; they raised sheep for wool for clothes; they raised flax to make linen. Jane McCollum was a good weaver and often sold her cloth to neighbors to help pay for her family's farm. William Wick, of Long Island, planted the first fruit-bearing apple trees in Austintown in 1810. The settlers purchased other goods elsewhere. Camden Cleaveland, the brother of Moses Cleaveland for whom Cleveland, Ohio, is named, settled in Austintown sometime before 1830. He would often ask his brother-in-law Aseal Adams, a mail carrier between Pittsburgh and Warren, to buy tobacco, gun powder, almanacs, and books for him in Pittsburgh.

Many settlers settled on lots containing streams, sometimes called runs, which provided a source of drinking water for themselves and their livestock and a source of power. On Bears Den

Run, Jacob Parkhurst built a small log mill to cut logs into boards. On Four Mile Run sometime after 1820, William Irvin built Austintown's first grist- or flour mill. In 1845, Andrew Brickley built a sawmill in the eastern part of the township, south of Mahoning Avenue, on a tributary of Bears Den Run. Ira Wilcox operated a sawmill on Axe Factory Run, not far from the present-day Woodside Lake, in 1845. Later Harvey McCollum built a sawmill on the same stream.

The 1820 census showed 728 residents, including 396 children, living in 108 houses in Austintown. While many of these settlers hailed from New England and Connecticut, the next wave of settlers came from Pennsylvania. These new settlers, with last names of Kistler, Weiss, Schumacher, Neff, Lodwick, Harshman, Fulks, Bailey, Flick, Dustman, Knappenberger, Sponseller, Brobst, Schnurrenberger, Habegger, Neff, and Fusselman, came to farm and grew meadow hay, clover hay, flax, wheat, rye, oats, barley, broom corn, tobacco, and sorghum. In 1840, the *Western Reserve Chronicle* reported Austintown farmers produced 14,246 bushels of wheat, 19,710 bushels of oats, 14,604 bushels of corn, and 3,355 pounds of sugar. Farmers owned 420 horses and mules, 1,970 cows, 4,222 sheep, and 1,513 hogs. Acreage of Austintown farms in 1845 was as follows: Henry Brobst, 80; Daniel Brobst, 80; Jacob Jr., Henry, Jacob, and John Brunstetter, 392; Jesse and John Corll, 80; John, Henry, and Mary Crum, 286; Archibald, Archibald Jr., and John Ewing, 237; Jacob Hammon, 300; John Handwork, 156; David Hood, 157; Abraham Jordan, 117; James and Scott Jordan, 98; Joshua and Henry Kyle, 259; Benjamin Leech, 100; John Lane, 100; John L. Lanterman, 797; Peter, William, John, and German Lanterman, 797; John McCollum, 130; Frederick, David, and Daniel Moherman, 1,521; George, Samuel, Henry Jr., Michael, and David Ohl, 335; Calwell Porter, 377; George Shively, 100; William and Samuel Strock, 173; Joseph Turner, 50; Vincent and Abner Webb, 393; and John Yeager, 60. Farming remained the major occupation for the next several decades. According to the 1860 census, 150 adult males over age 15 were farmers. By 1860, the farms became smaller; only 19 farmers listed in the 1860 census had farms larger than 150 acres.

One

Founding Austintown and the Austin Log Cabin

John McCollum settled in Austintown in 1798. After McCollum and his family set up housekeeping, others followed. By 1801, Austintown had 21 taxpayers, including William and Benjamin Bayard, John Duncan, Samuel Furguson, Wendell Grove, Robert Kirkpatrick, Alexander McAllister, Thomas Morgan, John McCollum, Samuel Miller, Fredrick Moherman, Thomas Packard, David Parkhurst, Calvin Pease, Gilbert Roberts, George Stanford, James and Benjamin Sisco, William Templeton, Nathaniel Walker, and William Whethington.

Mary and John H. Packard bought the lot on which the Austin Log Cabin is now located. Packard's grandsons Warren Doud Packard (born in 1861) and James Packard (born in 1863) founded Packard Electric Company (now Delphi) in 1890 and Packard Motor Car Company in 1899. Mary Packard died in 1826; John died in 1827. Their son William inherited the land. In 1828, William sold the log house and 30 acres to Samuel Dorwat (Dorworth) for $150. Dorwat married his neighbor Sarah "Ann" Burgett, for whom Burgett Road is named. In 1829, Dorwat sold 10 acres with the house on it to Henry and Polly Lawrence (Lorins) for $50. When Lawrence died in 1845, his wife and 15 heirs sold the land to Abraham and Rebecca Mauer Dustman for $406. Dustman added a barn and sold the property in 1850 to Henry and Margaret Wehr for $510. Wehr added a hog shed and dug two wells; one for humans, the other for livestock. Henry's nephew and wife, Levi and Emma Wehr, occupied the cabin next. In 1910, the barn burned to the ground, and Levi Wehr built a new barn. Archeologist Dr. John White, of Youngstown State University, discovered the barns' foundations during an archeological dig at the cabin in 1976–1977.

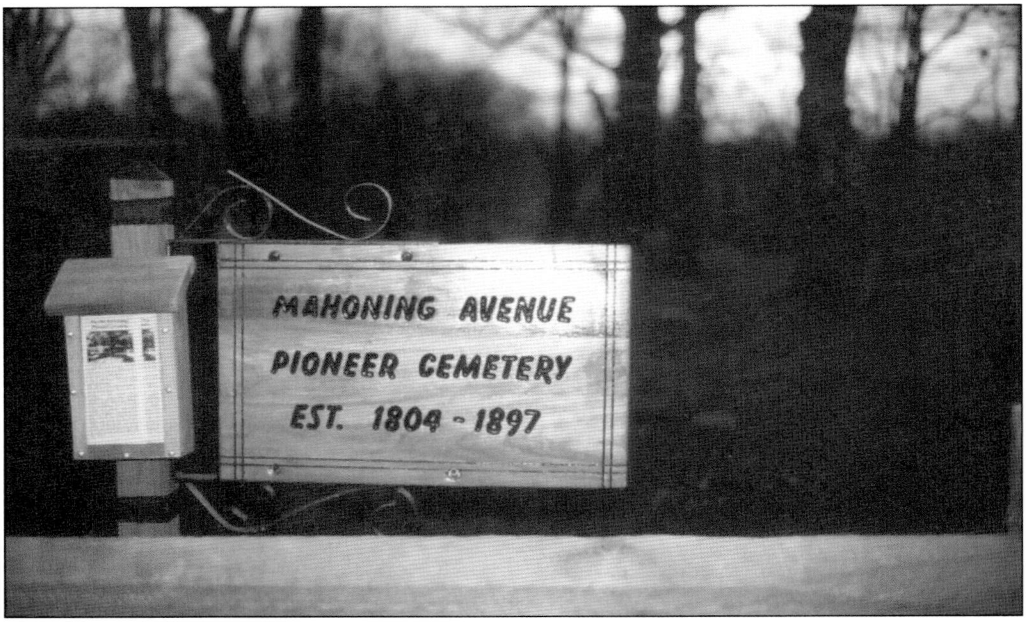

PIONEER CEMETERY AND CALVIN AUSTIN TOMBSTONE. Austintown is named for Calvin Austin, who was born on January 27, 1762, in Suffield, Hartford County, Connecticut, and moved to Warren after the death of his first wife, Rebecca Kent Austin, in 1800. Austin, a land agent for the Connecticut Land Company, sold the lot to John Packard where the Austin Log Cabin is located. Austin, a justice of the peace, became a judge of the Western Reserve, and, together with George Tod, Simon Perkins, Robert Parkman, Turhand Kirtland, John Ford, C. Mygatt, William Rayen, and John Kinsman, founded the Western Reserve Bank in 1811. Austin, a Mason, was treasurer of Erie Lodge 47. He died October 2, 1819, and is buried in Pioneer Cemetery in Warren. (Courtesy Joyce Pogany.)

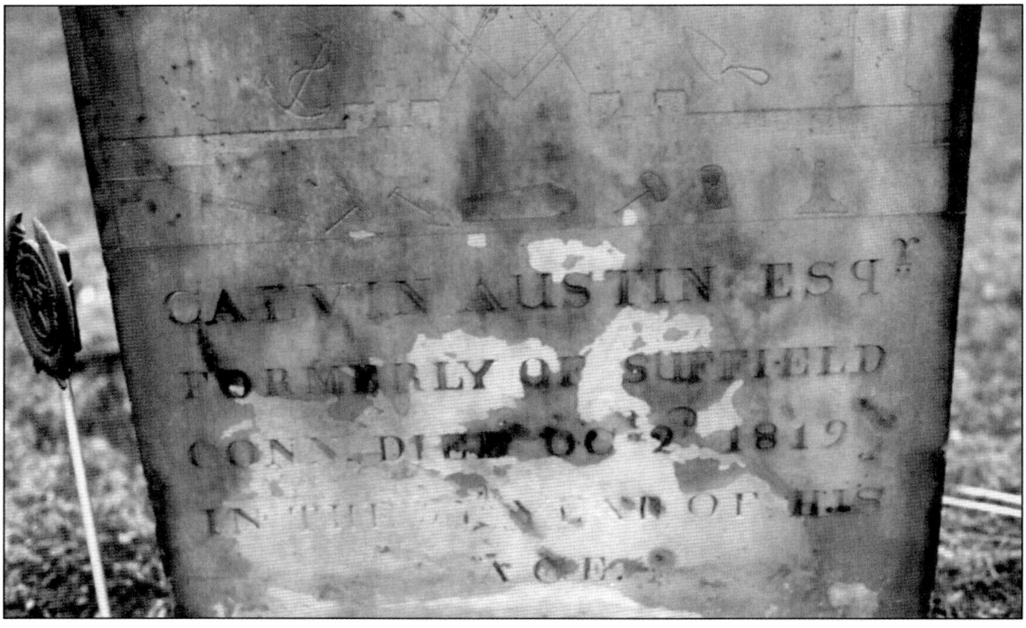

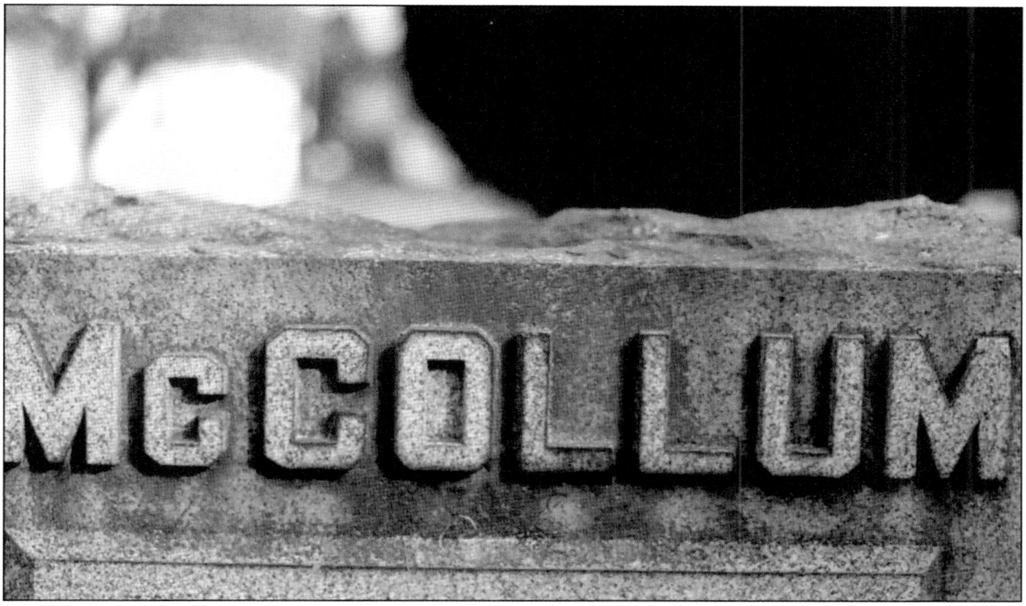

McCOLLUM TOMBSTONES. In 1798, John Henry McCollum built the first homestead in Austintown near the Salt Springs a half-mile west of the Youngstown line. A native of Basking Ridge, New Jersey, McCollum married Jane Ayres Hampson, a widow with five children. They had eight more children. In 1800, the entire family moved to Austintown. McCollum's son John, the first white child born in Austintown, married Mary Magdalene "Polly" Packard, of the log cabin Packards, in 1826. McCollum's stepdaughter Elizabeth Hampson married William Templeton. Templeton's family asserts Templeton was the first settler in Austintown. Township records are incomplete, but Templeton family records show Templeton carrying the mail between Pittsburgh and Warren in 1798, with his cabin in Austintown. John H. McCollum died on April 7, 1849, and is buried in Cornersburg Cemetery in row 16. (Courtesy Joyce Pogany.)

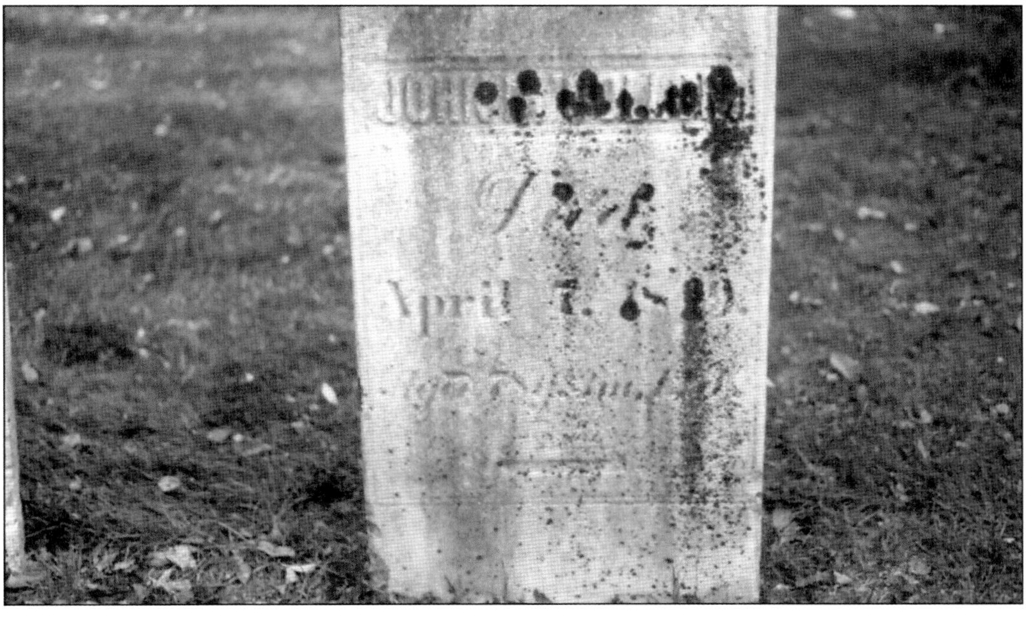

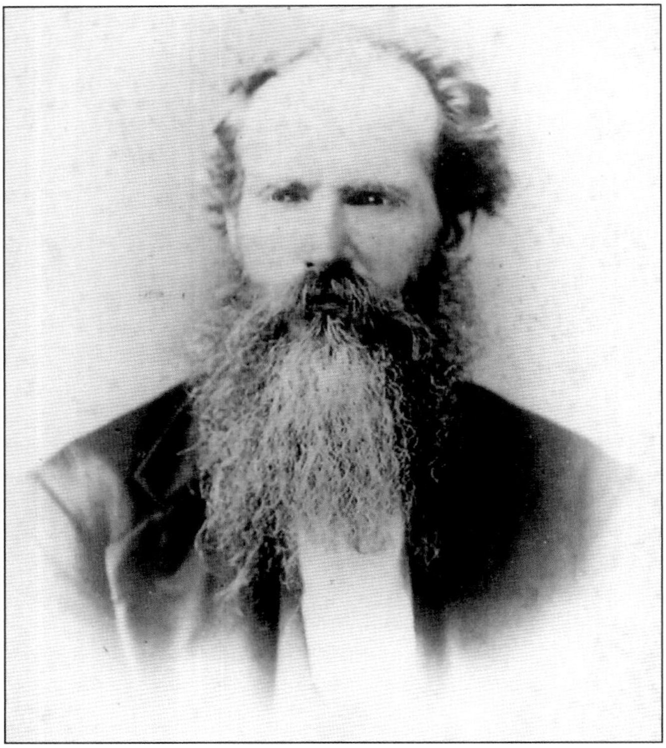

JAMES WOLFCALE. James Wolfcale was born in May 1832 to Abraham and Eliza Wilcox Wolfcale. Abraham Wolfcale, a carpenter and cabinet maker, settled in Austintown before 1811 with his brother. They settled in the area roughly bounded by Mahoning Avenue, Viall and South Raccoon Roads. (Courtesy Sue Allen.)

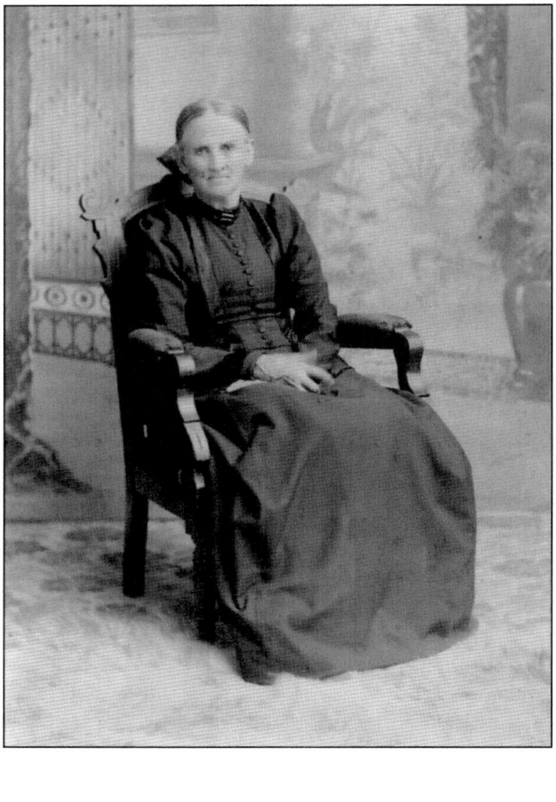

VICTORY COTTON SOWLE. Victory Cotton Sowle was born in Austintown in 1818 to Joshua and Elizabeth Williamson Cotton, who settled in Austintown in 1803. Joshua Cotton was captain of the 1st Regiment, 3rd Brigade, 4th Division Ohio Militia in the War of 1812. Sam Calhoon, Abraham Leach, Abraham Wintermute, John Russell, John and Isaac Parkhurst, and Henry Brunstetter were among many Austintown residents in this regiment. (Courtesy Sue Allen.)

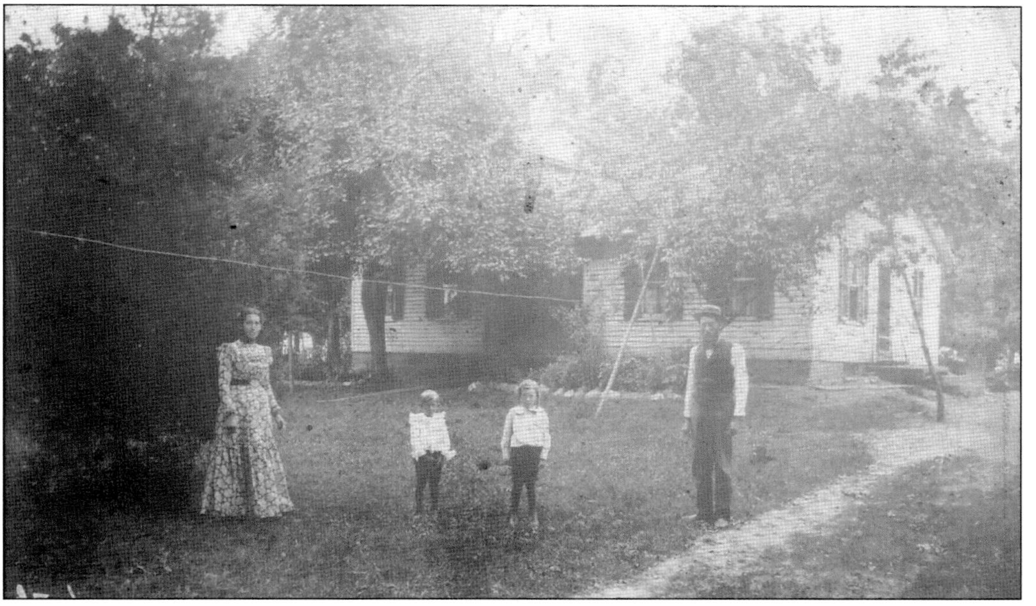

THOMAS ROBERT RUSSELL FAMILY, C. 1900. Thomas Robert Russell, born 1860 and died 1907, stands with his wife Pauline Caroline Mayer Russell and two sons, Thomas "Edmond" (on left) and George "Oliver" (on right) on their New Road farm. Thomas is the grandson of Robert Russell who settled on 200 acres along Turner Road in Austintown in 1806–1807. (Courtesy AHS.)

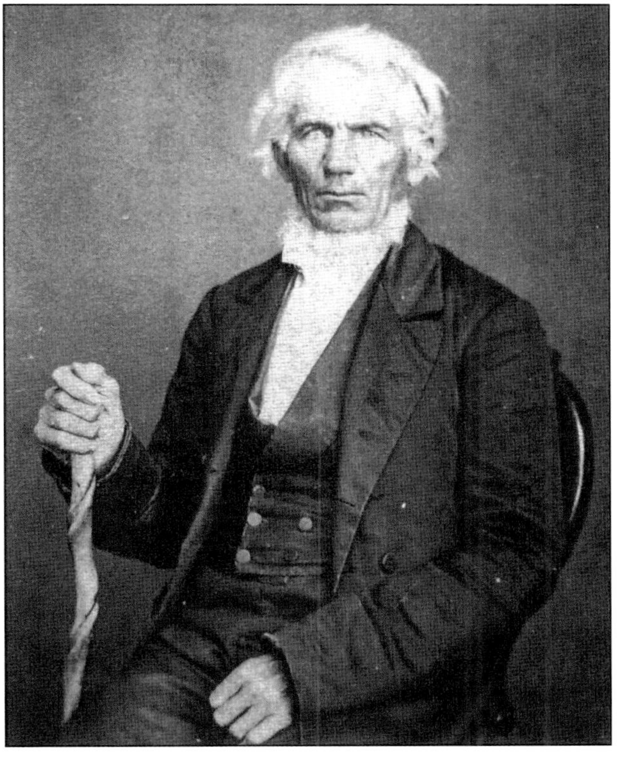

WILLIAM HAYDEN, FOUNDER OF HIRAM COLLEGE. An Austintown schoolteacher, William Hayden, and nine others founded Hiram College (then the Western Reserve Eclectic Institute) in March 1850. Born in Pennsylvania in 1799, Hayden moved to Poland in 1806. Hayden settled in Austintown after his 1818 marriage to Mary McCollum. He lived with his in-laws, John and Jane McCollum, and served the Disciples of Christ Church. (Courtesy Hiram College.)

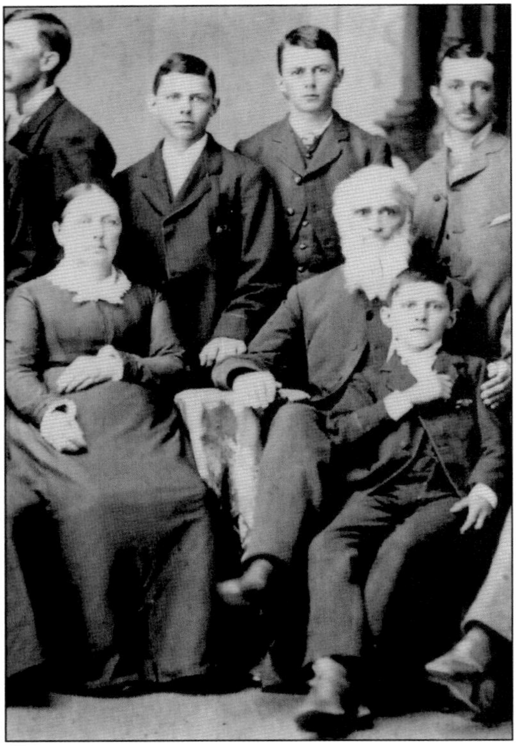

AUSTIN MOHERMAN, COFOUNDER AND FIRST TREASURER, ASHLAND UNIVERSITY. Austin Moherman, born on June 2, 1817, in Austintown, was the seventh child of Frederick and Mary Horn Moherman who settled in Austintown before 1801. In 1840, Moherman moved to Ashland County where he owned 1,258 acres known as Moherman Corners. He cofounded Ashland College, February 20, 1878, with 10 other members of the German Baptist Church. (Courtesy Ashland University Archives.)

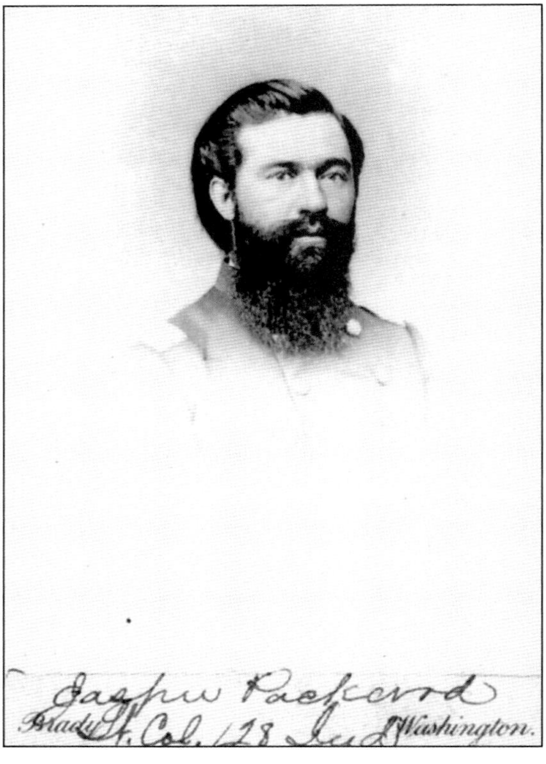

JASPER PACKARD. Jasper Packard, born in Austintown on February 1, 1832, to Thomas and Nancy Berry Packard, was the grandson of the Austin Log Cabin Packards. He fought with Indiana's 128th regiment during the Civil War and was brevetted brigadier general for his service at Vicksburg and Atlanta. He represented Indiana in the U.S. Congress from 1869 to 1875. (Courtesy Indiana State Library.)

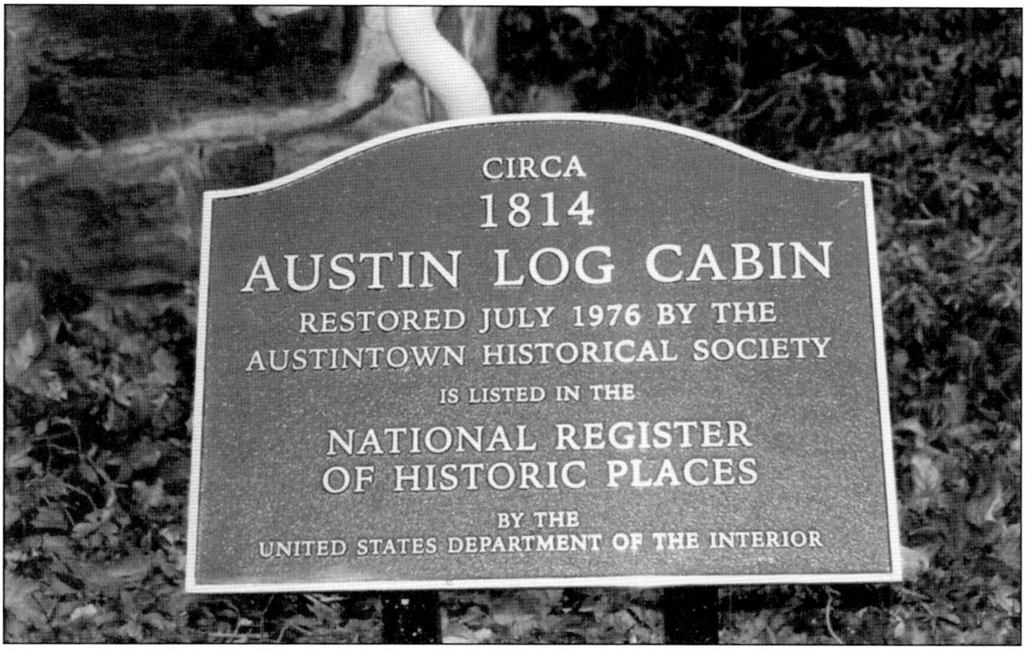

AUSTIN LOG CABIN. The Austin Log Cabin, on the corner of South Raccoon and Burgett Roads, is named for Calvin Austin, a Connecticut Land Company agent who sold 150.5 acres to John Packard on April 29, 1814, for $500. Historians assume Packard built the log cabin because the steeple notches on the log corners were not used after 1824. When Packard died in 1827, he willed the property to his son William. The cabin, restored by community volunteers, was dedicated on July 4, 1976. It was registered as a national historic landmark on July 30, 1974. The bronze plaque was donated by Dr. Fred and Judith Blue, members of the AHS. (Courtesy Joyce Pogany.)

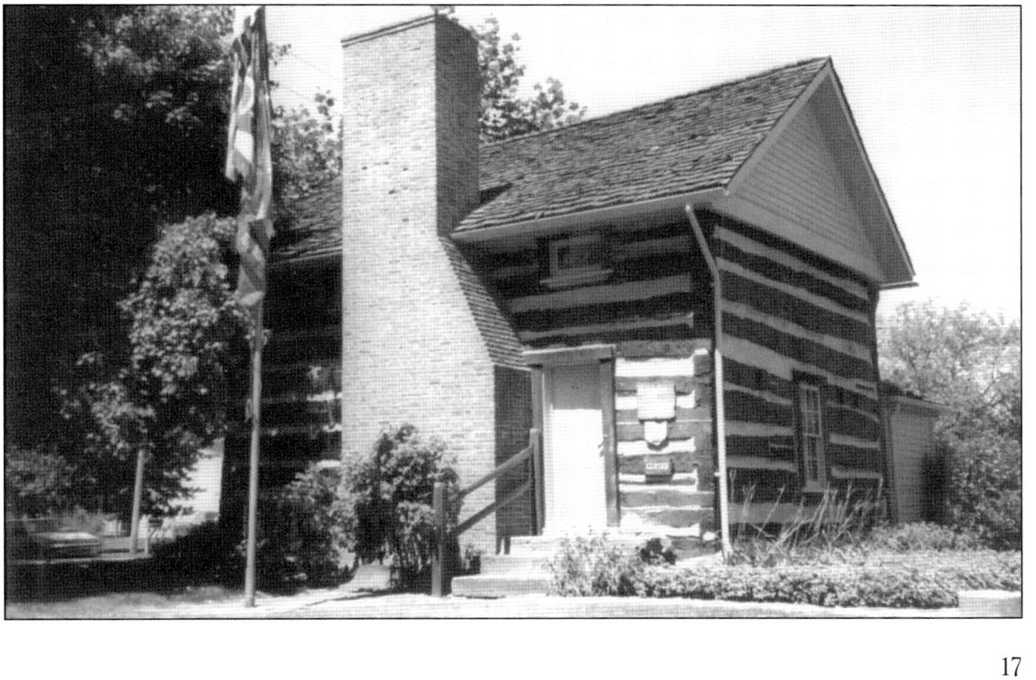

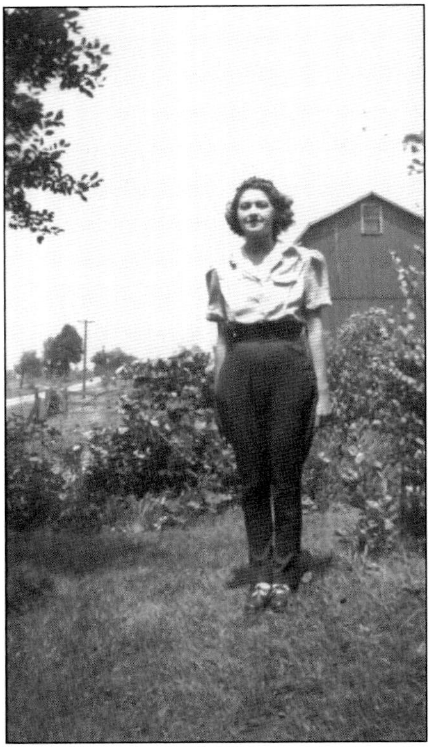

MARY "JANIE" HEINER STRICKLIN, 1943. Bob Stricklin's wife Janie stands between the Austin Log Cabin and the two-story red barn, which was 50 meters north of the cabin. In the background on the left is South Raccoon Road looking north toward the present-day Brookwood Estates. (Courtesy AHS.)

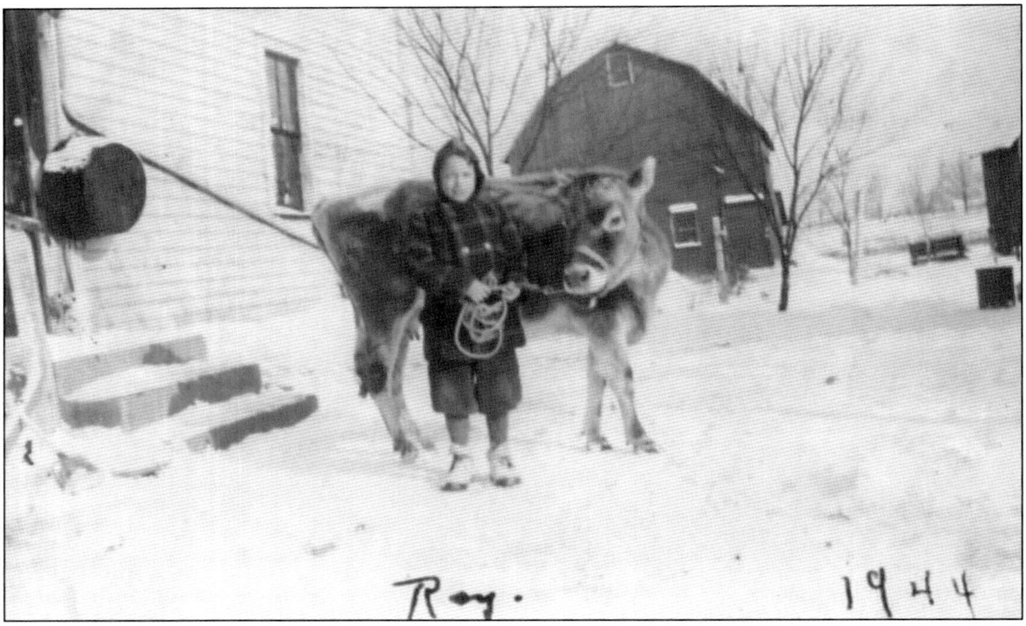

RAY STRICKLIN, WINTER 1944. Ray Stricklin, son of Mr. and Mrs. Willard Wesley Stricklin, poses with his cow Betsey next to the Austin Log Cabin. Wooden siding, perhaps added by Levi Wehr in the early 1900s, hides the Austin Log Cabin's logs. Later Joseph Hanko, the cabin's next occupant, covered the wooden siding with artificial brick siding. (Courtesy AHS.)

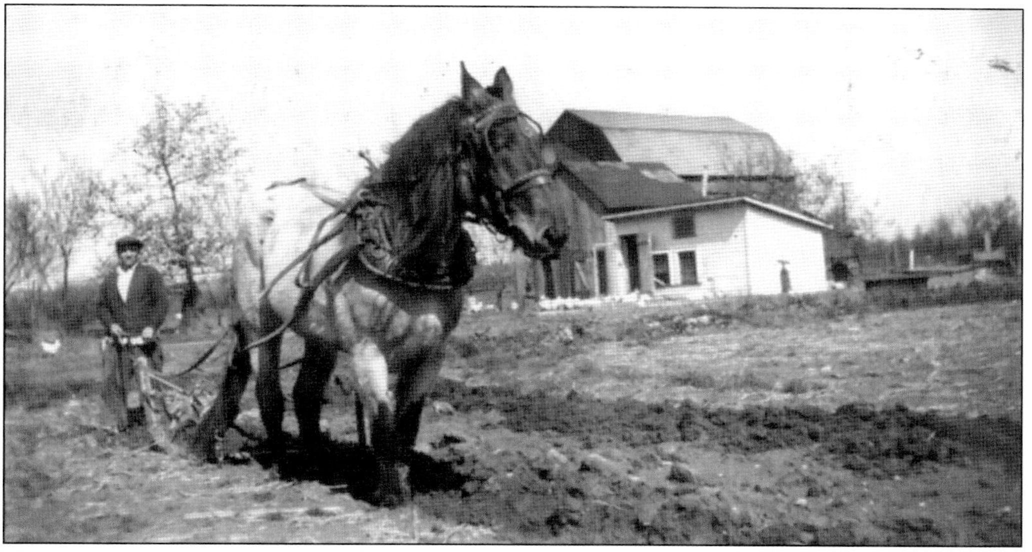

WILLARD STRICKLIN, 1943. Willard Stricklin, with his horse Bob, lived at the Austin Log Cabin with his wife and six children during World War II. The barn, pig pen, and chicken coop in the background were directly north of the log cabin along Raccoon Road. These buildings were built around 1910 by Levi Wehr and were destroyed sometime before the cabin's restoration. (Courtesy AHS.)

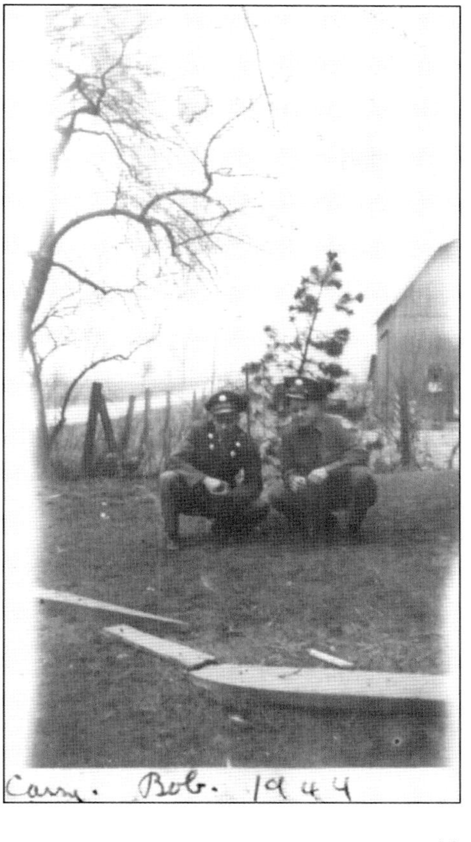

CARMEN QUESTRINO (LEFT) AND BOB STRICKLIN SR. ON LEAVE FROM WORLD WAR II. After World War II, Bob Stricklin; his father, Willard; and his brothers, Ray and Jim, dug by hand the root cellar under the Austin Log Cabin's kitchen. They carried the dirt out bucket by bucket. Joseph Hanko, the cabin's next occupant, finished the cellar. (Courtesy AHS.)

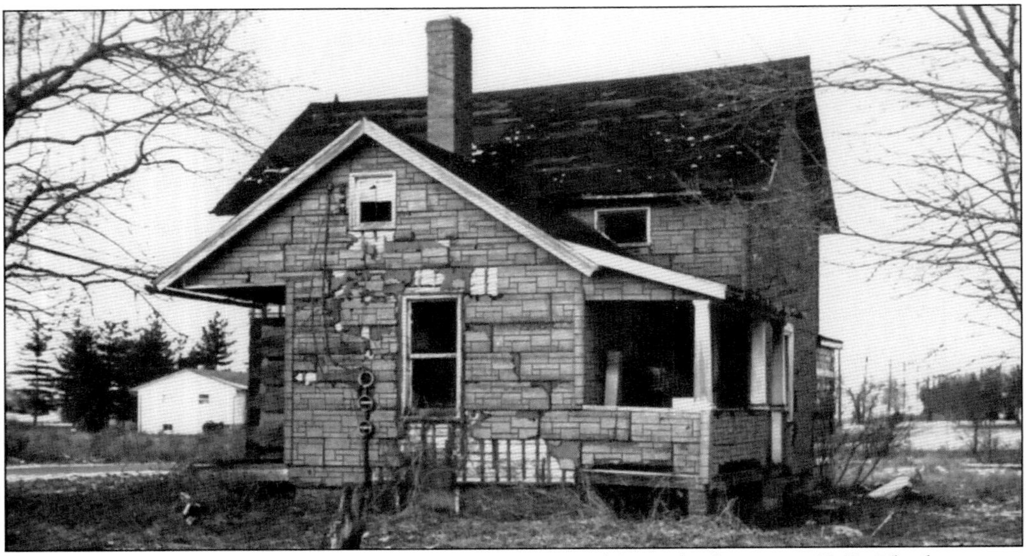

Discovery of a Log Cabin. The Hanko family moved from the house in 1963. The house sat vacant until 1973. The adjacent St. Andrew's Episcopal Church bought the eyesore and began demolishing it by removing the artificial brick and siding. When they discovered log beams, demolition stopped. Volunteers, led by the Austintown Community Council's Mike Antonoff and guided by a historic architect, removed the porch and kitchen, which were not original. They replaced the cabin's roof with wood shake, removed interior walls, and replaced windows with panes of glass from a 100-year-old schoolhouse. They sealed the logs with preservatives and replaced the chinking with a cement mixture to simulate the original clay, straw, mud, and rock chinking. They built a fireplace using century-old brick and a mantel from a barn beam. (Courtesy AHS.)

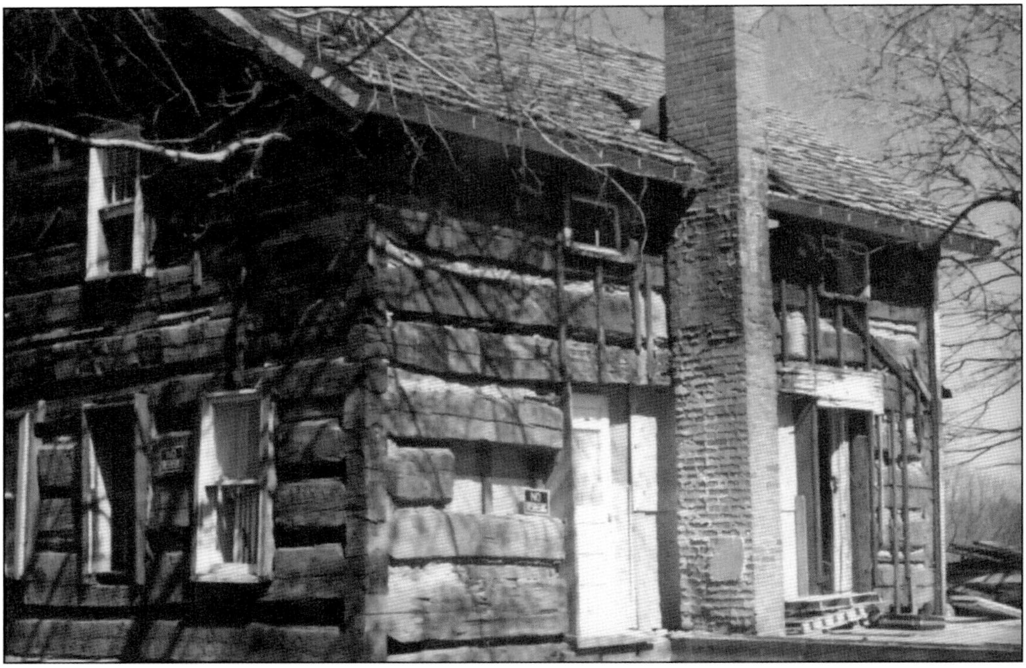

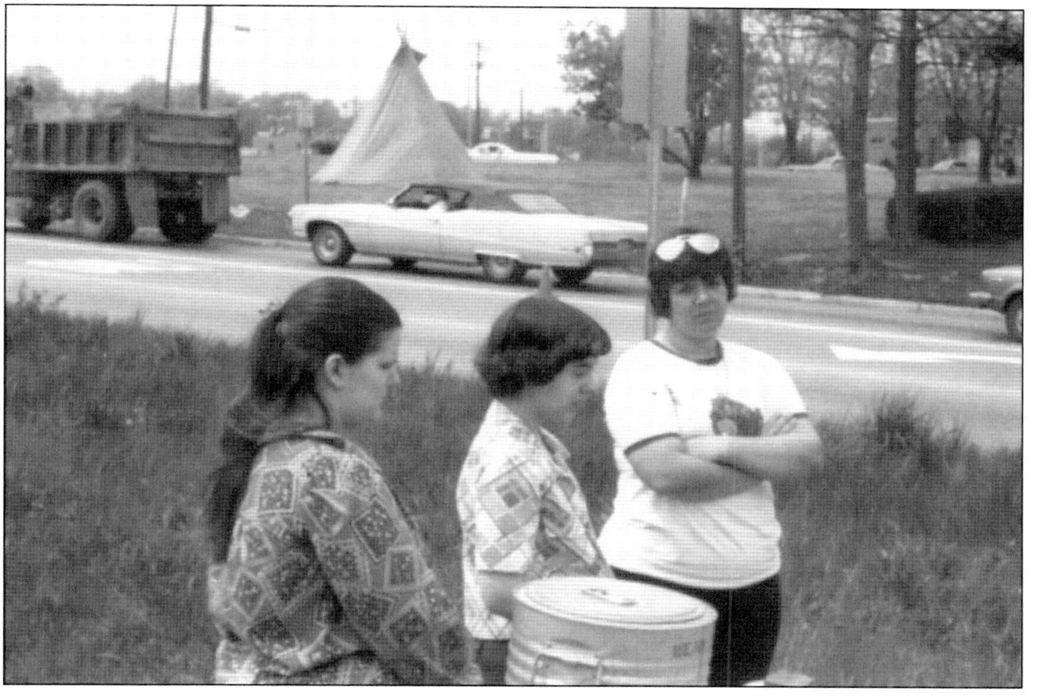

DONATIONS FOR THE AUSTIN LOG CABIN. On September 18, 1975, Charles Ditzler, Pat Bishop, Joyce Pogany, and Walt Duzzny coordinated a road toll collecting donations from drivers stopped at the intersection of Raccoon Road and Mahoning Avenue. Camp Fire Girls and a parent stand in front of the teepee erected on the corner of North Raccoon Road and Norquest Boulevard for the road toll. The road toll, coupled with donations from schools, students, PTAs, civic organization, and church groups; bake sales; book sales; a Log Cabin Dance featuring Freedom Sound; a night at the Youngstown Playhouse; a flea market; and a grant, yielded $50,000 to restore the log cabin. Dorothy Honey and Mike Antonoff count money raised for the log cabin. (Courtesy AHS.)

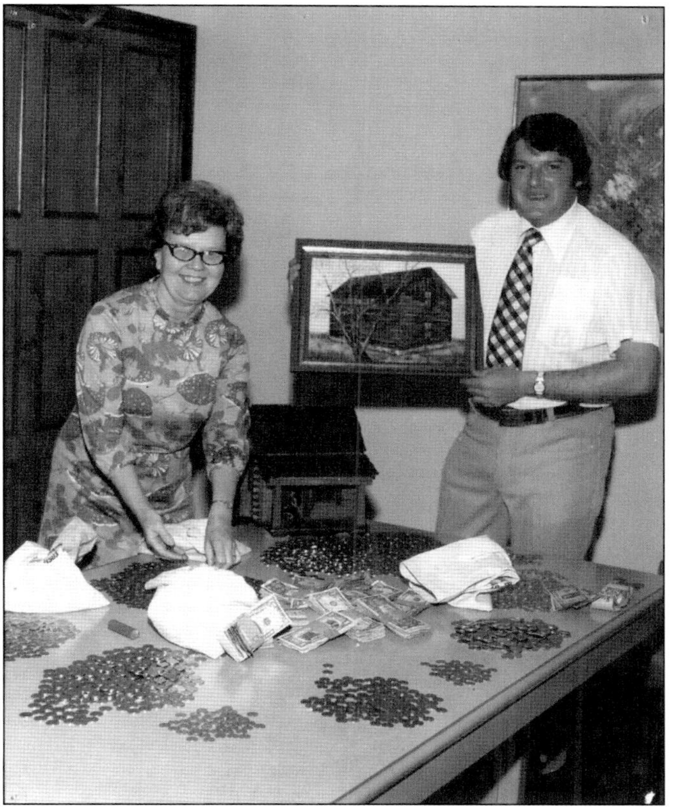

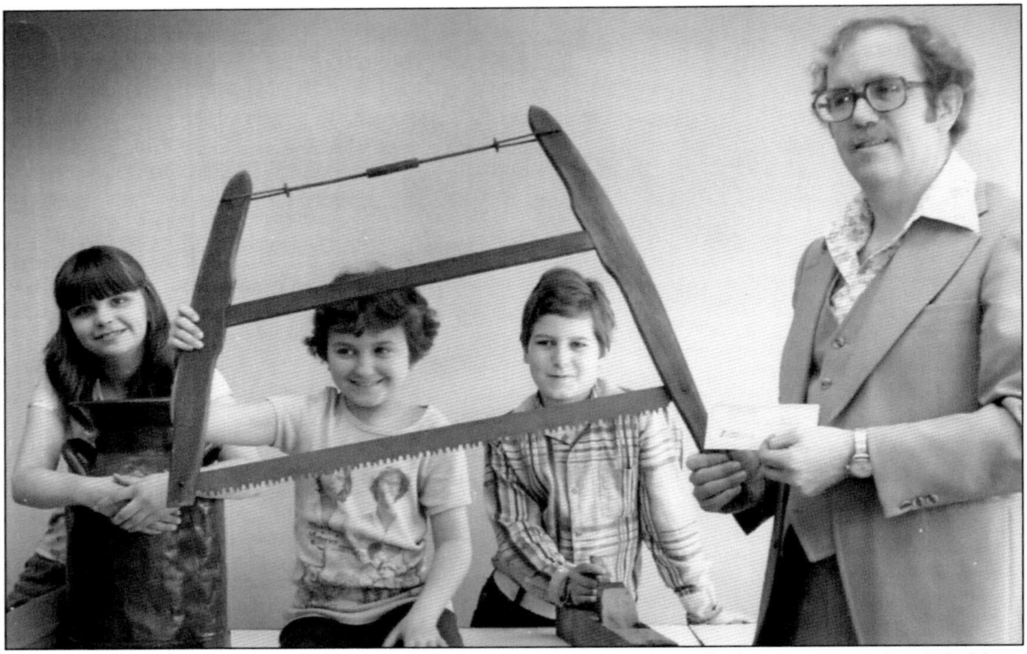

KEN ZINZ AND SCHOOLCHILDREN. Once the cabin was restored, Austintown schoolchildren and other community groups donated money and furnishings. Zinz, president of the AHS, receives a donation of a milk can, two-man saw, and wood plane. Community members continue to donate furniture and other historical items to the AHS. (Courtesy AHS.)

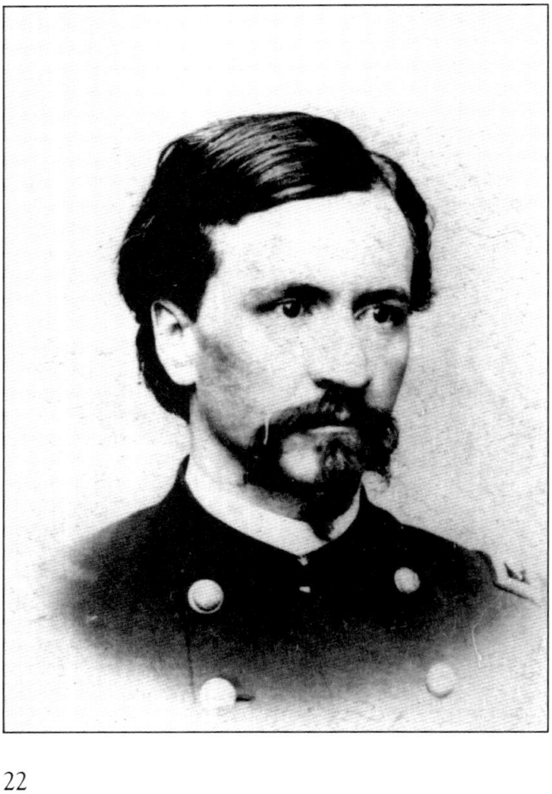

MAJ. HENRY LAWRENCE BURNETT. Maj. Henry Lawrence Burnett's biography lists his birthplace as Youngstown, but census records indicate his parents, Henry and Nancy Jones Burnett, lived in Austintown, near Weathersfield, when Henry was born December 26, 1838. Following Abraham Lincoln's assassination, Burnett was appointed special judge advocate and was a member of the team who tried John Wilkes Booth and his coconspirators. (Courtesy Roger D. Hunt Collection, U.S. Army Military History Institute.)

Two

West Austintown

Visitors to Austintown might drive through West Austintown without realizing it was once the most populous spot in Austintown. West Austintown is seven miles west of downtown Youngstown (hence the name of the once popular night spot, the "7 Mile Inn") and is in the vicinity of the intersection of Mahoning Avenue and Turner Road. In 1870, approximately 500 of Austintown's 1,948 residents lived within two miles of this intersection.

West Austintown included, at one time or another, a hotel, a post office, a school, several churches, a train depot, several saloons, James Campbell's store, Silas Anderson's store, Ripple's blacksmith, James Booker's hardware, a drugstore, and Mary Painter Bowman' s millinery store. Austintown's first physician, Dr. J. T. McKinley, a relative of Pres. William McKinley, opened his office and a drugstore in 1870. McKinley was followed by Dr. Rose, Dr. Kline, and Dr. Ruhelman.

West Austintown's 39 coal mines fueled the iron and steel industry in Youngstown. Some mines, such as the Austin mine on the Henry Kyle farm near the Mahoning County line, produced 150 tons of coal per day. The coal mines were either slope/surface or shaft mines. Under the coal, miners often found a 10-inch-thick vein of black band iron ore, which they sent to the Meander Furnace. Most of West Austintown's coal was mined out by 1888.

In 1876, David Brown (D. B.) Robertson was born in West Austintown to Robert and Jane Brown Robertson. He attended Austintown schools until he quit at age 12 to work on the railroad. In 1922, Robertson was elected president of the Brotherhood of Locomotive Firemen and Enginemen, then the second-largest railway union. He continued to work on railroad issues until his death in 1961.

After the demise of the coal mines, the population of West Austintown decreased by half. With the advent of the car and closing of the post office, West Austintown lost its identity as a separate town. Many West Austintown buildings were razed with the 1955 widening of Mahoning Avenue. The once thriving town became merely another intersection with a traffic light.

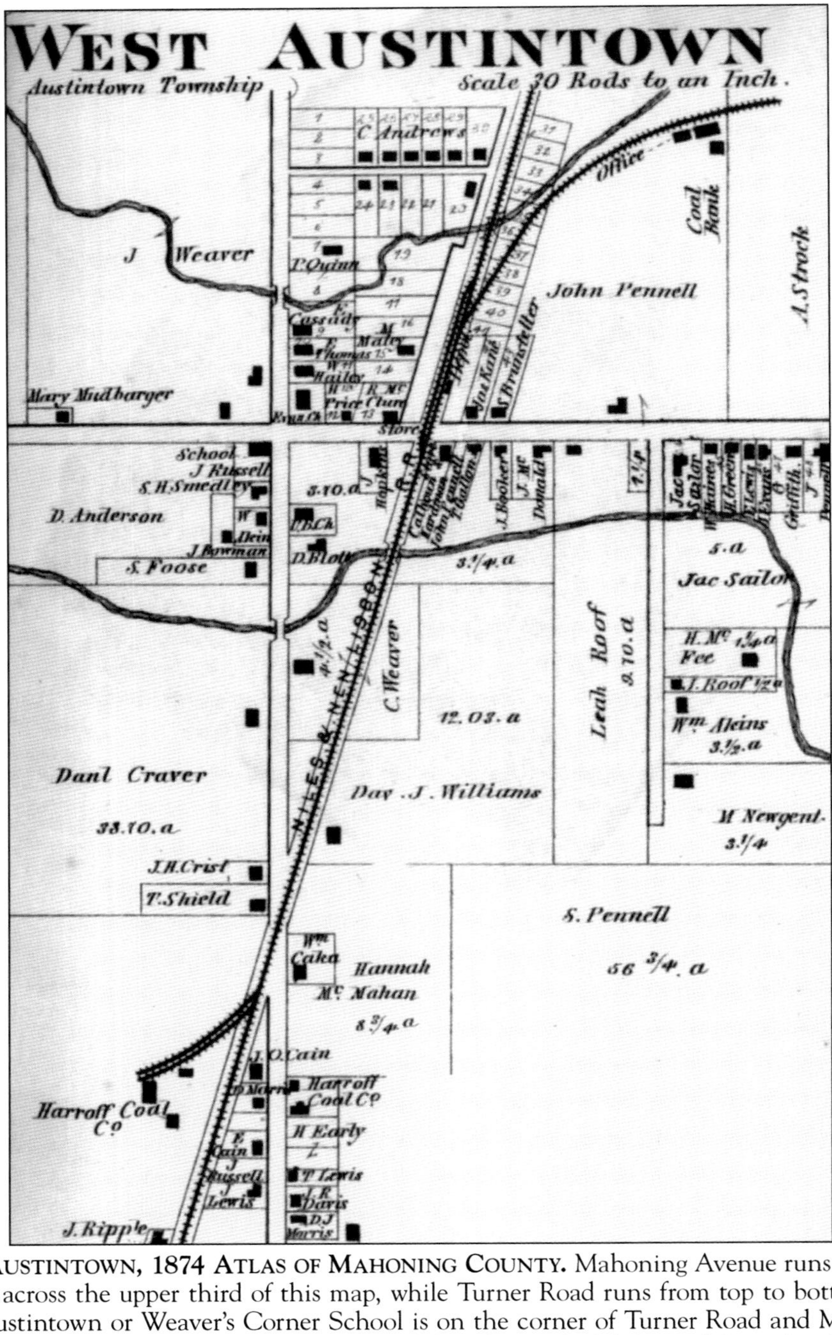

West Austintown, 1874 Atlas of Mahoning County. Mahoning Avenue runs from left to right across the upper third of this map, while Turner Road runs from top to bottom. The West Austintown or Weaver's Corner School is on the corner of Turner Road and Mahoning Avenue. Wesley Ohl and Daniel Blott operated the Blott and Ohl General Store (marked *store*) located at the corner of Mahoning Avenue and the railroad tracks; Ohl was postmaster from February 10, 1874 to 1885. The West Austintown Depot and James Kane's saloon and restaurant are on the east side of the tracks near Mahoning Avenue. James B. Jones was the "top boss" at the Harroff Coal Company, which operated the coal mine west of the railroad tracks on the bottom left. (Courtesy AHS.)

WEST AUSTINTOWN POST OFFICE AND DEHOFF GENERAL STORE. From left to right are Herbert Festus DeHoff, Ida Bauman DeHoff (in doorway), George W. DeHoff, Mabel DeHoff, and William DeHoff. George DeHoff owned the store from 1914 to 1929 and served as postmaster. He caught the incoming mail when it was thrown off the train and threw the outgoing mail onto the train as it passed by. (Courtesy West Austintown United Methodist Church.)

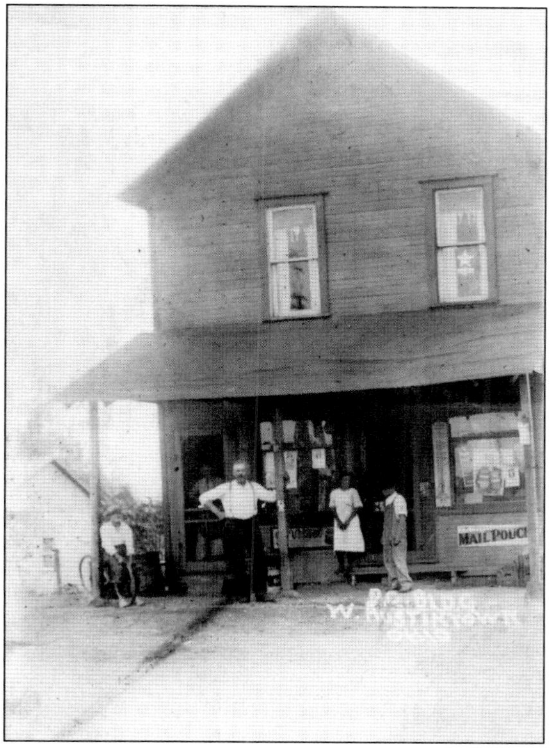

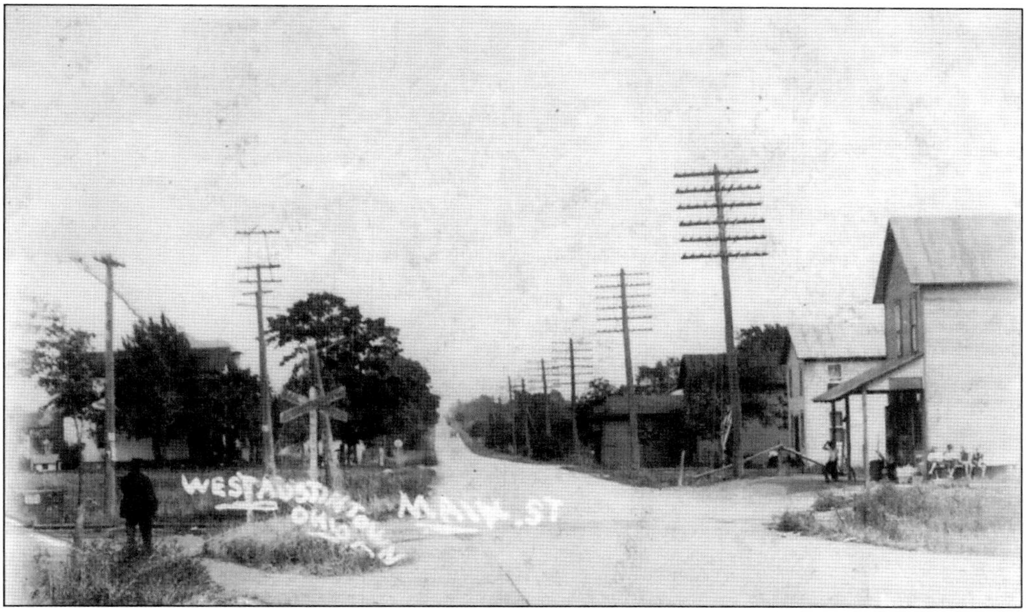

LOOKING EAST ON MAHONING AVENUE IN WEST AUSTINTOWN. On the right are the West Austintown Post Office and DeHoff General Store. On the left, just beyond the railroad crossing sign, is the Ohl house. The four children are unidentified. The macadam road was applied in 1905 by the Howley Contracting Company from Pittsburgh. (Courtesy West Austintown United Methodist Church.)

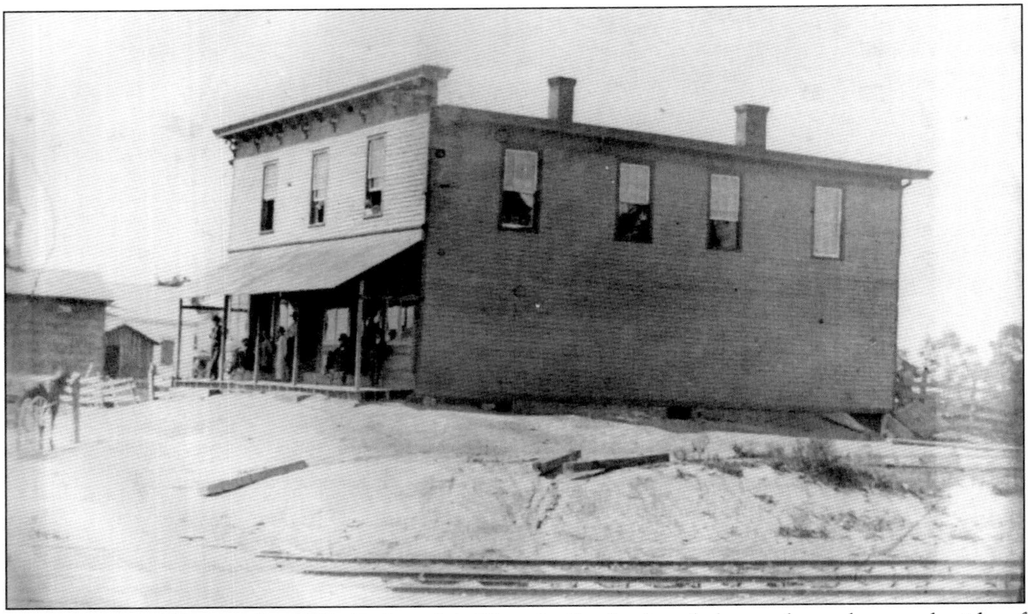

BISHOP FLAT HOTEL. In 1871, Robert McClure built the hotel, located on the north side of Mahoning Avenue just west of the railroad tracks. In 1877, English immigrant Harry Bishop bought the hotel, renaming it Bishop Flat Hotel. *Flat* is English for "rooms for rent." In 1907, Peter Schrum bought the hotel and enlarged it. It was razed in 1955 when Mahoning Avenue was widened. (Courtesy Advanced Marking.)

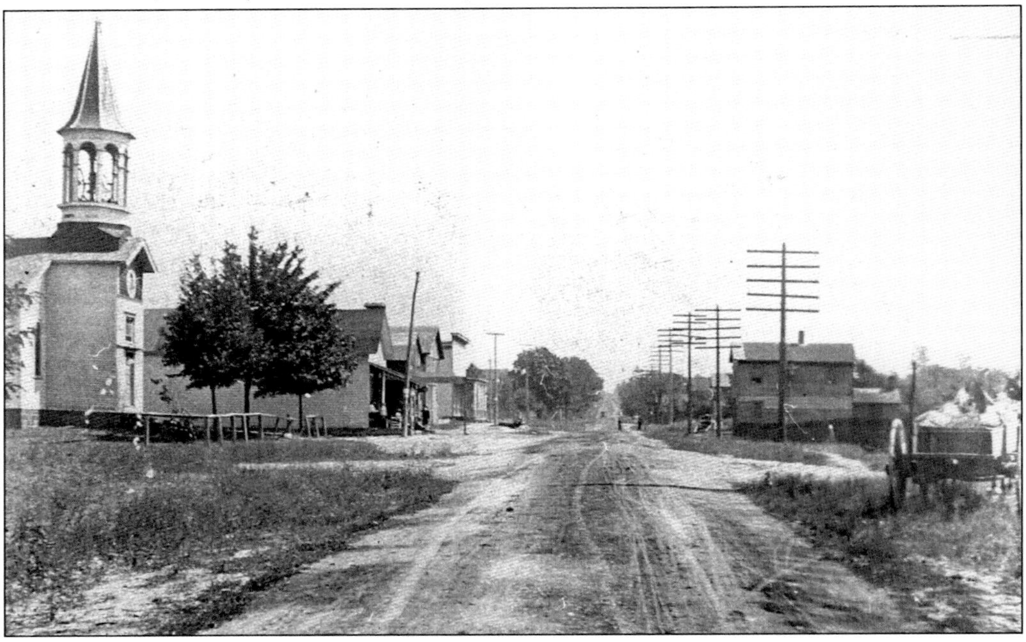

INTERSECTION OF MAHONING AVENUE AND TURNER ROAD, C. 1900. On Mahoning Avenue just west of Turner Road and looking east toward Austintown Center, the photograph shows wagon wheel marks on the dirt road. Notice the loaded wagon parked on the southwest corner of Turner Road and Mahoning Avenue. (Courtesy AHS.)

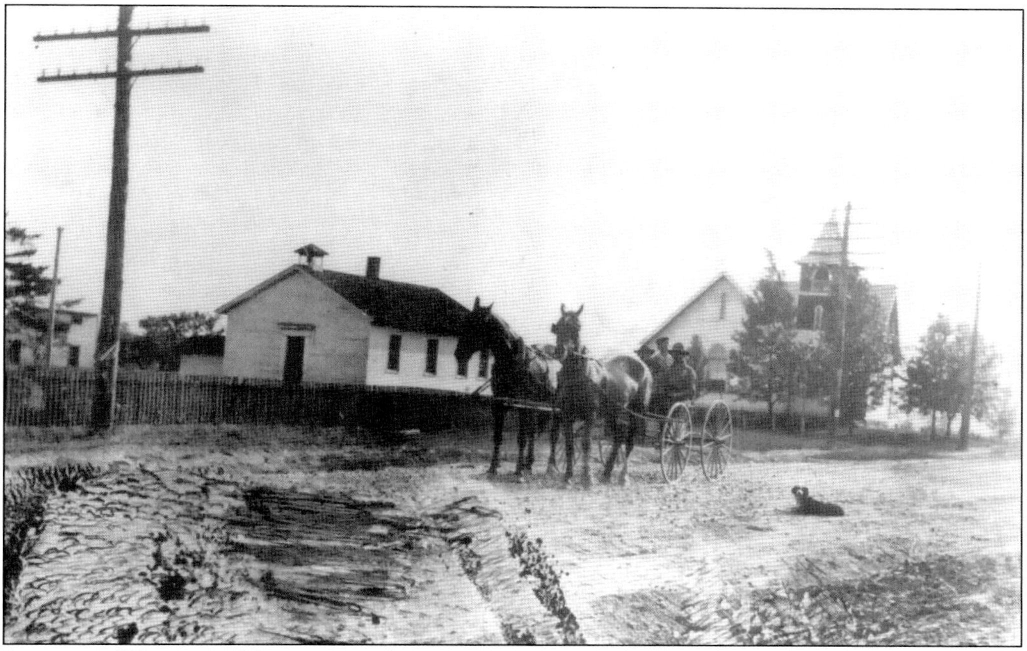

LOOKING WEST ON MAHONING AVENUE IN WEST AUSTINTOWN. The West Austintown one-room schoolhouse, in the background on the left, was on the southwest corner of the intersection of Turner Road and Mahoning Avenue. The West Austintown Evangelical Church is in the background on the right. The telephone lines and poles were installed in 1896. (Courtesy West Austintown United Methodist Church.)

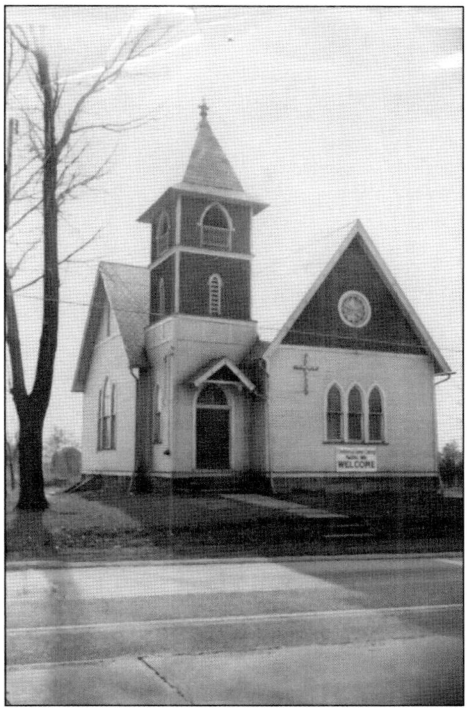

WEST AUSTINTOWN METHODIST CHURCH. This church, built in 1899, was located on the southwest corner of Mahoning Avenue and South Turner Road on a lot purchased from Little Welsh Congregational Church. The West Austintown Methodist Church was founded in 1853. In 1968, it merged with Grace Evangelical United Brethren to become West Austintown First United Methodist Church. It was razed in 2006. (Courtesy AHS.)

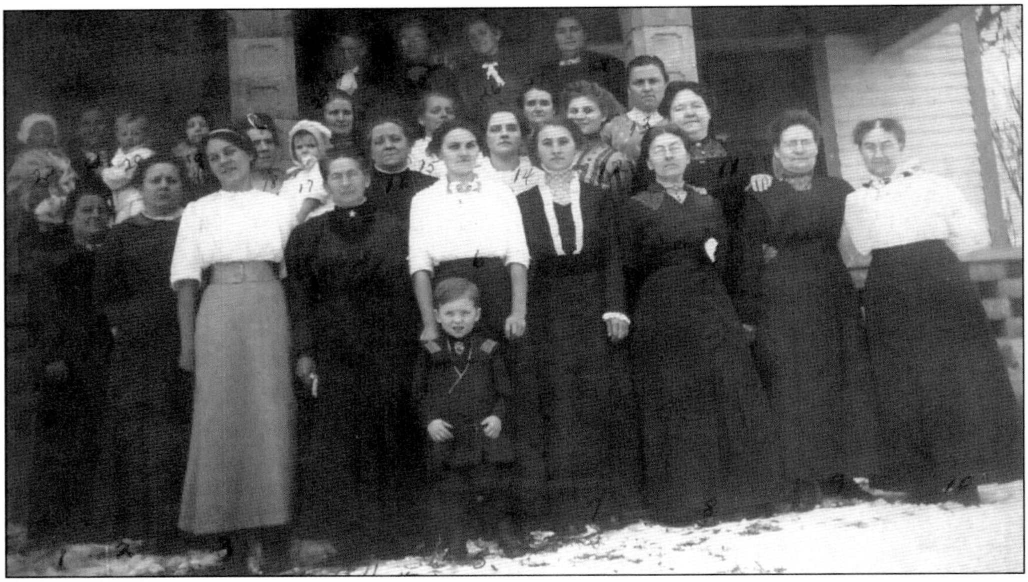

West Austintown Evangelical Ladies Aid Society, December 31, 1913. Members of the West Austintown Evangelical Ladies Aid Society from left to right include (first row) Gertie Anderson, Bertie Ripple Crum, Laura Wodnickel, Nealy Brobst, Mary Schrum Ripple, Junior Wilcox, Margaret Schrum, Grace Schrum Davis, Lizzie Jordan, and Kate McDonald; (second row) Martha Wilcox holding Wilcox children, Ethel May Richmond, Mrs. Wilcox holding her son, Sis Anderson, Edna Crum, Dot Boyer, and Lottie Ohl; (third row) Mildred Knight, Mary Bowman, Minnie Haefke, Doll Knight, and Ellen Bishop; (fourth row) Sara Lawrence, Sara Ellen Ripple, Sara Tessan, and unidentified. (Courtesy West Austintown United Methodist Church.)

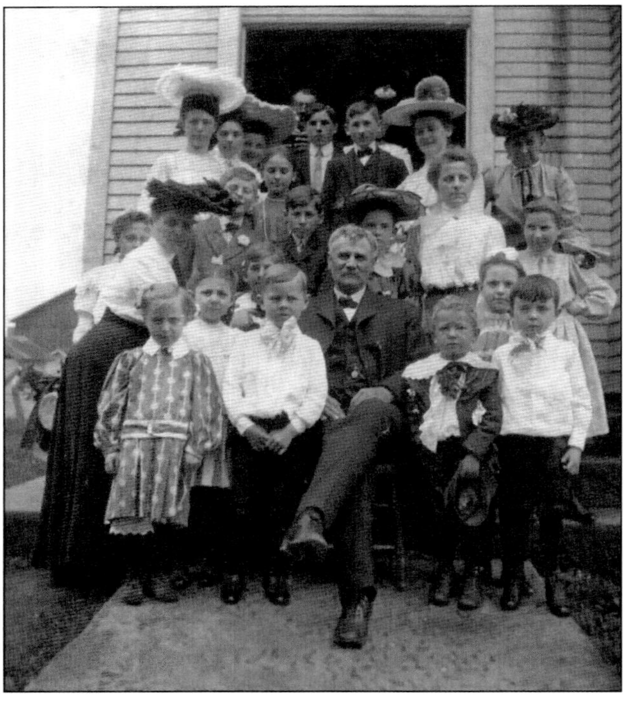

Early Sunday School Class, West Austintown Evangelical Church. This early Sunday school class, from left to right, includes (first row) Margaret Jones, Myron Crum, teacher George Jordan, Nelson Kech, and Danny Ripple; (second row) Lizzie Jordan, Vada Bowman, Sam Schrum, and Elsie Kech; (third row) Mabel DeHoff (partially hidden), Harmon Brobst, Todd Jordan, Grace Schrum, Edna Bowman, and Gertrude Anderson; (fourth row) Blanche Pelo, Dora Bowman, Dolly Brandyberry, unidentified, Tom Schrum, Clyde Schrum, George Ripple, Daisy Kroeck, and Mrs. Ripple. (Courtesy West Austintown United Methodist Church.)

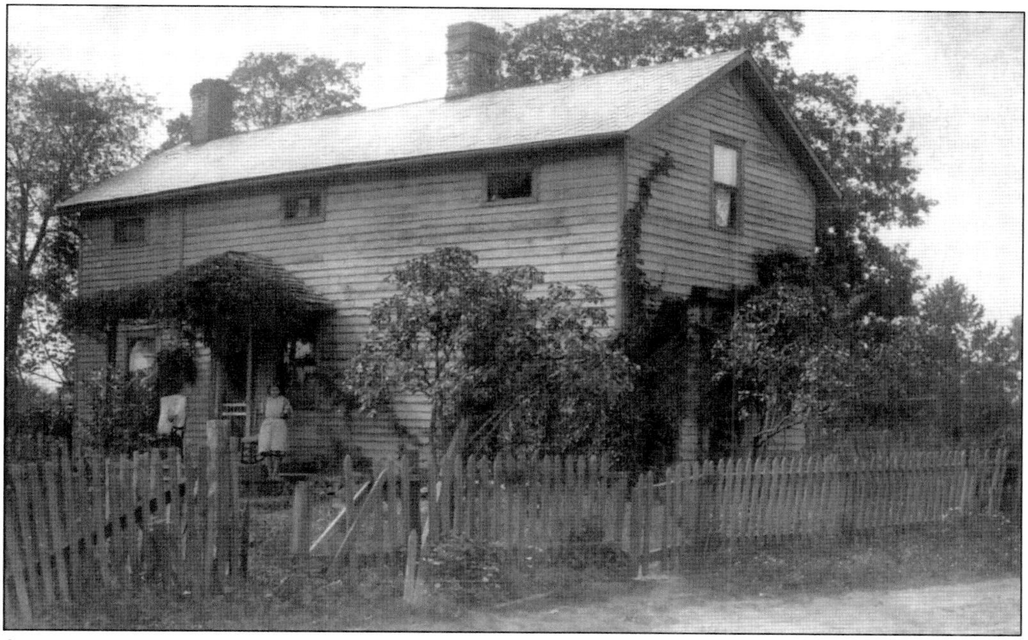

SMEDLEY HOUSE ON RAILROAD STREET. William and Sarah Smedley, born in England in 1826 and 1830 respectively, lived on Railroad Street, which was on the north side of Mahoning Avenue west of the railroad tracks. The Smedleys raised their granddaughter Edna Boyd, pictured, born about 1893. (Courtesy West Austintown United Methodist Church.)

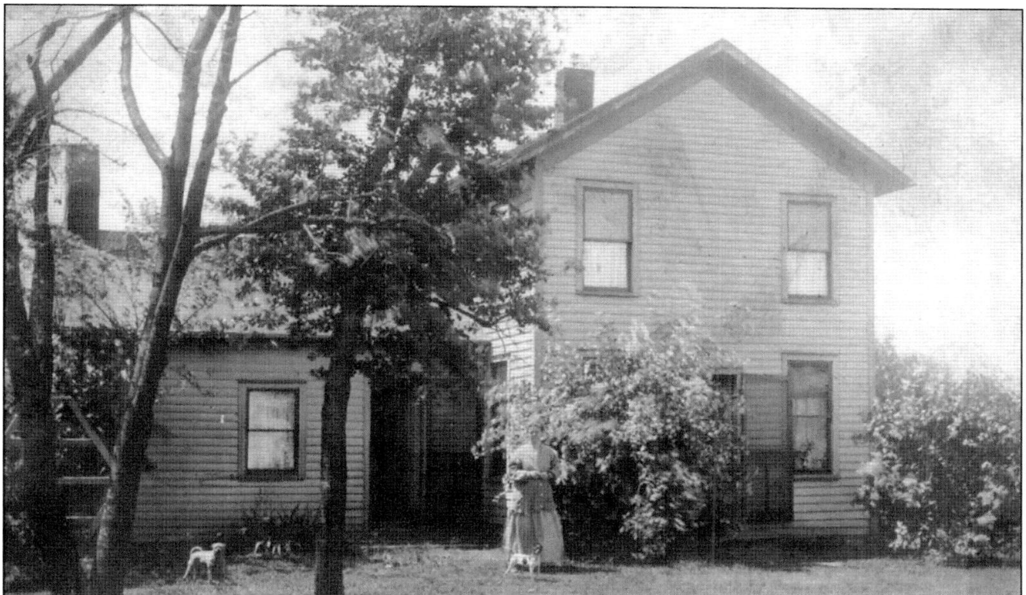

GEORGE ANDERSON HOUSE. Sarah Anderson (born about 1877) and dogs pose in front of her house, just east of the railroad tracks on Youngstown-Jackson Road (Mahoning Avenue) next to the West Austintown Post Office and DeHoff Store. Their neighbors included the Fryfogles, Haefkes, and O'Rourkes. George Anderson, born about 1876, managed a coal mine. (Courtesy West Austintown United Methodist Church.)

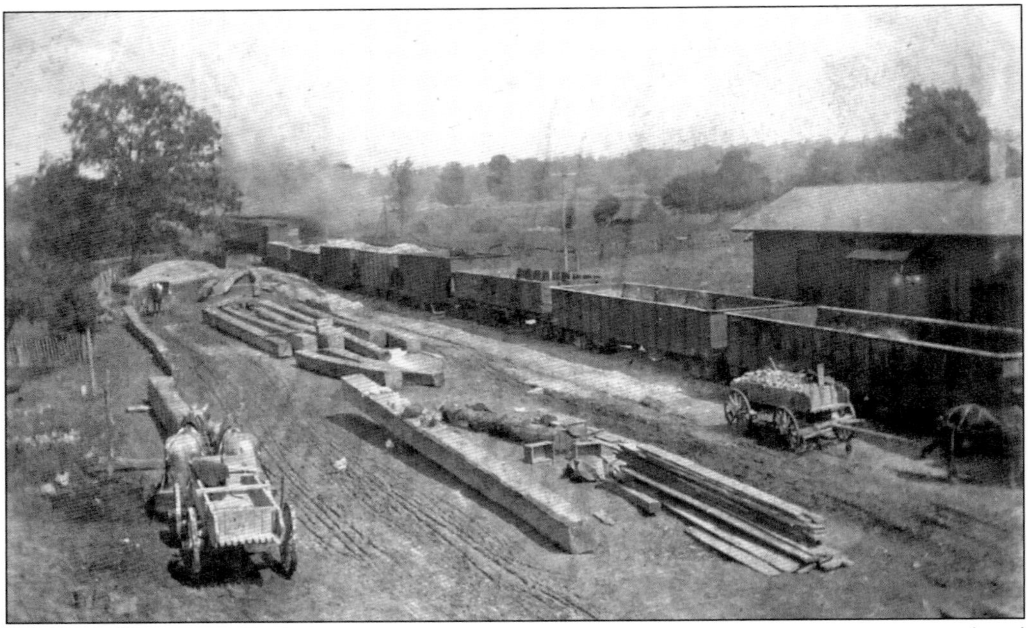

THE NILES-NEW LISBON RAILROAD. Chauncey Andrews built the Niles-New Lisbon Railroad in 1857. The train made two trips a day between Niles and New Lisbon (now called Lisbon). The train stopped at the West Austintown Depot, built 1869, at 11:08 a.m. (going north to Niles) and at 3:44 p.m. (going south to New Lisbon). The station agent pictured, believed to be David Childs, signaled the train to stop. Ross Rourke operated the depot's telegraph. Additional cars loaded with coal, ore, lumber, and other freight are on the siding. The West Austintown depot was razed in 1911. Regular passenger service stopped in the mid-1920s; regular freight routes stopped in 1951. The tracks were converted to a bike trail in 2000. (Courtesy Advanced Marking and West Austintown United Methodist Church.)

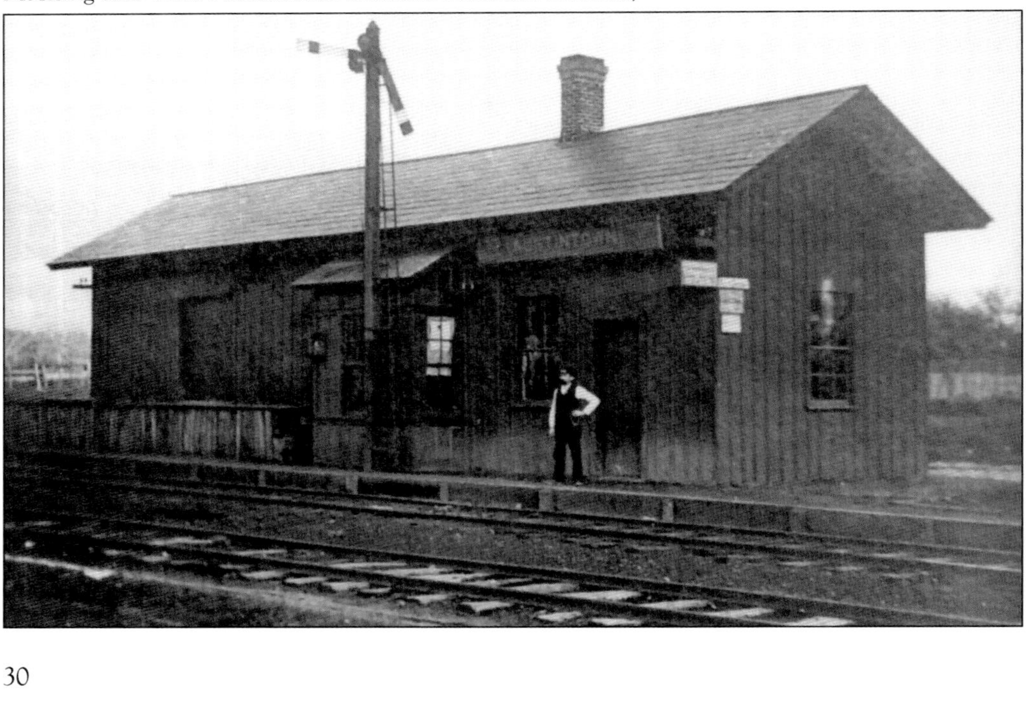

PERRY AND CORA OHL, C. 1918. From left to right are Mrs. Klingerman, her daughter Cora Ohl (born about 1874), and son-in-law Perry Ohl (born about 1875) seated in front of a grape arbor. They lived on Youngstown-Jackson Road, east of the railroad tracks, across the street from DeHoff Store. (Courtesy West Austintown United Methodist Church.)

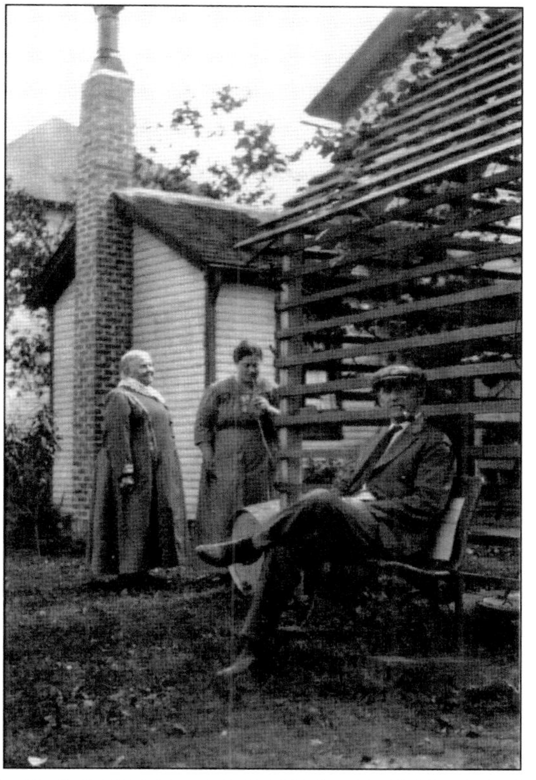

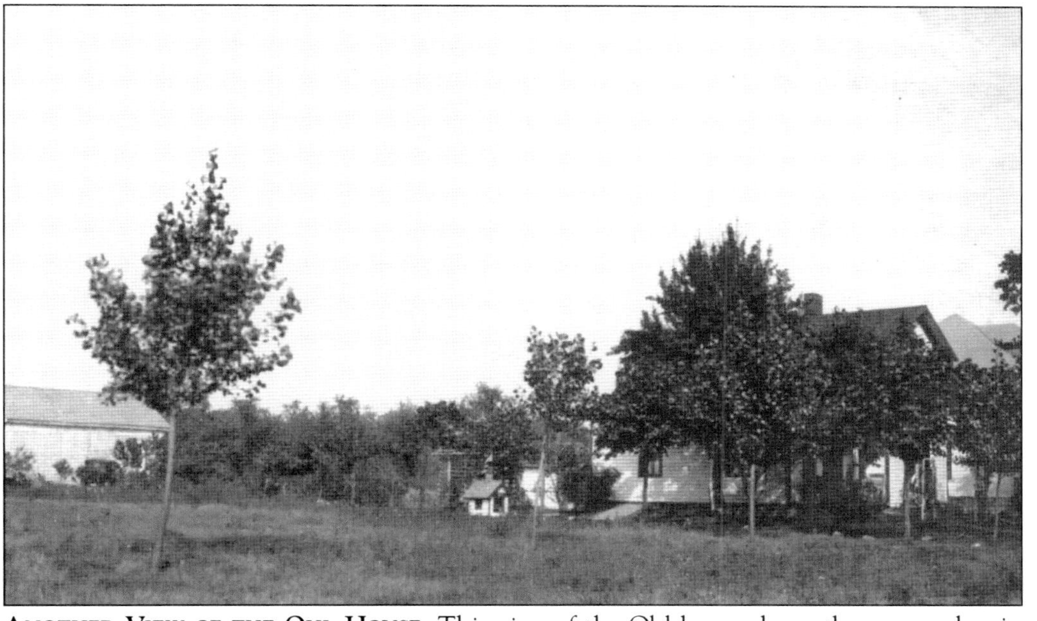

ANOTHER VIEW OF THE OHL HOUSE. This view of the Ohl house shows the grape arbor in the center of the picture and a barn in the background. Near the back of the house, at ground level, are the outside cellar doors, typical of the houses built in the late 1800s. (Courtesy West Austintown United Methodist Church.)

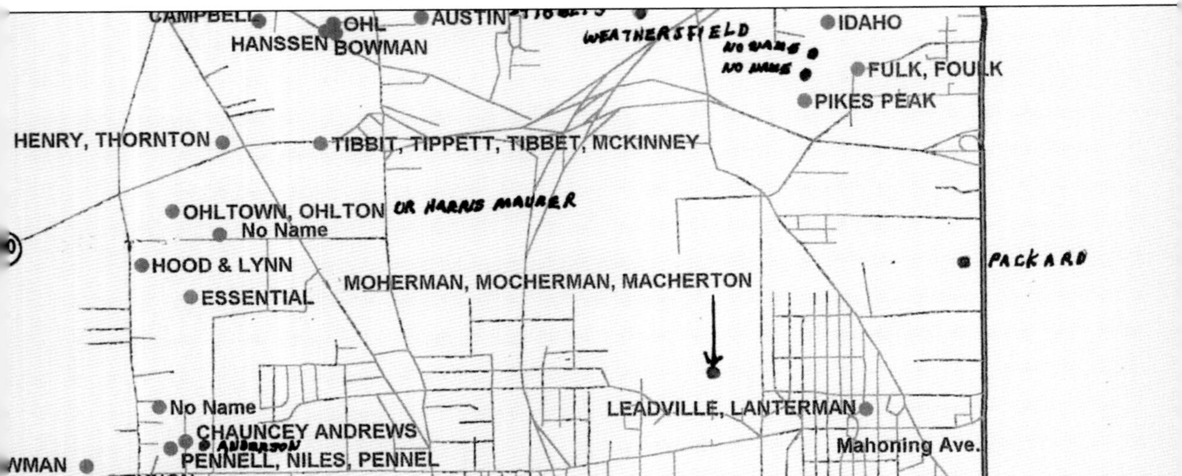

MAP OF AUSTINTOWN COAL MINES. Austintown was the geological center of a coal seam crossing the Mahoning Valley. The first coal mine in Austintown opened in 1835 on Michael Ohl's farm. During the 1870s and 1880s, 39 coal mines operated in Austintown. In 1886, Mahoning County produced 313,040 tons of coal, most of this from Austintown. In 1850, just 53 Austintown men were coal miners; by 1880, 359 Austintown men and boys were coal miners. The majority of these miners immigrated from Wales, Scotland, and England. The miners and families lived in South Ridge, West Austintown, and in two-story block houses on the northeast corner of Turner Road and on South Turner Road by New Road. Miners, some as young as 12, worked from 7:00 a.m. to 5:00 p.m. with an hour lunch break. They used their own equipment and earned 45¢ per ton for seams six feet thick; some earned $1 per ton if the seams were thin and difficult to reach. (Courtesy Greg A. Ricker and Ann G. Harris.)

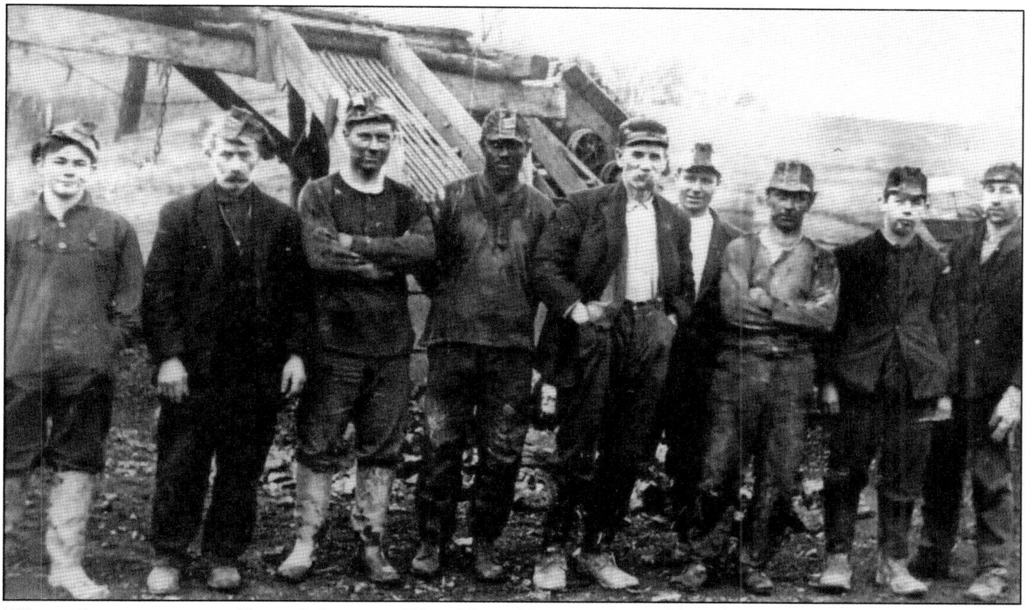

West Austintown Coal Miners. The 25-to-30-acre Harroff coal mine, a slope mine located on the west side of South Turner Road near Fairview Road, operated from 1870 to 1880. Miners include, from left to right, Bobby Cramer, Charley Cramer, Roy Schisler, William Wagner, Leander Wagner, unidentified, Charlie Schisler, Freeman Ripple, and Floyd Ripple. (Courtesy Lois Ripple Peterson.)

Iron ore. Two "paint works" ground West Austintown iron ore into powder to make red barn paint. One paint works, on Wilcox Road just south of Old Brunstetter Cemetery, employed 12 men, including Howard Harroff, Emery Lawrence, and Floyd Ripple. William Crayton operated the paint works on the southeast corner of Turner Road and Fairview Road. The paint works closed during the 1920s. (Courtesy Janet Keich McHenry.)

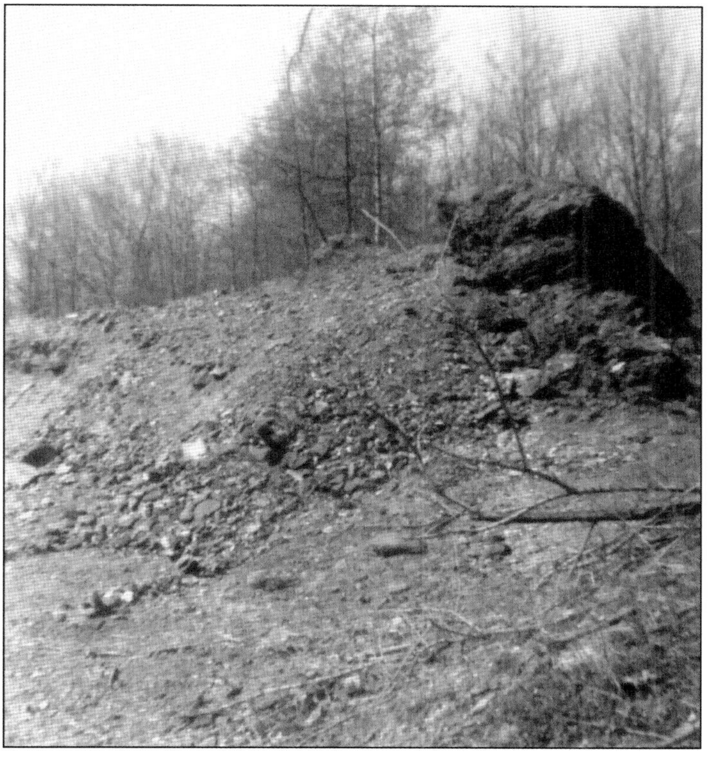

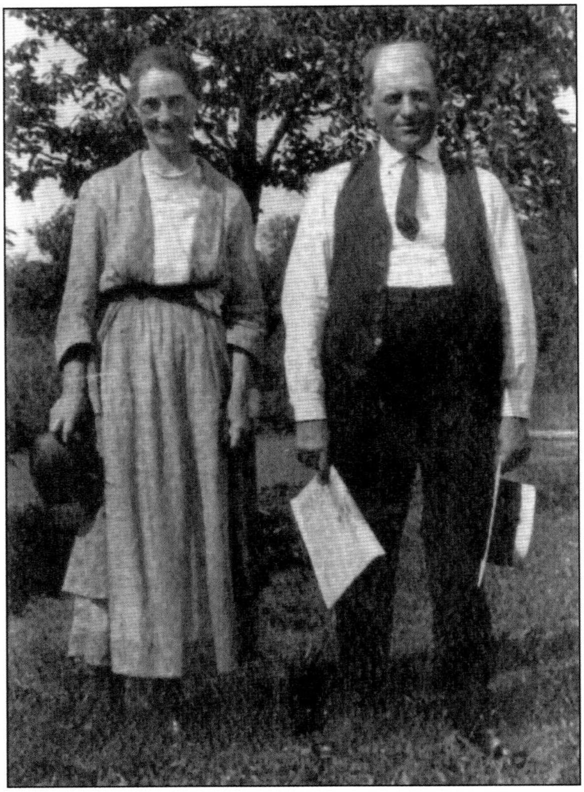

West Austintown Natives John and Sarah Ballard Bishop. John Bishop was West Austintown's postmaster from 1907 to 1914. In 1870, residents applied for a post office and debated its name. Those who bought lots from John Pennell preferred Pennelton; others preferred Weaver's Corners because it was in Weaver's Corners. The U.S. Postal Service named it West Austintown Post Office. It closed in 1929. (Courtesy Bob Bishop.)

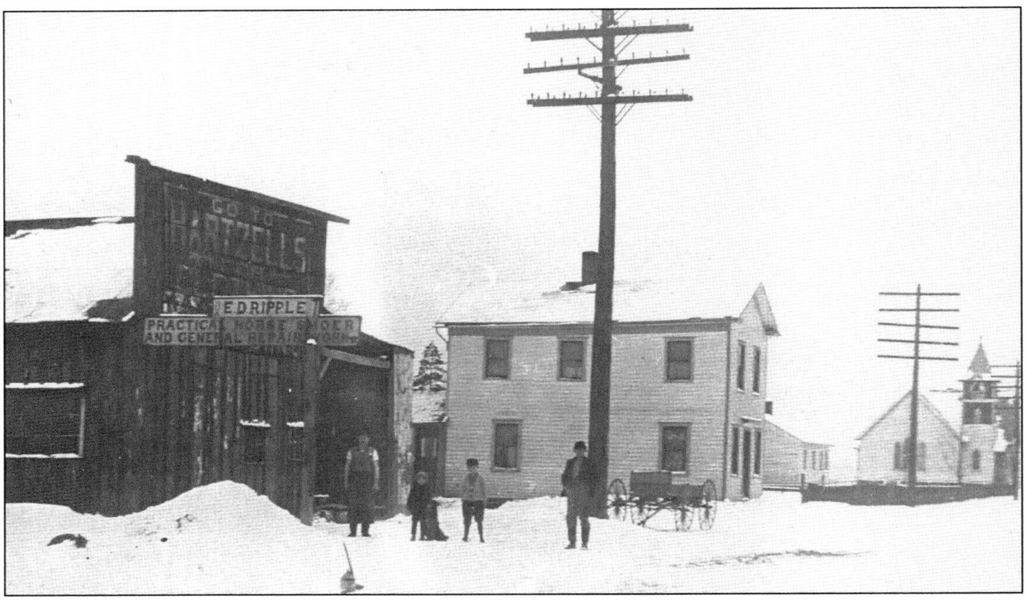

Side View of Ripple Blacksmith Shop. Dow Ripple, on the left, poses with some unidentified neighbors and a dog in front of his blacksmith shop on Mahoning Avenue. Although winter, Ripple wears short sleeves and a vest. Beyond the large white house are the West Austintown one-room schoolhouse and the West Austintown church. (Courtesy AHS.)

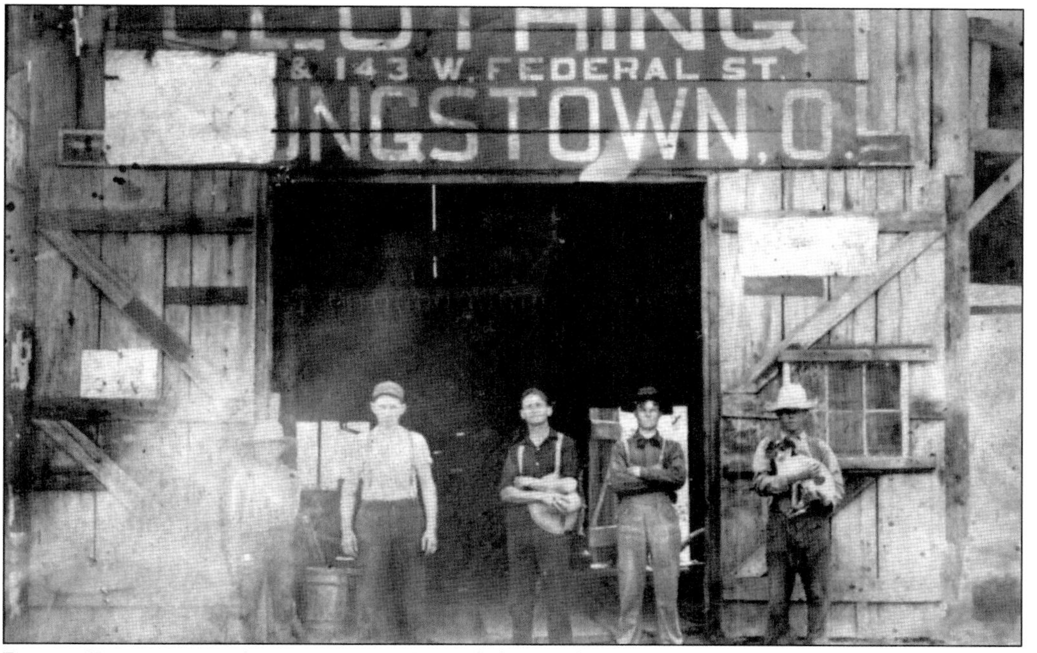

RIPPLE BLACKSMITH SHOP, C. 1910. From left to right are Emery Ripple, Dow Ripple, Abner Williams, Elmer Schisler, and Honey Shoffner. The shop, located on the south side of Mahoning Avenue, west of the railroad tracks, was across the street from the Bishop Flat Hotel. The Ripple family moved to Austintown in 1827. (Courtesy West Austintown United Methodist Church.)

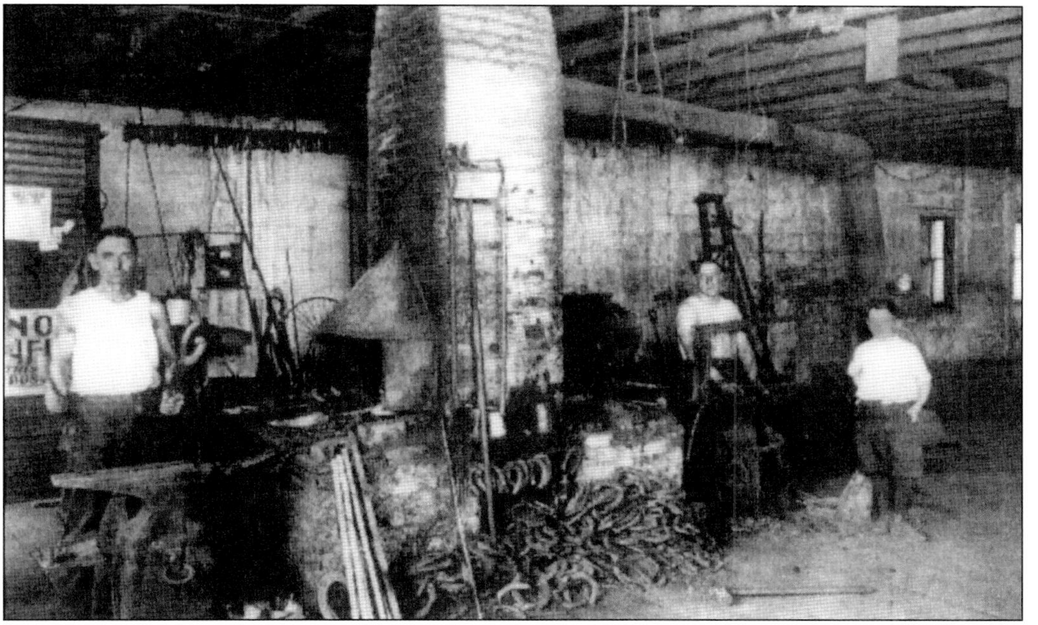

INSIDE RIPPLE BLACKSMITH SHOP. Near the forge at Ripple Blacksmith Shop are, from left to right, blacksmith Dow Ripple, standing by the anvil; an unnamed apprentice; and Emery Ripple. In the center are some of the many horseshoes produced at the shop. (Courtesy Lois Ripple Peterson.)

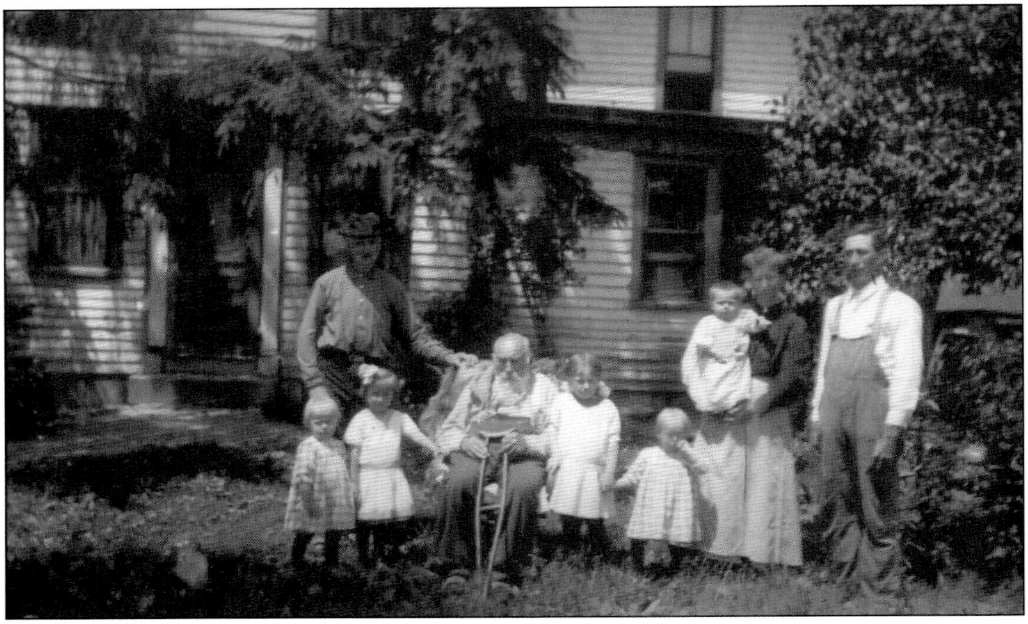

John Ripple Family. Pictured here are Bernice Ripple, Ethel Ripple, John Ripple, Hazel Ripple, Beatrice Ripple, Irene Wagner Ripple holding Randall Ripple, Floyd Ripple, and friend Tom in front of John and Sarah Jane Lawrence Ripple's home, built in 1890 on 60 acres along Fairview Road purchased from the Harroff Coal Company for $50. Limestone from the farm was burned at several Austintown lime kilns to make fertilizer, chalk, and whitewash. (Courtesy Lois Ripple Peterson.)

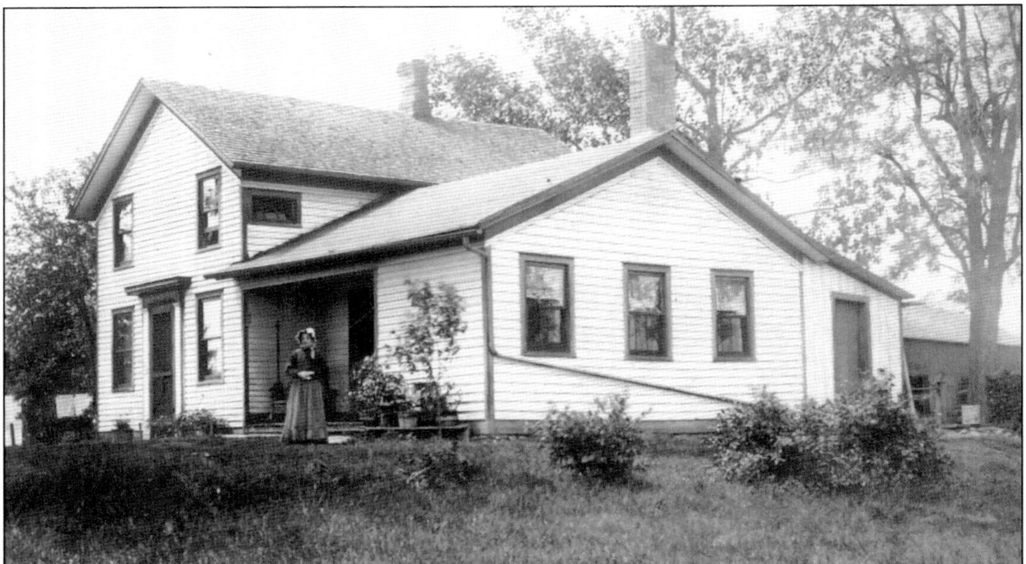

Foos House, 206 South Turner Road. This house, on the west side of South Turner Road, north of Fairview Road, was built in 1876. Julia Hewitt Foos, born about 1850, and her husband, Simon Foos, born about 1835, were farmers. Julia's brothers, Eli and Andrew Hewitt, lived here too and helped farm. (Courtesy West Austintown United Methodist Church.)

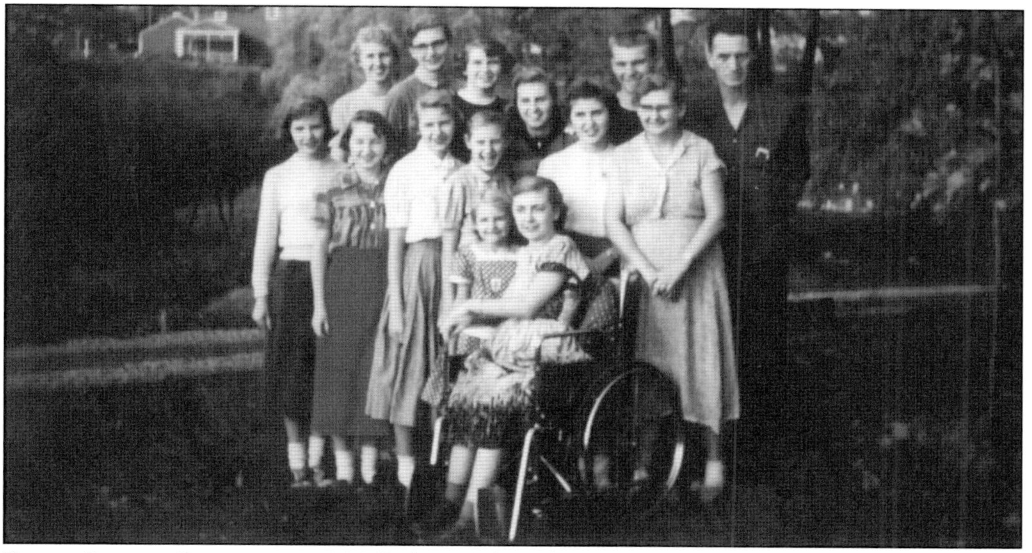

BOYER FAMILY, SEPTEMBER 1956. Robert "Ed" and Anna Louise Yates Boyer and five children moved into the Foos house in 1936 and had seven more children. The Boyer family from left to right includes (first row) Kareene, 8, and Claire Mae, 26; (second row) Judy, 17; Barbara, 15; Anna Ruth, 14; Alice, 12; Lillian, 25; and Anna Louise, 48; (third row) Nancy, 19; Kathryn, 20; Janice, 21; Betty Ann, 22; Robert Jr., 24; and Ed, 49. Claire Mae began school in Austintown in 1935; Kareene graduated in 1966, marking 30 consecutive years with a Boyer in Austintown schools. (Courtesy Boyer family.)

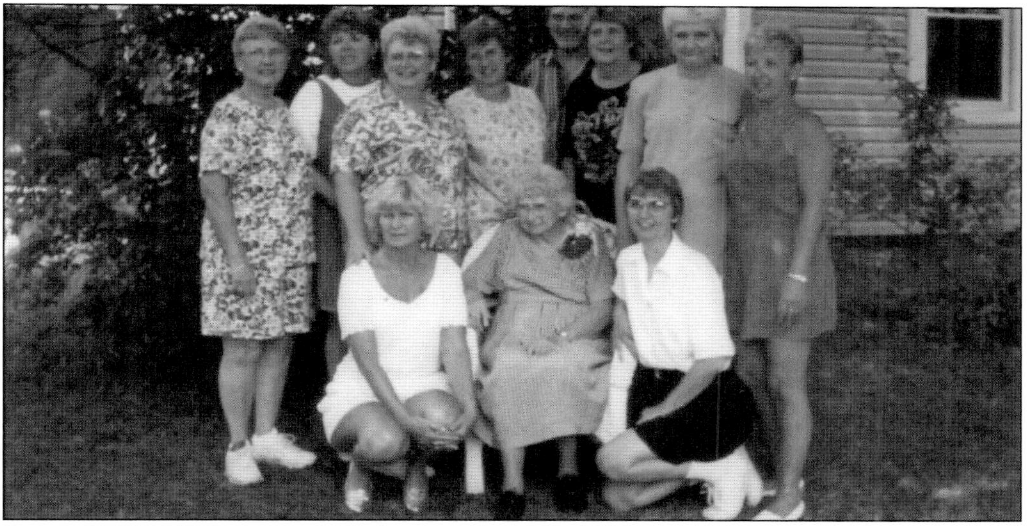

BOYER FAMILY, AUGUST 1998. At the Boyer home from left to right are (first row) Alice Kochera, Anna Louise Boyer, and Kareene Conway; (second row) Lillian Divelbiss, Judy Kaiser, Janice Kunkle, Betty Ann Genetta, Robert Jr., Nancy Welch, Kathryn Johnson, and Barbara Phillips. Married 58 years, Ed died in 1988 at age 81; Anna Louise died in 2002 at age 93. Claire Mae died in 1991; Anna Ruth Boyer Rick died in 1993. In 2003, Howard Divelbiss III, the eldest grandson, bought the house. In 2006, the family included 31 grandchildren, 47 great-grandchildren, and one great-great-grandchild. Twenty-two grandchildren graduated from Fitch High School; in 2006, 16 grandchildren attended Austintown Schools. (Courtesy Boyer family.)

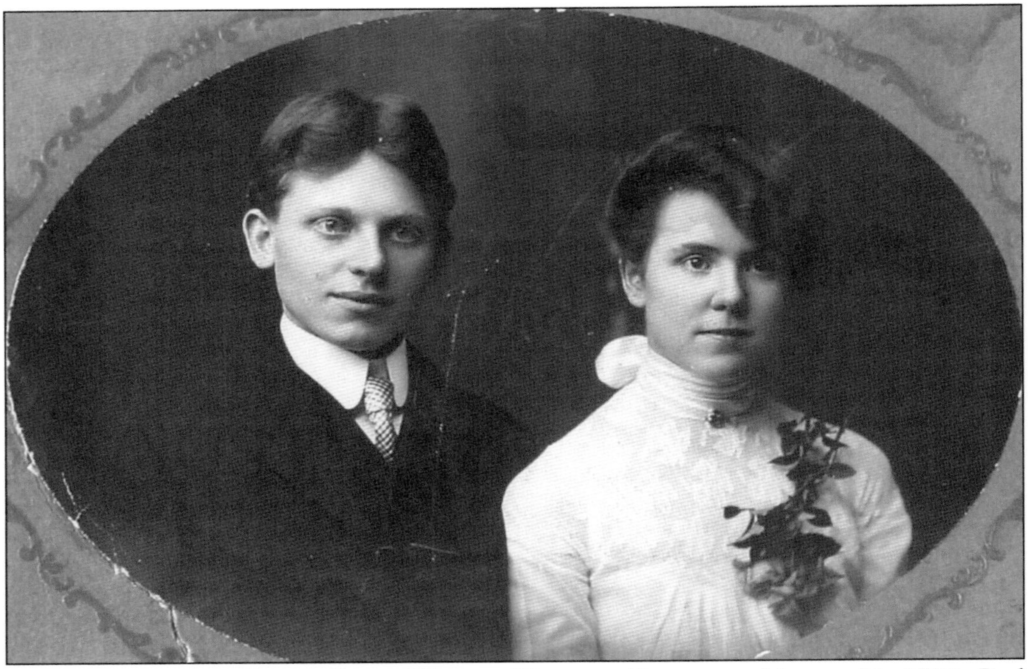

PAUL AND MARTHA BELLE KLING WILCOX WEDDING PORTRAIT, MARCH 11, 1903. Paul and Martha Wilcox had three children, Alda, Ralph Donald, and Margaret. Paul was born in Austintown in 1881, one of seven children of Isaac and Elizabeth Paynter Wilcox. Isaac Wilcox, boss at the Chauncey Andrews coal mine, was postmaster from 1893 to 1897. (Courtesy Marjorie Jane Brown Hephner.)

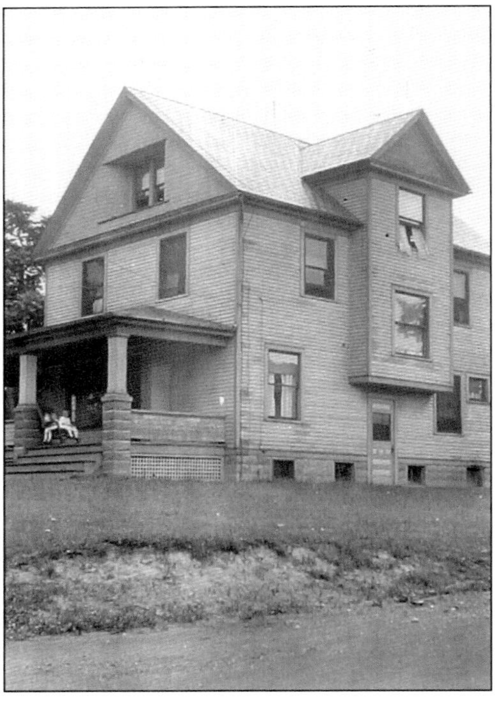

PAUL AND MARTHA WILCOX HOUSE, C. 1921. The house on the corner of Wilcox Road and Mahoning Avenue, built in 1914, included electric wiring even though electricity was not available in Austintown. In the winter, Paul Wilcox cut ice from the pond behind the house for the icehouse where he stored meat for his meat delivery business. (Courtesy Marjorie Jane Brown Hephner.)

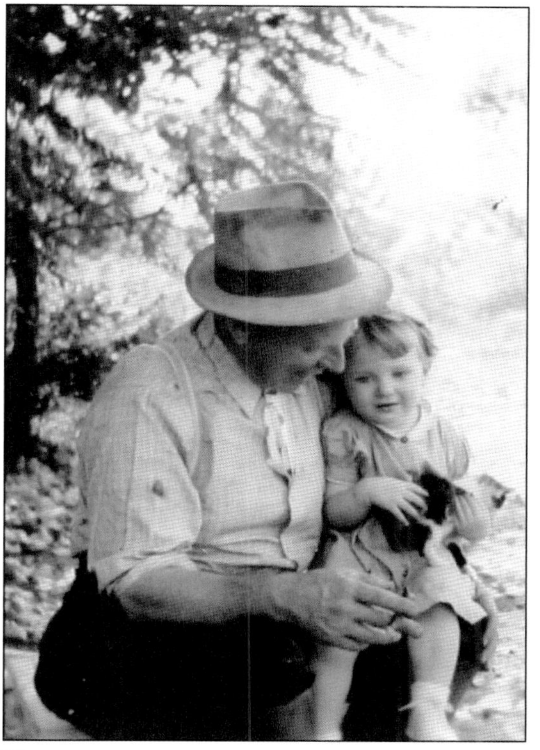

PAUL WILCOX AND FIRST GRANDCHILD, C. 1937. Paul Wilcox, with the first of six grandchildren, Marjorie Jane Brown, was elected to the Austintown School Board in 1916, serving as school board clerk. Wilcox owned his own school bus, No. 9, and drove it for the Austintown schools. Wilcox Road, formerly known as Brunstetter Cemetery Road, is named for the Wilcox family. (Courtesy Marjorie Jane Brown Hephner.)

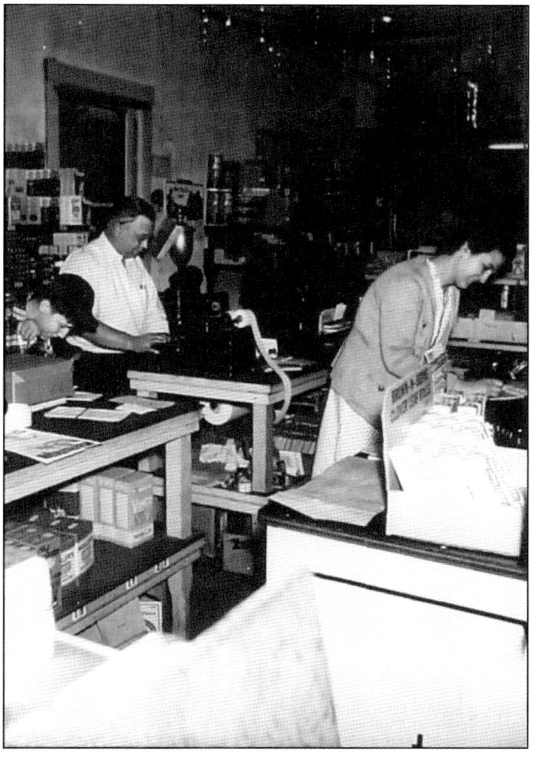

WILCOX FOOD MARKET. Paul Wilcox opened the Wilcox Butcher Shop on the south side of Mahoning Avenue, west of the family home, in 1919. His son, Donald, joined the store after World War II. The store was renamed Wilcox and Son Food Market. At the market are Don Wilcox, his wife Marianna, and son John Paul. (Courtesy Ken and John Wilcox and Marjorie Jane Brown Hephner.)

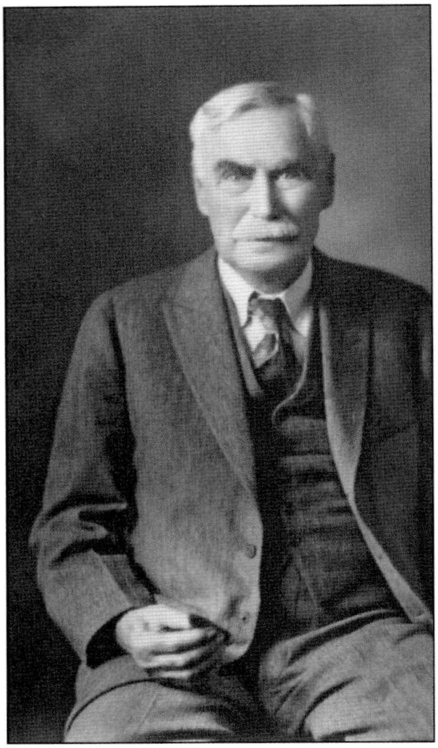

James Campbell, President of Youngstown Sheet and Tube. James Campbell, born in Ohltown on September 11, 1854, to James and Caroline Campbell, was reared in West Austintown where his parents operated a store. In 1900, he incorporated Youngstown Sheet and Tube, the largest independently owned steel company with $1 million in assets in 1920, and was president from 1904 to 1930. In 1926, East Youngstown was renamed Campbell after him. (Courtesy Mahoning Valley Historical Society.)

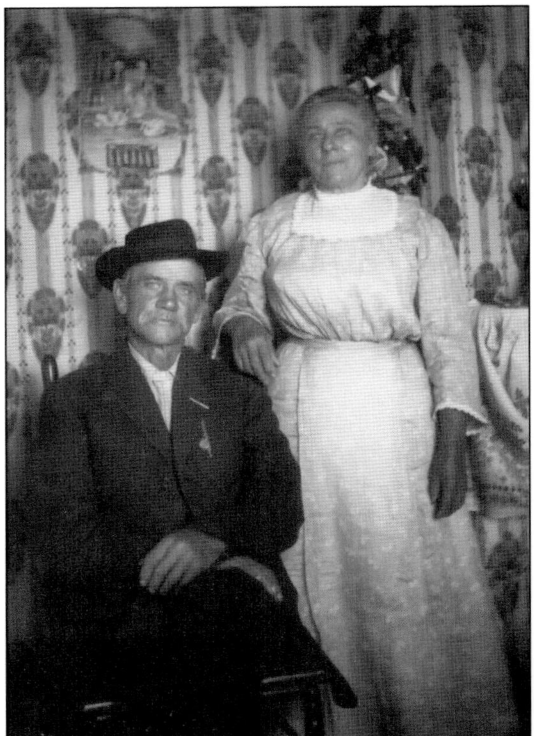

Leander and Caroline Cramer Wagner. In 1903, the Stoney Ridge one-room school was moved from the southeast corner of South Turner and Fairview Roads to the northwest corner of South Turner and New Roads. In 1916, the Wagners purchased the schoolhouse for $35 for their home. Their grandson Stewart Wagner served as the superintendent of Austintown Local Schools from 1971 to 1974. (Courtesy Lois Ripple Peterson.)

Three

Austintown Center

It is hard to imagine the bustling intersection of Mahoning Avenue and Canfield-Niles Road, known as Austintown Center, as taking a back seat to any area. Yet historically, Austintown Center was less developed than West Austintown. In 1895, it had only 391 residents. The southeast corner of Austintown Center was home to the town hall, built sometime before 1874, the primary voting center for Austintown as well as headquarters for the trustees and justice of the peace. The center one-room schoolhouse, built in the 1850s, was located an eighth of a mile east of the southeast corner on Mahoning Avenue, and was sometimes called "Skunk's Misery School" because of the many skunks trapped in that area. Beyond the Center School were Smith's ice pond and icehouse. Eli Corll located his hotel and tavern, the Meander House Hotel, on the northeast corner. By 1880, Alvin Anderson ran this tavern. In 1881, Eli Creps, undertaker and furniture dealer, lived on the northwest corner. Austintown's first post office, called Austin Post Office, opened in Austintown Center in 1816 with Theophilus Cotton as postmaster. In 1817, the post office's name changed to Orange. Orange postmasters included Thomas Cotton, Cornelius Thompson, Henry Snyder, Joseph McCaughtry, Zachariah Strock, David Corll, and John Campbell. In 1872, at the request of then postmaster John Fitch, the post office's name changed to Austintown. The Austintown Center post office closed in 1917. Austintown Center was also home to one of Austintown's three airports. The Austintown Airport, owned by the Wheeler family, was on the east side of South Canfield-Niles Road near Willow Crest Drive. DuRell or Jones' Airfield was on South Raccoon Road near Yorkshire Boulevard. Andrews Field was on the west side of Meridian Road in the Wickliffe area.

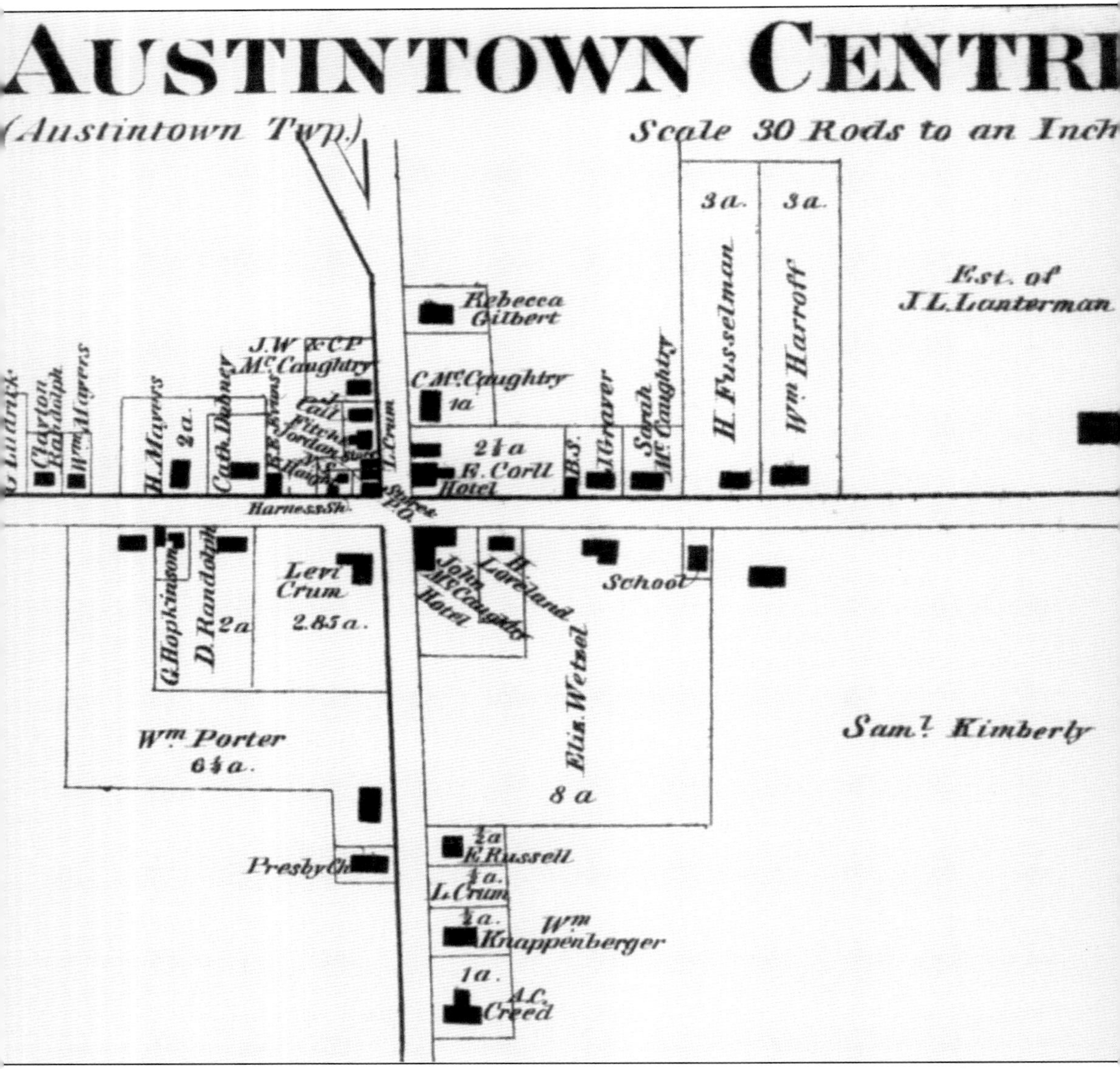

AUSTINTOWN CENTER, 1874. Mahoning Avenue runs from left to right across the center. Canfield-Niles Road runs from top to bottom. Fitch's general store was on North Canfield-Niles Road four buildings from the center. John McCaughtry's Indian Queen Hotel on the southeast corner of the center, later called Imperial Hotel, was the stagecoach relay station between Salem and Warren. The town water pump was behind the hotel. Levi Crum's store was on the southwest corner of the center. Eli Corll's Meander House hotel and saloon was on the northeast corner. Nelson Haight's harness shop was on Mahoning Avenue west of the center; Haight was postmaster from 1894 to 1897. The Presbyterian church located on Canfield-Niles Road is now called Austintown Community Church. (Courtesy AHS.)

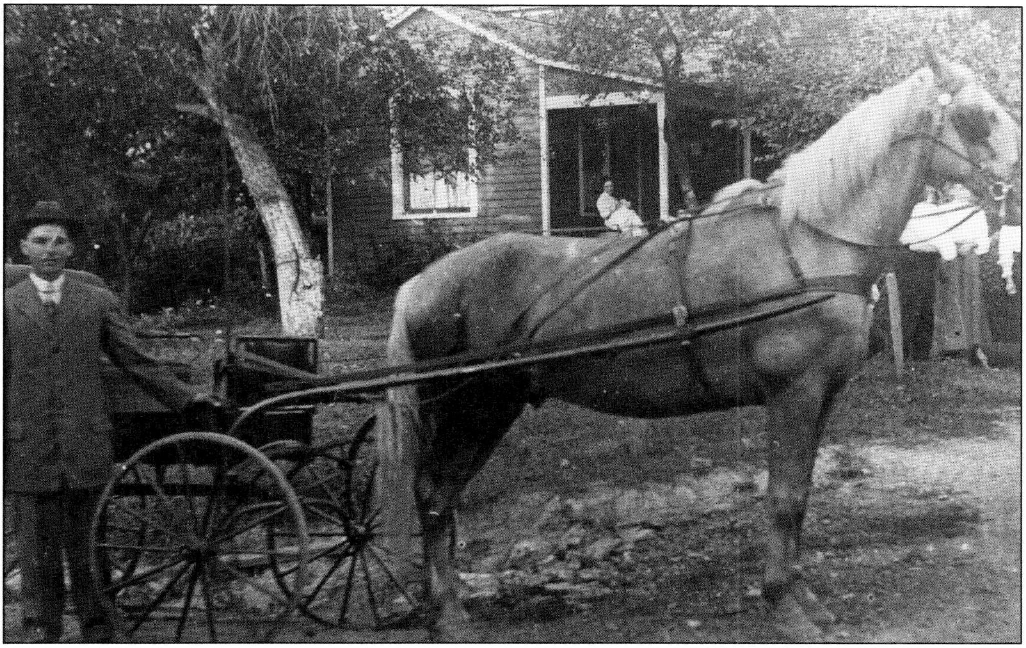

Charles V. Baker. Charles V. Baker stands in front of his home near Austintown Center on the east side of North Canfield-Niles Road, which was a dirt road at the time. Baker's wife, Mary "Jennie" Baker, is on the front porch feeding their child who is presumed to be Merrill, born about 1892. (Courtesy AHS.)

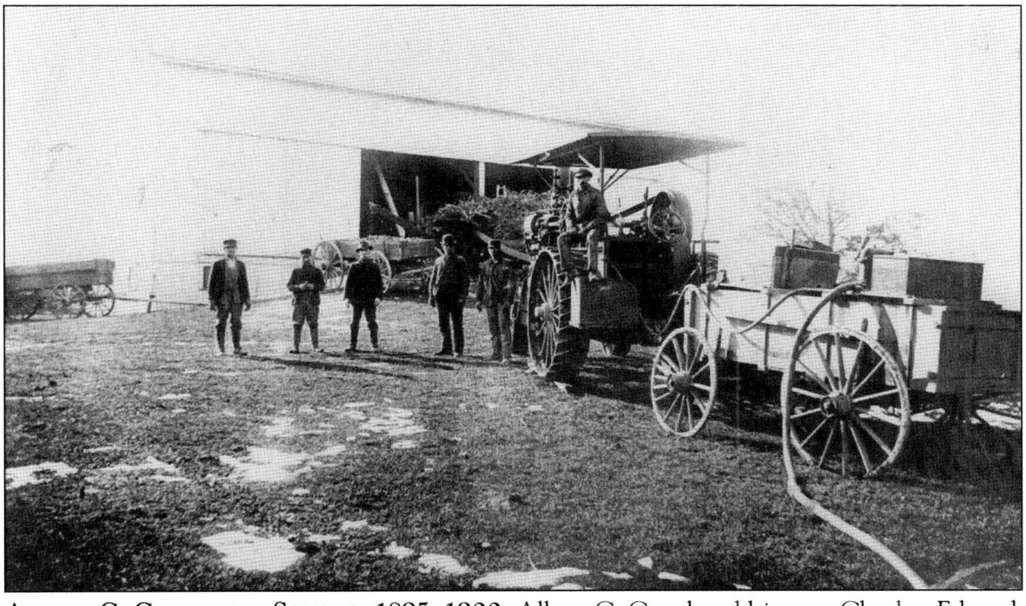

Albert C. Creed and Sons, c. 1895–1900. Albert C. Creed and his sons Charles, Edward, and Albert pose with their steam-powered corn shredder on William and Rachel May's dairy farm. The Creed and May farms were on the east side of South Canfield-Niles Road near Austintown Center. In 1900, 354 of the 406 families (87 percent) in Austintown were farmers. (Courtesy AHS.)

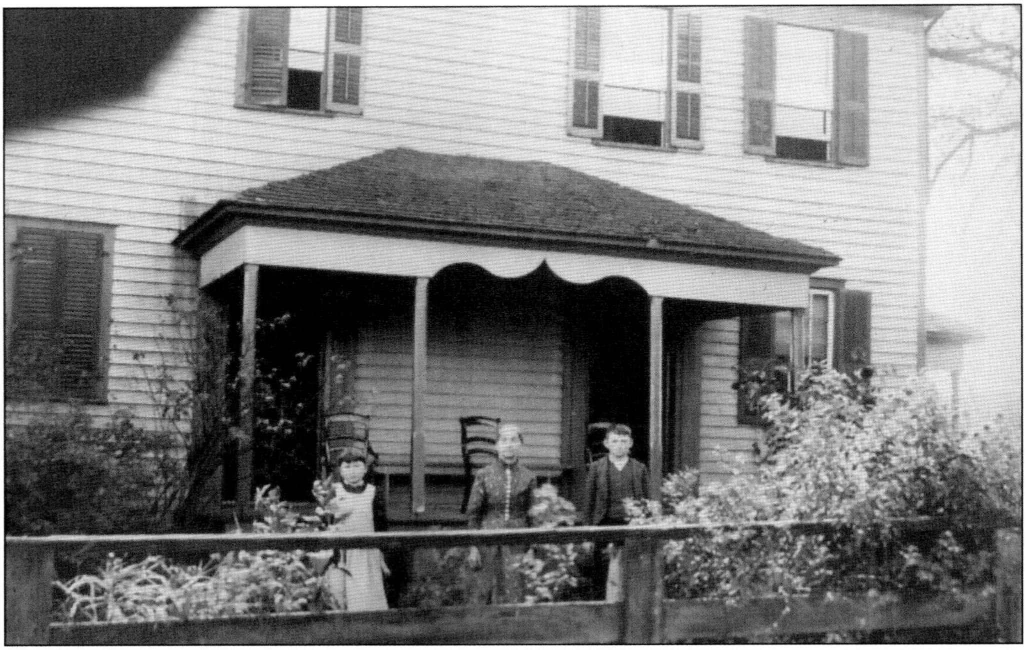

ELIZABETH CARNS WETZEL, C. 1887. Elizabeth Wetzel (born 1825), her granddaughter Maude Van Wye Mehlo (born 1881 and died 1956), and an unidentified boy stand in front of their home. Wetzel and her husband Jacob operated a hotel and tavern on the northeast corner of Mahoning Avenue and Canfield-Niles Road in the 1860s. (Courtesy Jean Ong.)

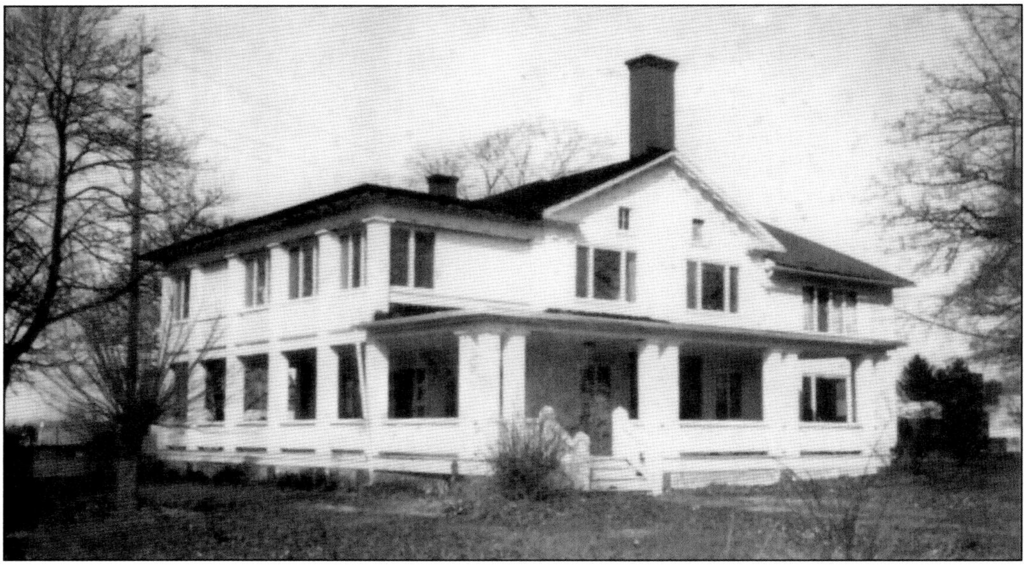

JOHN H. FITCH SUMMER HOME. The three-story, 4,500-square-foot Fitch summer home was at Ohltown and North Canfield-Niles Roads. Fitch's business holdings included Fitch Grocery Store, Fitch Coffee Company, Youngstown Ice Company, and Ohio Merchandise Company. Fitch married Alice Packard and had four children. Dr. Herbert Clarence and Betty Patterson Blackann purchased the house in 1957. The home was razed in 1989. (Courtesy John and Gay Lynn Bishop Blackann.)

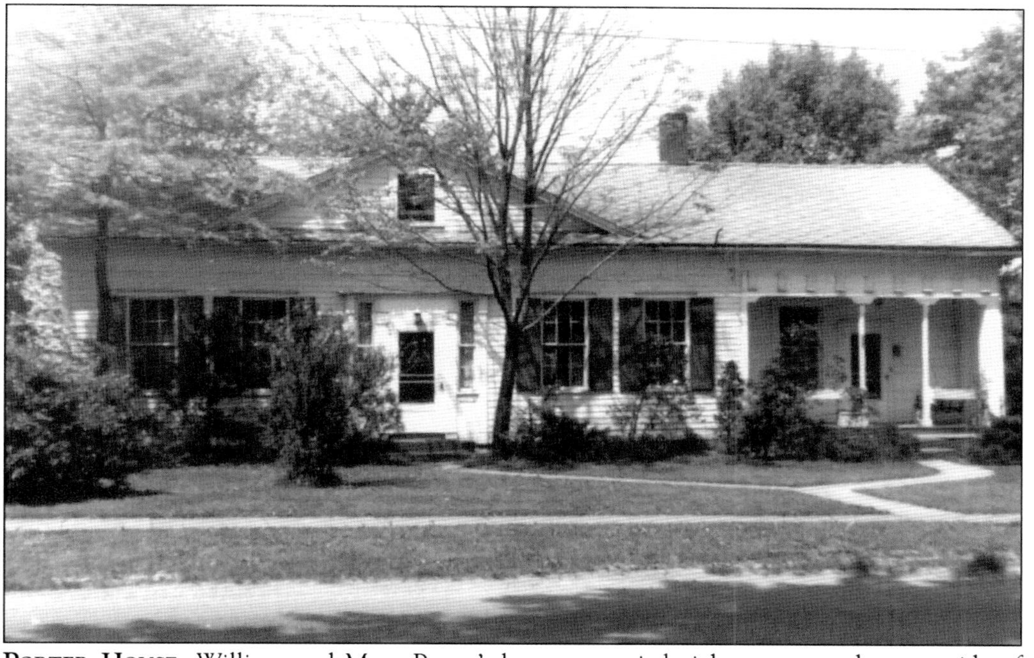

PORTER HOUSE. William and Mary Porter's house occupied eight acres on the west side of Canfield-Niles Road just south of the center. Porter sold the house, after he lost his fortune on the Meander Furnace, to Daniel and Amanda Priscilla Corll Shoff, who bought the house for $600 using the salary Daniel earned while fighting the Civil War. (Courtesy Dan and Charen Bishop Fink.)

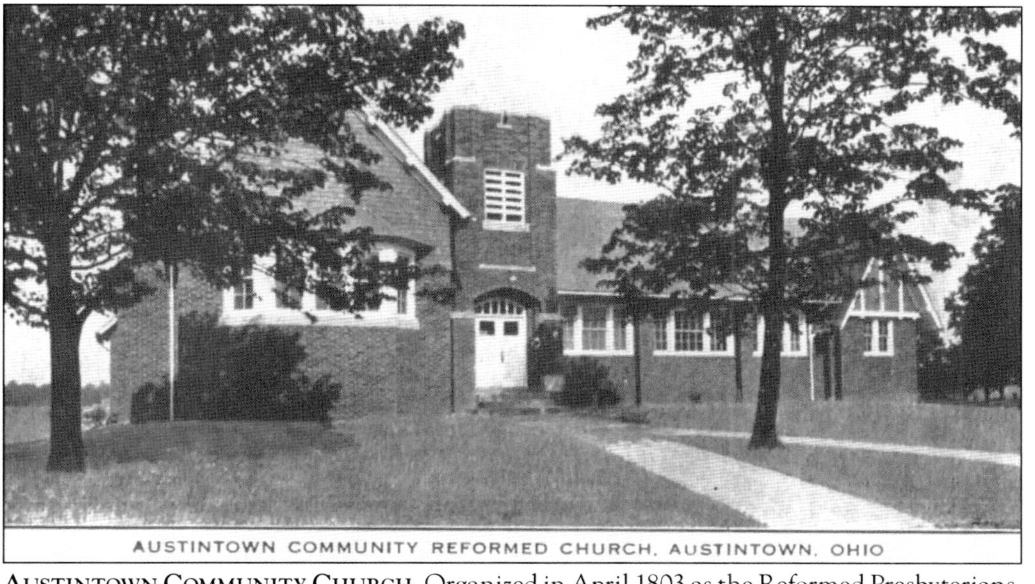

AUSTINTOWN COMMUNITY CHURCH. Organized in April 1803 as the Reformed Presbyterians, the original church was a log cabin built in 1815 on land owned by Robert Fullerton. In 1862, the church bought land at 242 South Canfield-Niles Road and built a new building. The church pictured was built in 1924. The green space behind the church is now Capital Estates. (Courtesy AHS.)

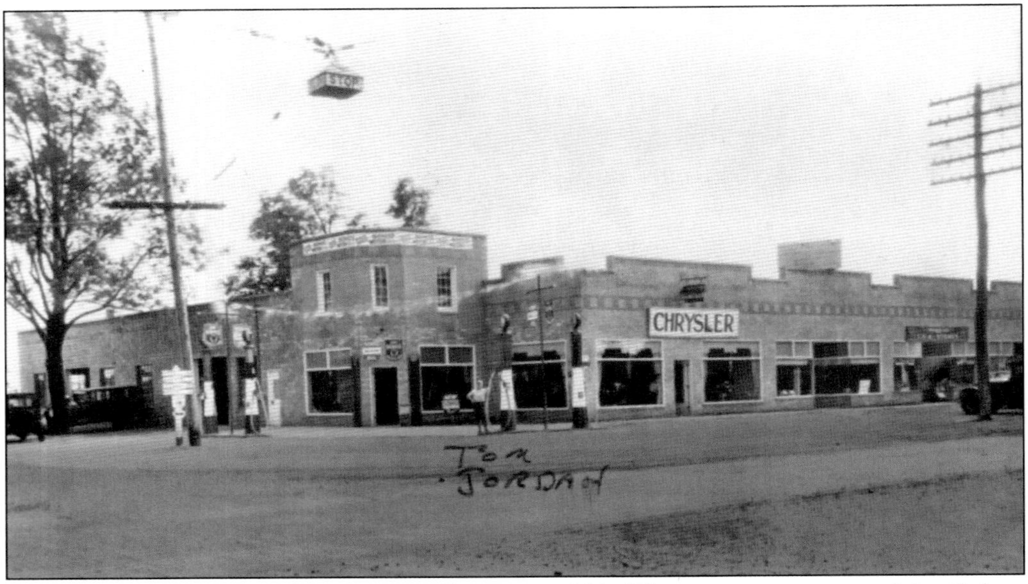

AUSTINTOWN CENTER, SOUTHWEST CORNER, 1929. This corner was owned by Robert Fullerton in 1829; by Davis Randolph, attorney and shoemaker, in 1860; and by Levi Crum in 1874. The Jordan-Akins building, pictured with Tommy Jordan, was built in 1928 by Todd Jordan and Ray Akins. It housed a Chrysler dealership, automobile repair shop, Standard Oil of Ohio station, and IGA grocery store. Notice the traffic signal. (Courtesy Advanced Marking.)

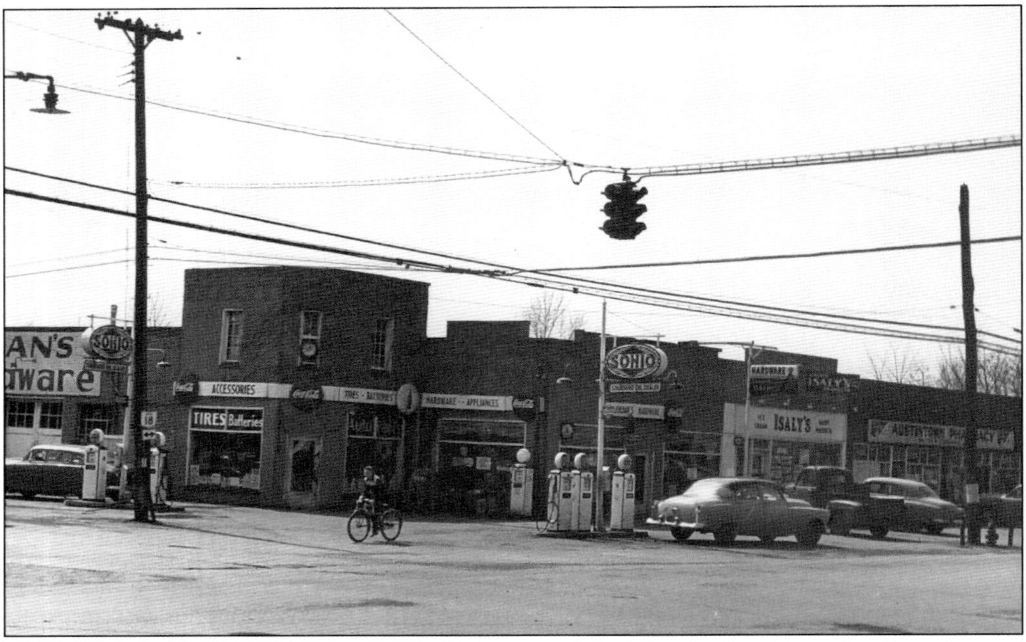

AUSTINTOWN CENTER, SOUTHWEST CORNER, 1954. The Jordan-Akins building housed Zimmerman's Rexall pharmacy, Isaly's, Jordan's Hardware, and Sohio gas station. The Harris Market, founded by Fred Harris and sons Bill and Jim, moved here from Crum and Four Mile Run Roads in 1931. During the Depression, they distributed government staples. The Harris Market later moved to South Aldrich Road and Mahoning Avenue. (Courtesy AHS.)

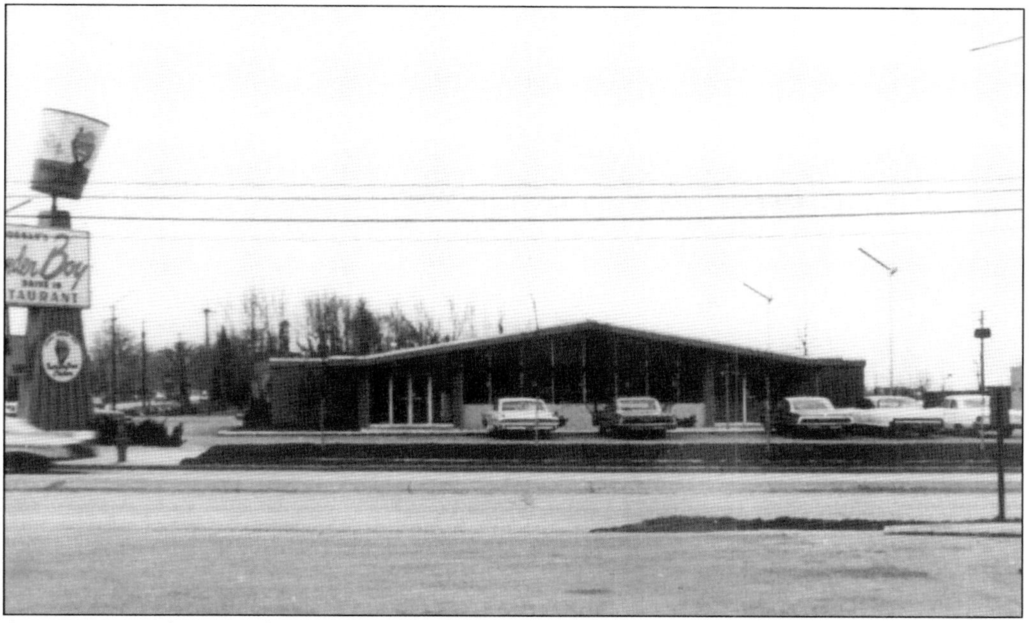

AUSTINTOWN CENTER, SOUTHWEST CORNER, 1960S. When Mahoning Avenue was widened in 1955, the gas station in front of the Jordan-Akins building closed. In the 1960s, the Jordan-Akins building was razed and replaced by Morgan's Wonder Boy Restaurant, which offered drive-in curbside service for in-the-car dining. (Courtesy Advanced Marking.)

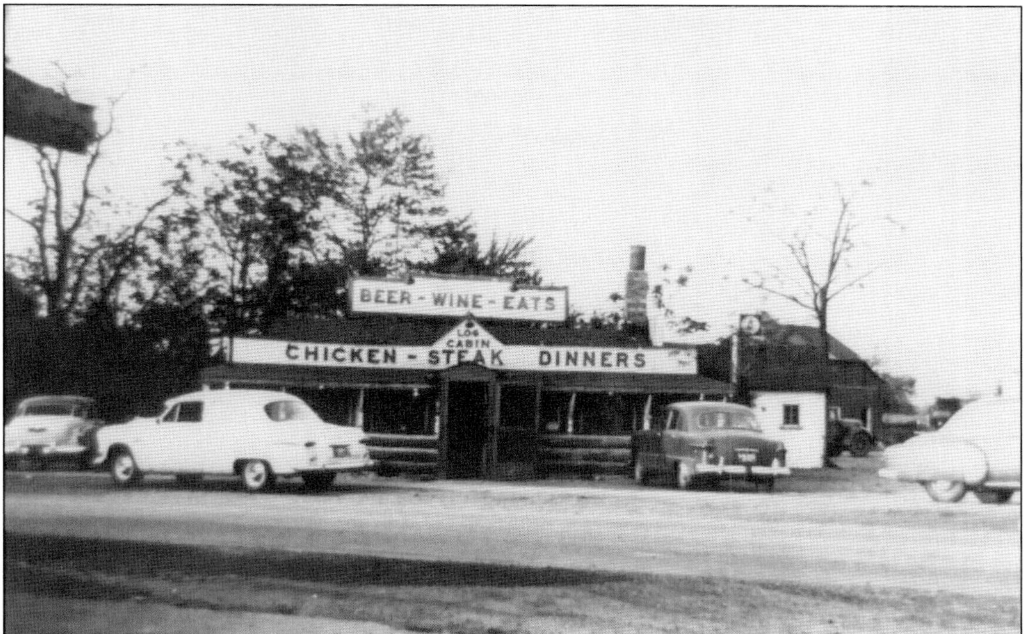

LOG CABIN RESTAURANT, 1950S. Located on the northwest corner of Austintown Center, the Log Cabin Restaurant opened about 1937. Owned by Peter Schrum and later by Shorty Parker, it was renowned for its steak dinners. The restaurant got its name from the exterior logs. (Courtesy Advanced Marking.)

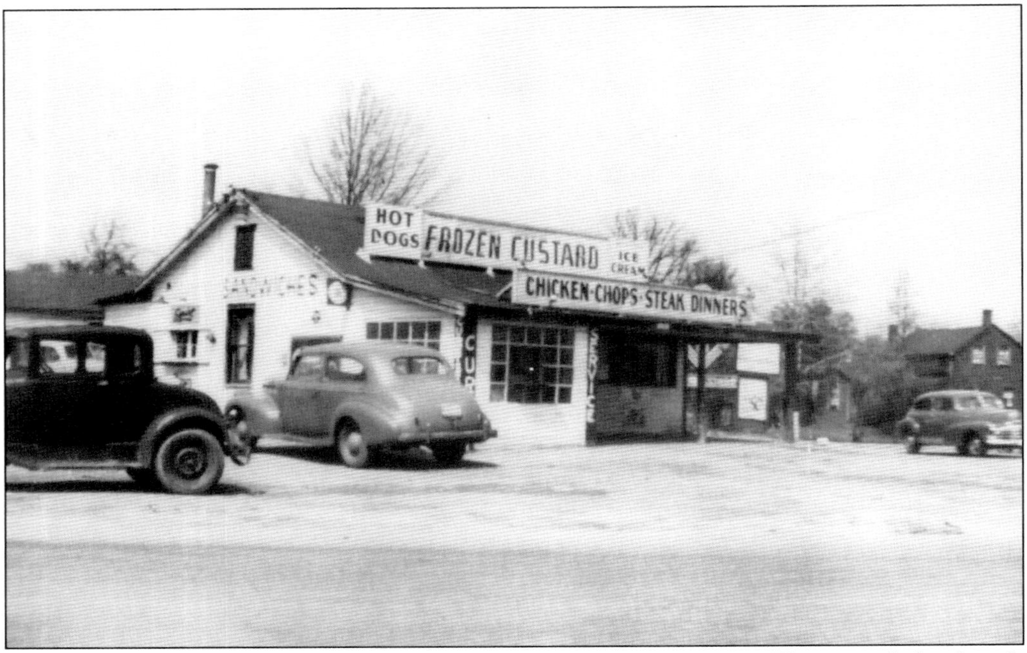

AUSTINTOWN CENTER, NORTHWEST CORNER, 1940S AND 1954. The site of the Joseph McCaughtery store in 1860, the northwest corner housed a fruit stand in the 1920s and the restaurant pictured in the 1940s. The 1954 photograph, taken by George Whetson, shows the Austintown Drive-Inn Restaurant, 5502 Mahoning Avenue. The cars are driving on the two-lane North Canfield-Niles Road. In 1954, Standard Oil of Ohio razed the restaurant and house and built a Sohio station there to capitalize on the turnpike traffic. (Courtesy AHS.)

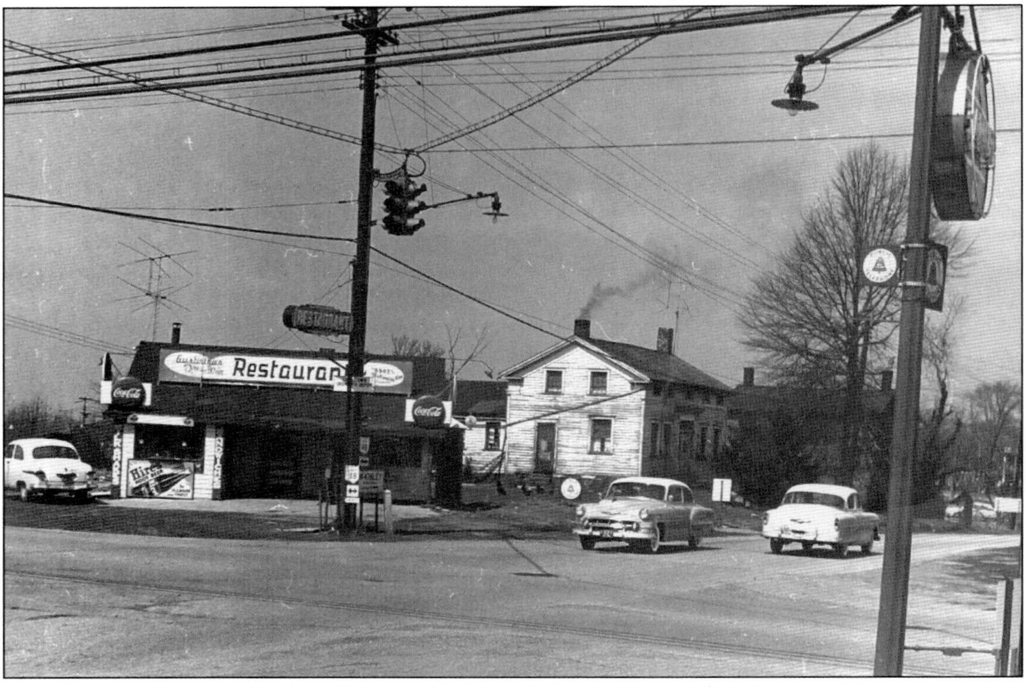

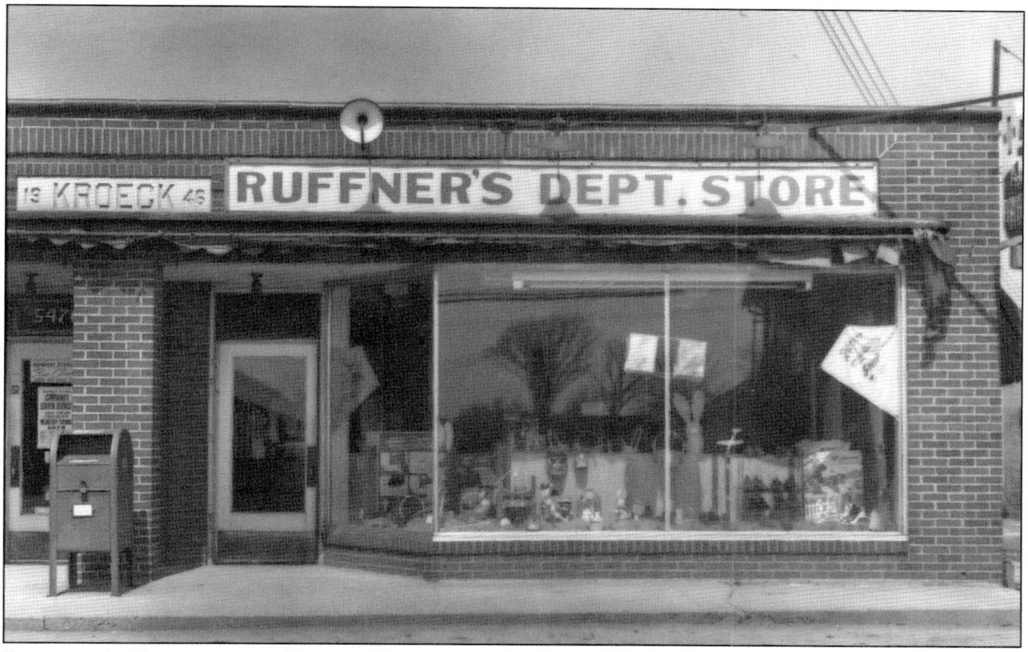

RUFFNER'S DEPARTMENT STORE, EASTER 1954. Owned by Jack Ruffner, the store was located in the Kroeck building constructed in 1946 east of Austintown Center on the north side of Mahoning Avenue. The Kroeck building also housed a pharmacy. The Kroeck building still stands in 2007. (Courtesy AHS.)

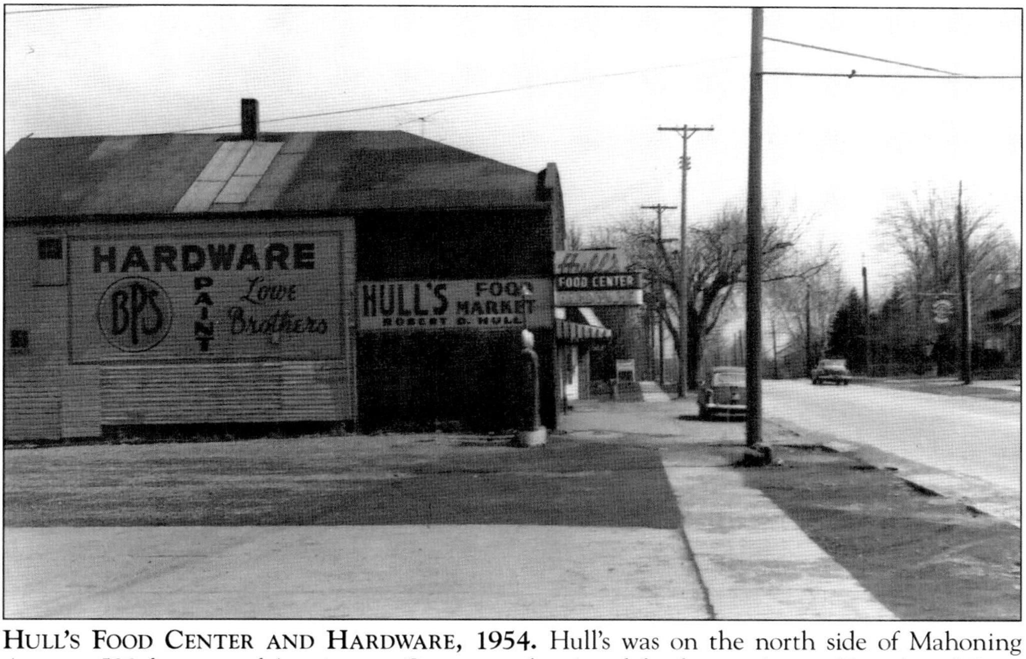

HULL'S FOOD CENTER AND HARDWARE, 1954. Hull's was on the north side of Mahoning Avenue, 500 feet east of Austintown Center on the site of the former August Kroeck and Sons General Store, which opened in 1880. Kroeck and his sons Andrew, Charles, and Lewis, also owned a 22-room hotel. Kroeck Avenue is named after August Kroeck. (Courtesy AHS.)

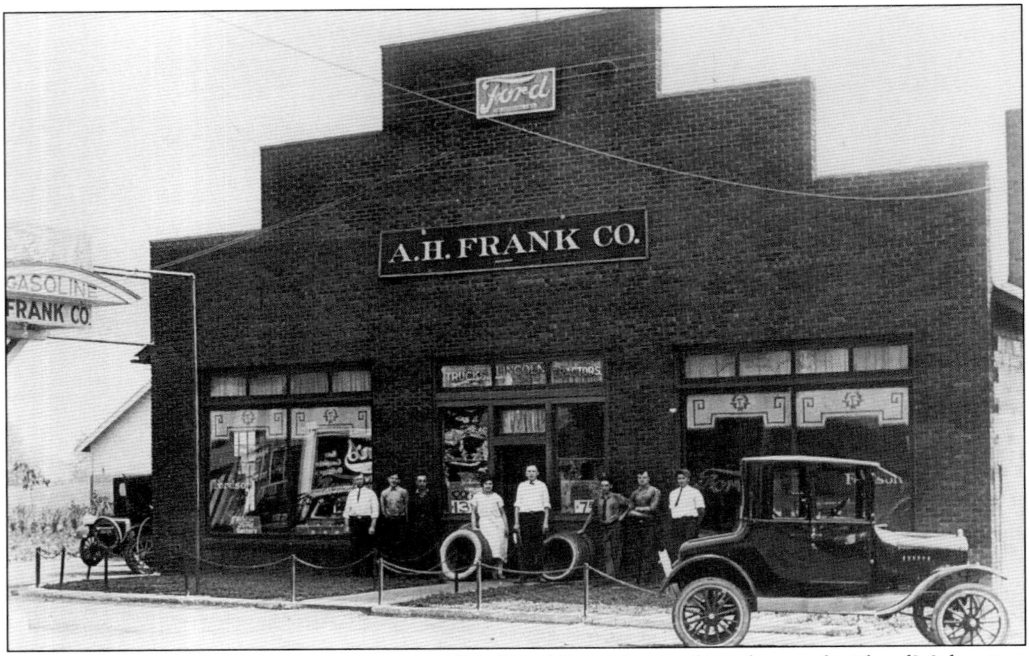

Abe H. Frank's Ford Dealership, c. 1920. Frank's was located on the south side of Mahoning Avenue (4021) east of Canfield-Niles Road. From left to right are Harry Knight, Pete Schisler, Paul Parshall, Dorothy Frank Carr (Abe's sister), Abe Frank, Bert Couche, Howard Detchon, Todd Jordan. Frank also sold tractors, Lincoln cars, and gasoline. (Courtesy AHS.)

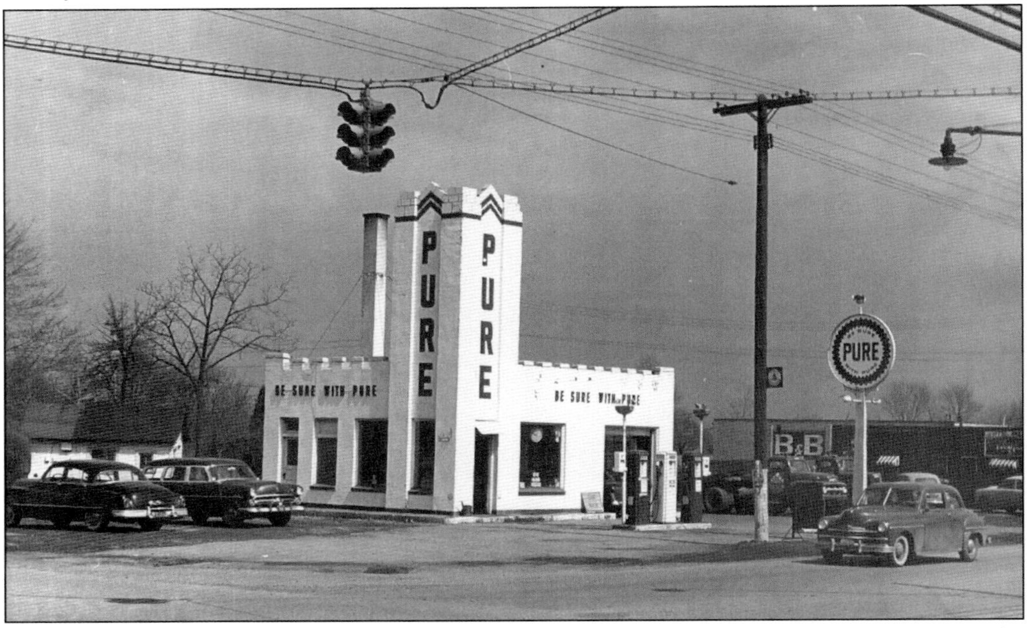

Austintown Center, Northeast Corner, 1954. George Whetson's photograph shows the Pure gas station located on the northeast corner of Austintown Center. Like many gas stations during this era, the Pure station offered garage, repair, and towing services. The car pictured is driving on Mahoning Avenue. (Courtesy AHS.)

Four

Ohltown and the Mahoning Valley Sanitary District

Ohltown, sometimes called Ohl's Town, Ohlton, or Ohltown Station, was founded in 1816 by Michael Ohl. Part of Ohltown was in Weathersfield Township, but an 1874 map clearly shows some of the 30 acres encompassing Ohltown were in Austintown Township between North Turner and Ohltown Roads. Michael Ohl was born in Pennsylvania in 1784. In 1815, Ohl and his wife, Eve Lasta Ohl, built one of the first homes in the Meander area for their family of 15 children. About 1820, the stagecoach route from Cleveland to the Ohio River ran through Ohltown. Ohl opened a store in his house and sold goods to the stagecoach passengers and later built an inn. Passengers consumed whiskey produced in Ohl's distillery. The records for liquor production have not been located, but Simon Hood, who made the kegs for the liquor, employed 29 people at his cooper's shop. The stagecoach delivered mail. A post office, unofficially called Meander Post Office, was established on Ohltown Road just north of I-80, with Michael Ohl as postmaster. From 1841 to 1882, the post office was named Ohl's Town. In 1882, it was renamed Ohltown; it closed in 1902. By 1880, the town had 400 residents, Moore's general store, Rumsey's general store, three large blocks containing 30 houses, three churches, and a cemetery. Michael Ohl's granddaughter Jessie Ohl, born in Ohltown in 1852, was the first wife of attorney Clarence Darrow. Col. William Christy, born in Ohltown in 1841, founded and became president of Valley Bank of Phoenix, Arizona. Dr. Robert Murray, born in Ohltown in 1845, became acting assistant surgeon of the U.S. Navy and an expert on yellow fever.

Ohltown became a ghost town with the creation of Meander Reservoir in 1929. Despite lawsuits from residents, the Mahoning Valley Sanitary District (MVSD) appropriated most of the town. The Strock Stone House, one of the few homes left standing in the Meander basin, housed the MVSD chief engineer.

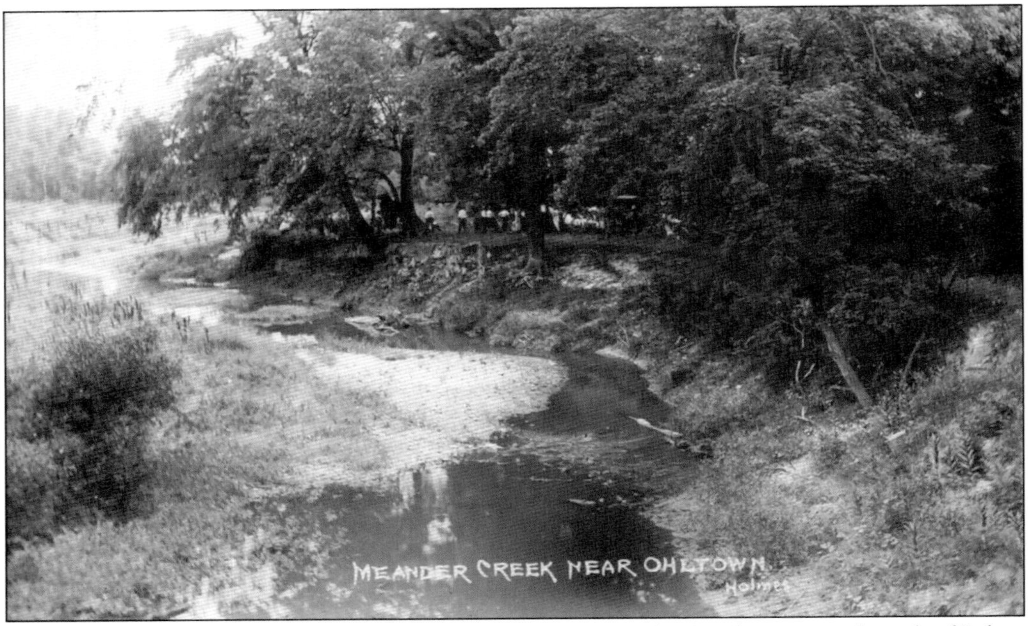

MEANDER CREEK, NEAR OHLTOWN. The 11-mile-long Meander Creek originated north of Salem and meandered through western Mahoning County. Under the shade trees, Ohltown residents are picnicking. Further downstream, a 132-foot-long dam on the Meander Creek powered a lumber and gristmill originally built in 1815 by Michael Ohl. In 1880, Tom and William Flick operated the mill. (Courtesy Walt and Genevieve Shively.)

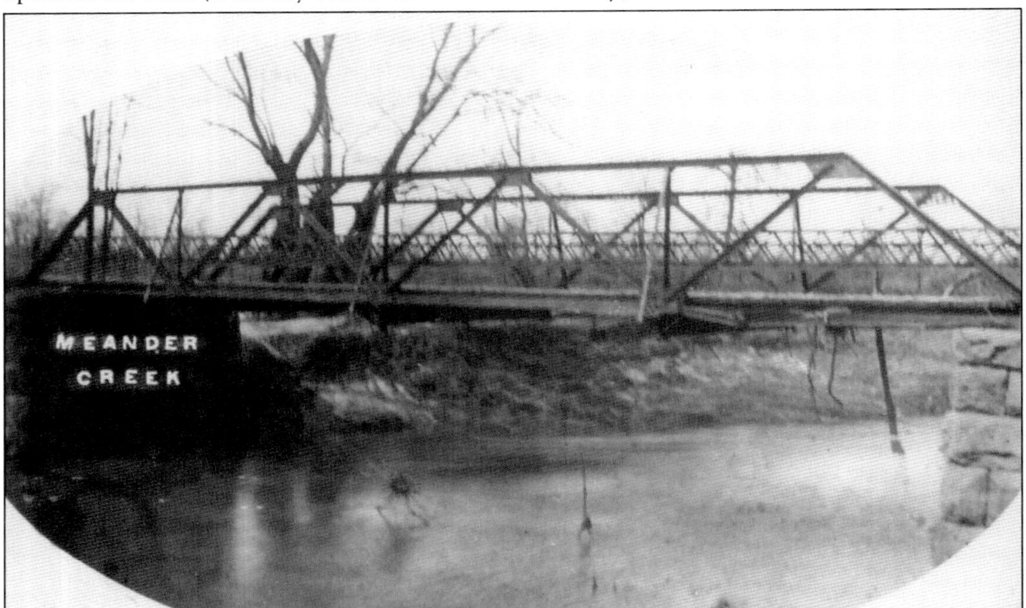

MEANDER CREEK BRIDGE, 1916. This iron bridge in Ohltown was near the original wooden bridge constructed by Michael Ohl in 1820. Ohl charged stagecoaches traveling from Cleveland to Wellsville a nickel to use his bridge. After Meander Creek flooded in 1878, this iron span replaced the wooden bridge. (Courtesy Walt and Genevieve Shively.)

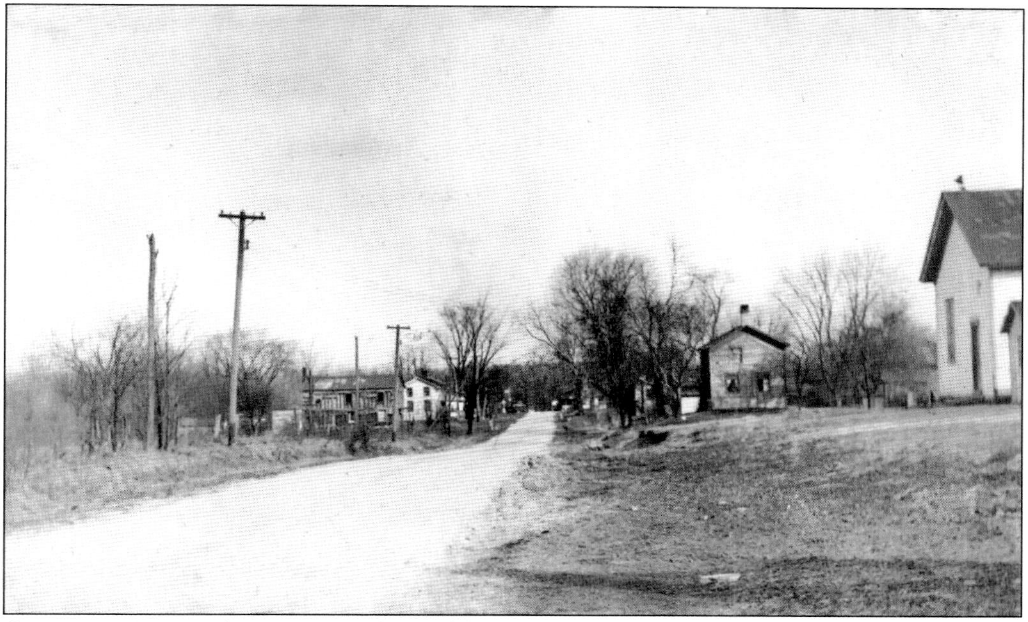

OHLTOWN ROAD. These pictures show Ohltown Road prior to the construction of the MVSD. The first scene, showing Ohltown Road north of the current County Line Road, is now covered by Meander Reservoir. The second picture is taken from the same spot, looking southward. Alva Cole's home (on the left side) and the homes of Mary Rose, Abe Coble, Phillip Smith, Addie Bingham, Simon and E. G. Hood, Charles Hudson, and Hatty Clemens were moved on rollers to North Turner, Webb, or south on Ohltown Roads in 1929. Rose's store and the homes of Joseph Phillips, John Dunlap, Peter Rummell, Abraham Mathews, Fred Evans, Ben Sutton, Anna Hudson, Mike Chuey, Mike Kerchner, and others were razed. (Courtesy Walt and Genevieve Shively.)

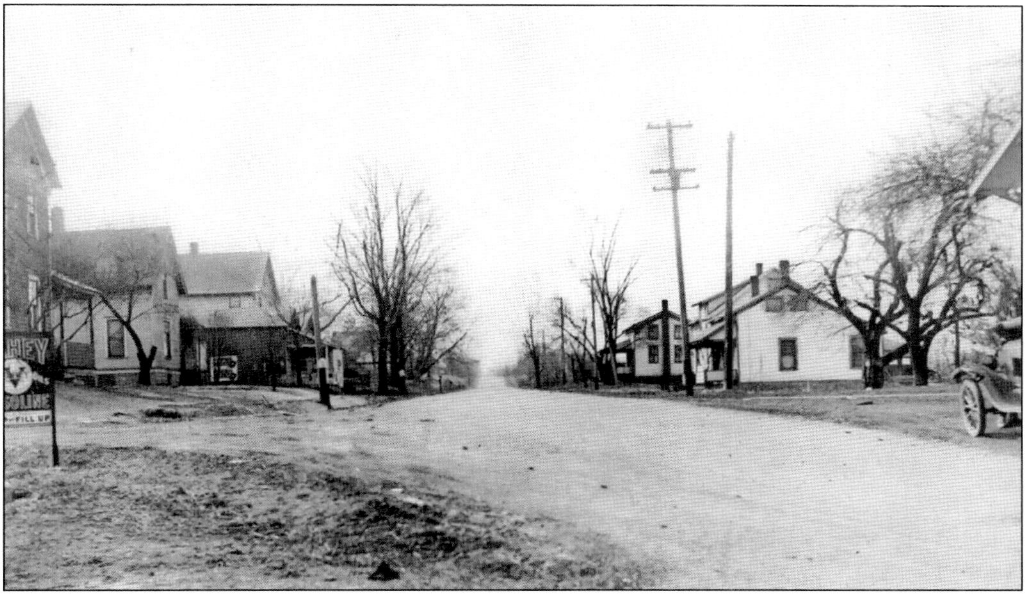

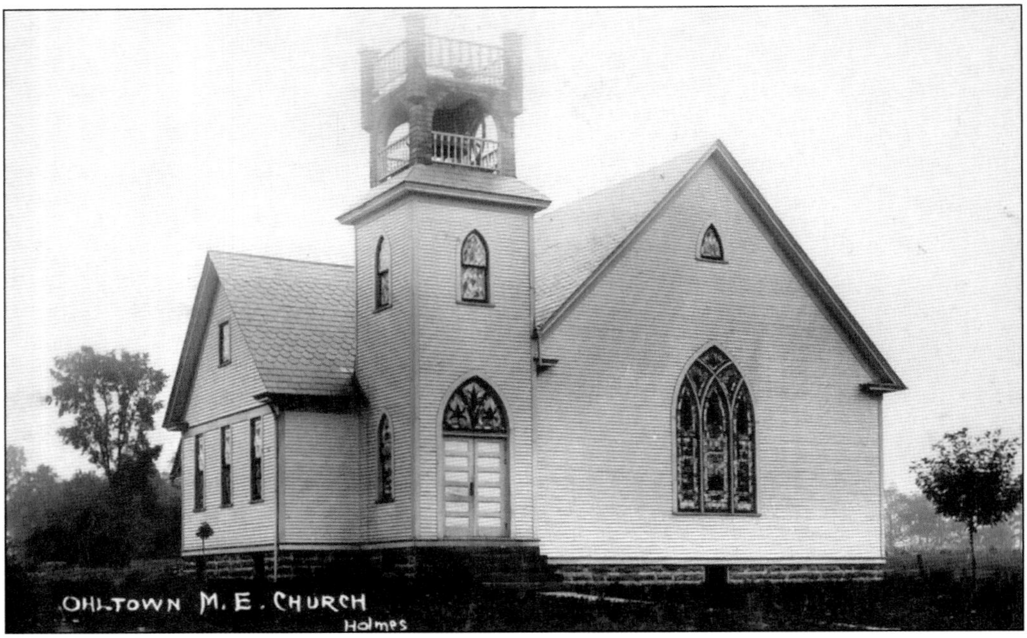

Ohltown United Methodist Church. This church, at the intersection of Ohltown and County Line Roads, was founded in 1838 as the Ohltown Methodist Episcopal Church by 15 members including Joseph Turner. The church first met in Michael Ohl's gristmill. This church was built in 1904 using wood that church members harvested from the church site and planed at Hood's lumber mill in Ohltown. The church caught fire in August 1953, but the bell tower, in the upper right-hand corner, was not destroyed. Members of the Ladies Aid Society examine the damage to the church. The church was rebuilt. (Courtesy Walt and Genevieve Shively.)

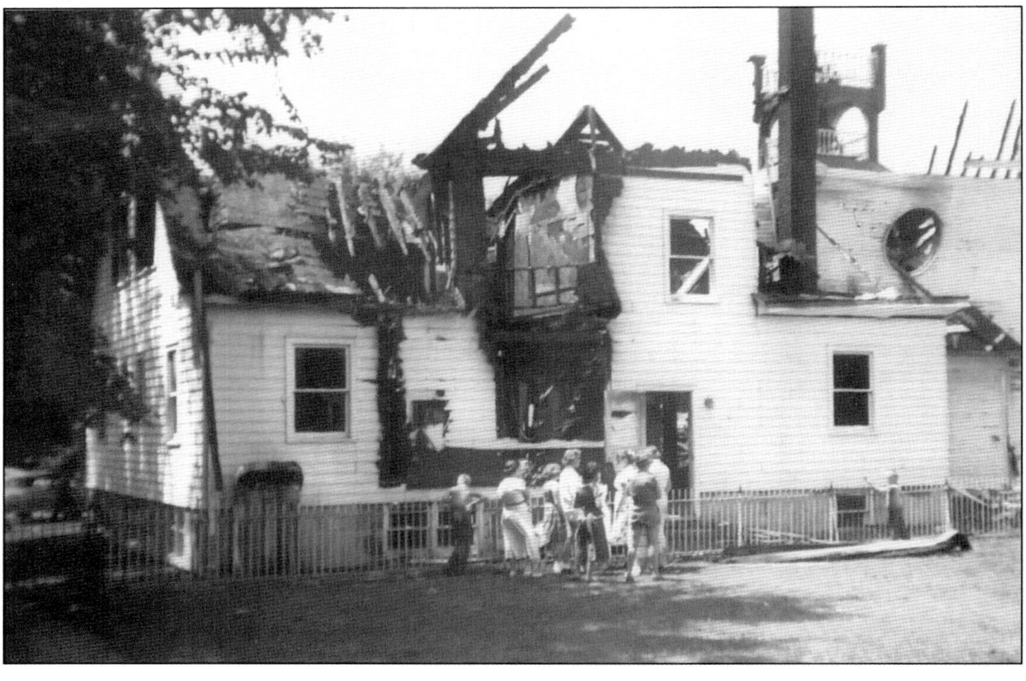

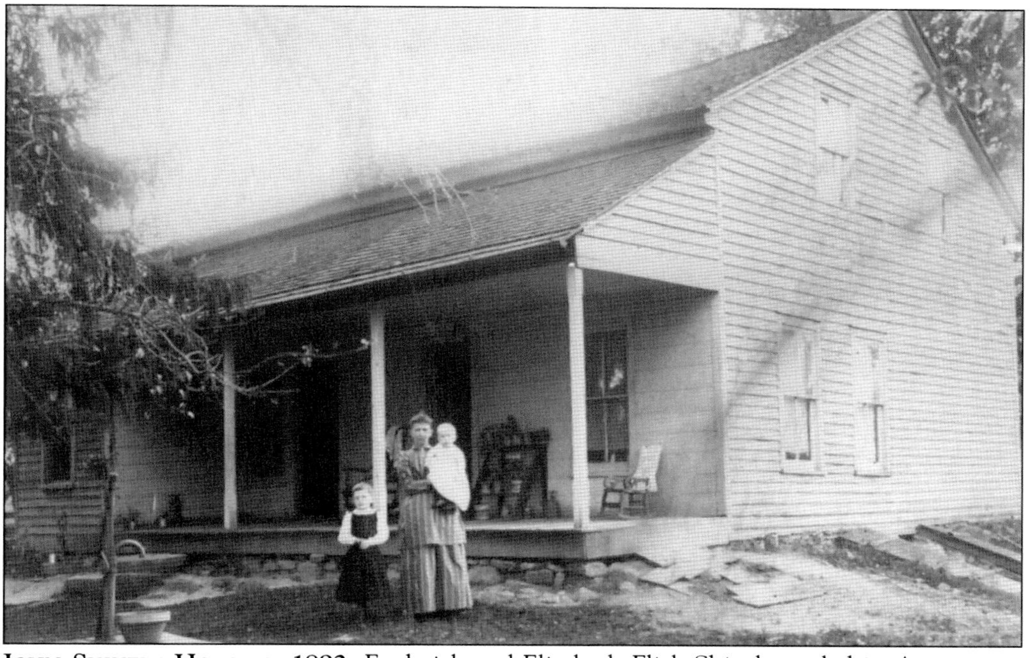

JOHN SHIVELY HOME, C. 1892. Frederick and Elizabeth Flick Shively settled in Austintown in 1812 or 1813. Elizabeth Wolfcale Shively (1851–1895) holds her son Wright (1891–1975) and stands with her daughter Emily Maria Shively Thomas (1887–1986). The house, located on the west side of Ohltown Road, anchored the 90-acre John Shively farm. (Courtesy Walt and Genevieve Shively.)

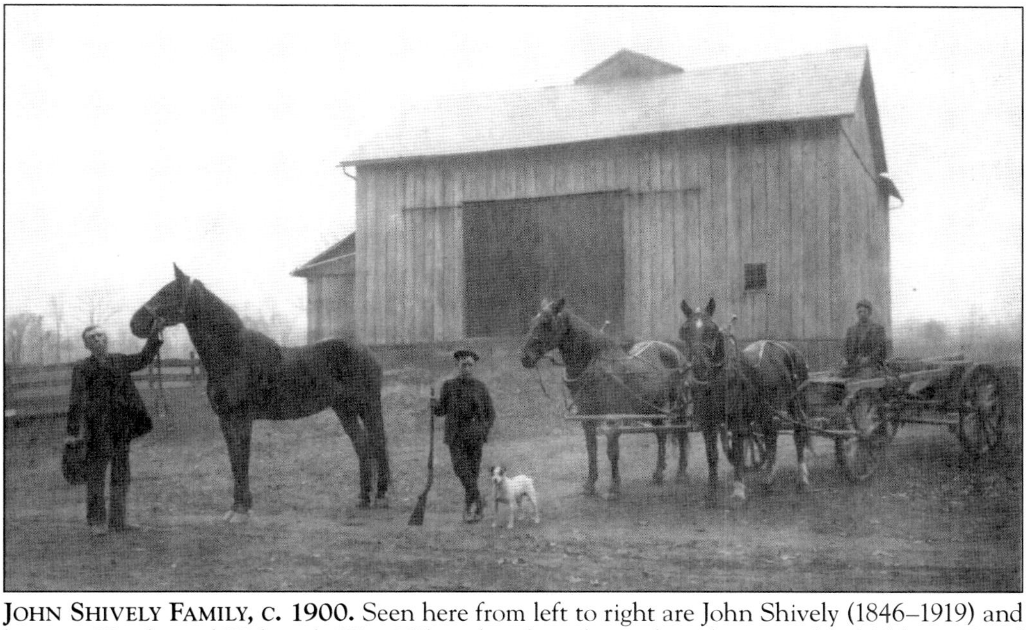

JOHN SHIVELY FAMILY, C. 1900. Seen here from left to right are John Shively (1846–1919) and his sons Wright and Walton (1875–1959) at their barn located on the east side of Ohltown Road where the Humility House of Mary is now located. Shively's Corners, at the intersection of Silica and Ohltown Roads, was named after John Shively. (Courtesy Walt and Genevieve Shively.)

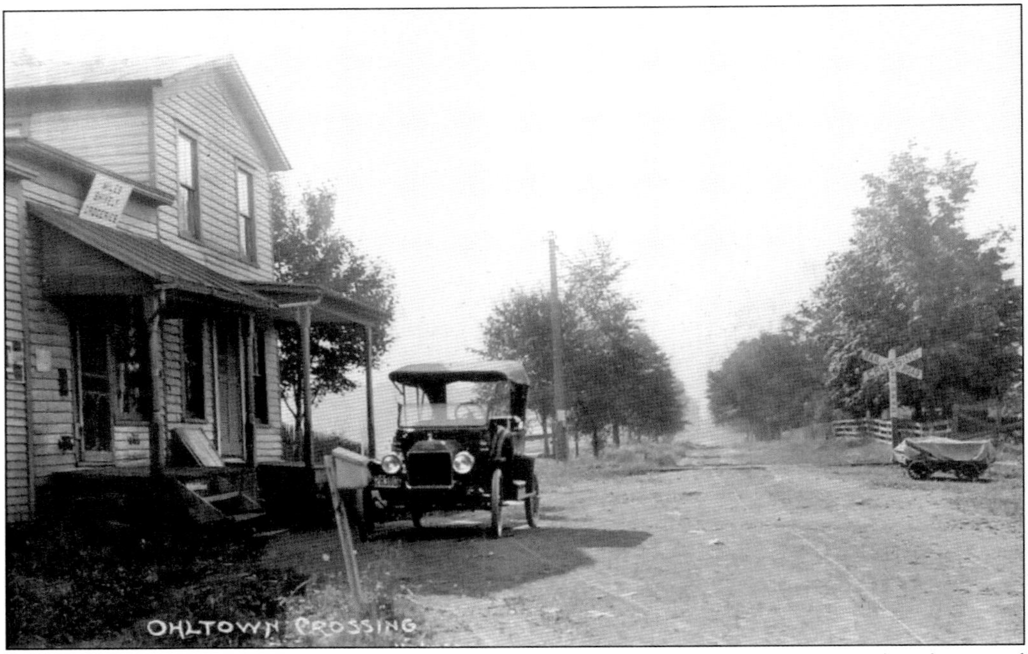

MILES SHIVELY STORE AT OHLTOWN CROSSING. The Niles-New Lisbon Railroad crossed Ohltown Road north of Silica Road. The Miles Shively grocery store was located next to the railroad tracks on the other side of the crossing on Ohltown Road. Sarah Miles Shively operated the store. The store occupied the left side of the building. The Shively family lived on the right. R. Walton Shively, first principal of Lloyd Elementary School, was born here. Cars, like the one parked in front of the store, were rare sights. These pictures were taken by Mr. Holmes and sold as postcards in the Miles Shively store. Mr. Hamlin bought the store in 1930. (Courtesy Walt and Genevieve Shively.)

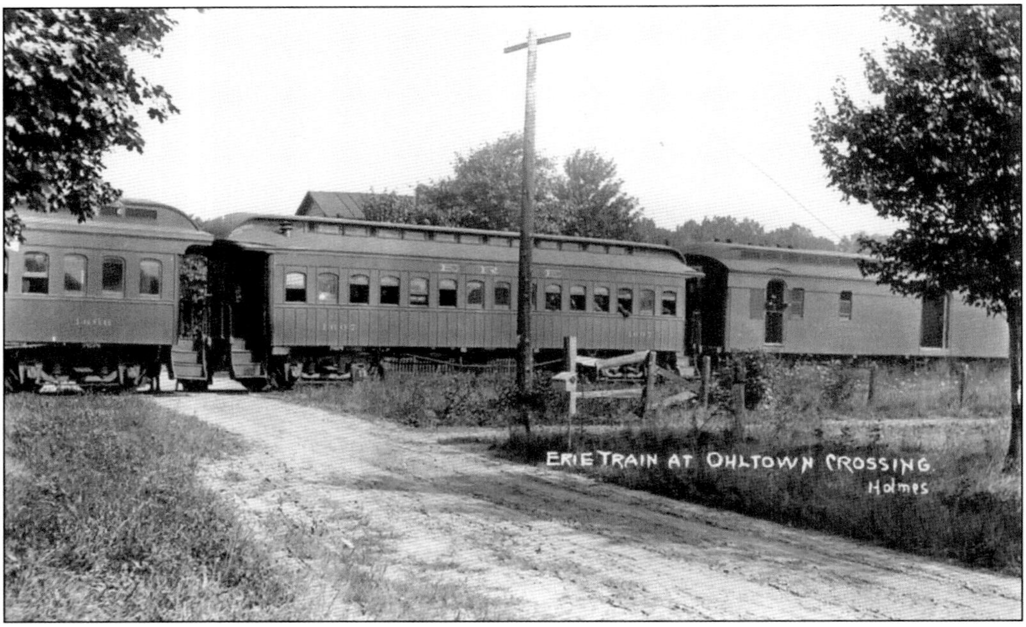

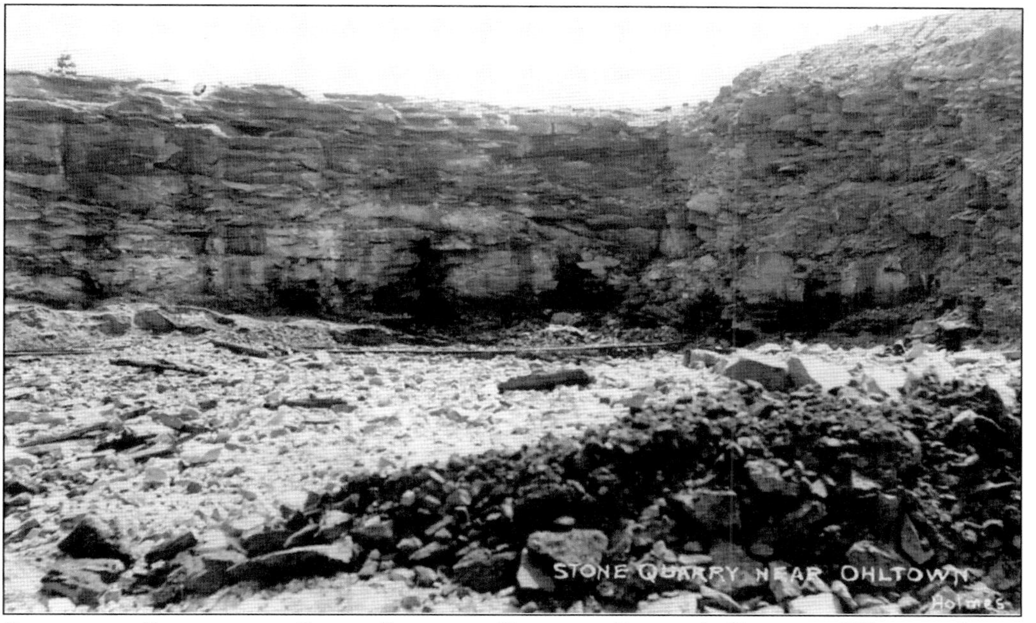

SANDSTONE QUARRY AND STONE CRUSHING PLANT IN SHIVELY'S CORNERS. White sandstone from beds 43 feet thick was mined from the Silica Sand Quarry on the southeast corner of Ohltown and Silica Roads. In 1910, the mine employed George Anderson, manager; Charles Creed, engineer; and miners Henry Witzen, Charles Bean, Thomas Baker, Edward Stuhldreker, and George Sutton. Mule-drawn wagons transported the sandstone to the stone-crushing plant, opened in 1891, on the southwest corner. The resulting white sand or silica was sent to the Fostoria Glass Company in Niles. The GE Company bought Fostoria in 1911 and made lightbulbs with the sand. Eighteen Hungarian miners lived in George and Julia Vass's boardinghouse, the former stagecoach stop, on Ohltown Road. (Courtesy Walt and Genevieve Shively and Bob Bishop.)

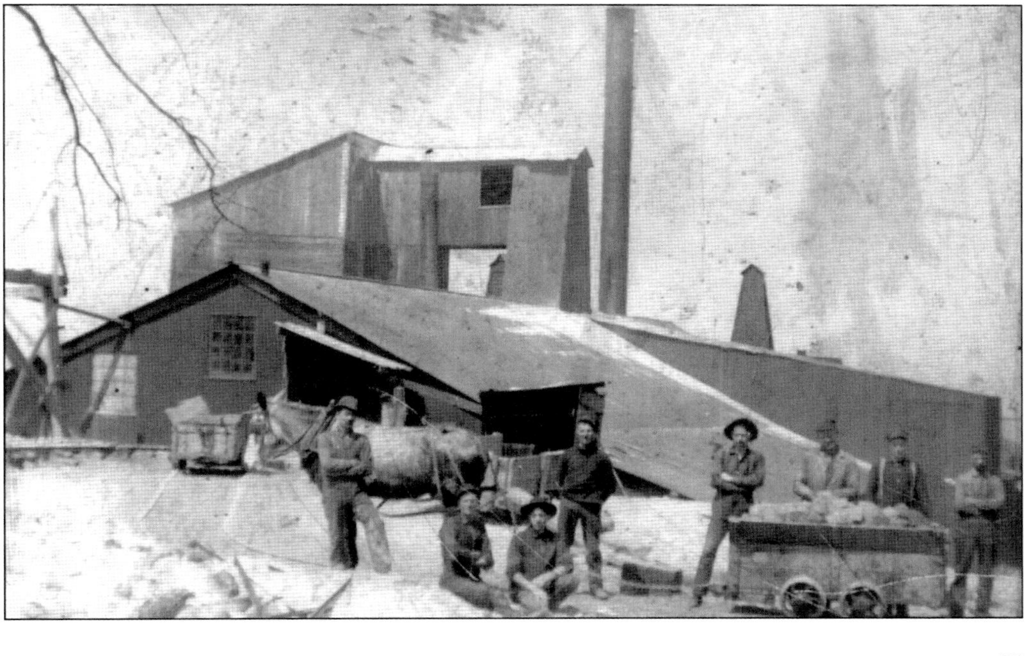

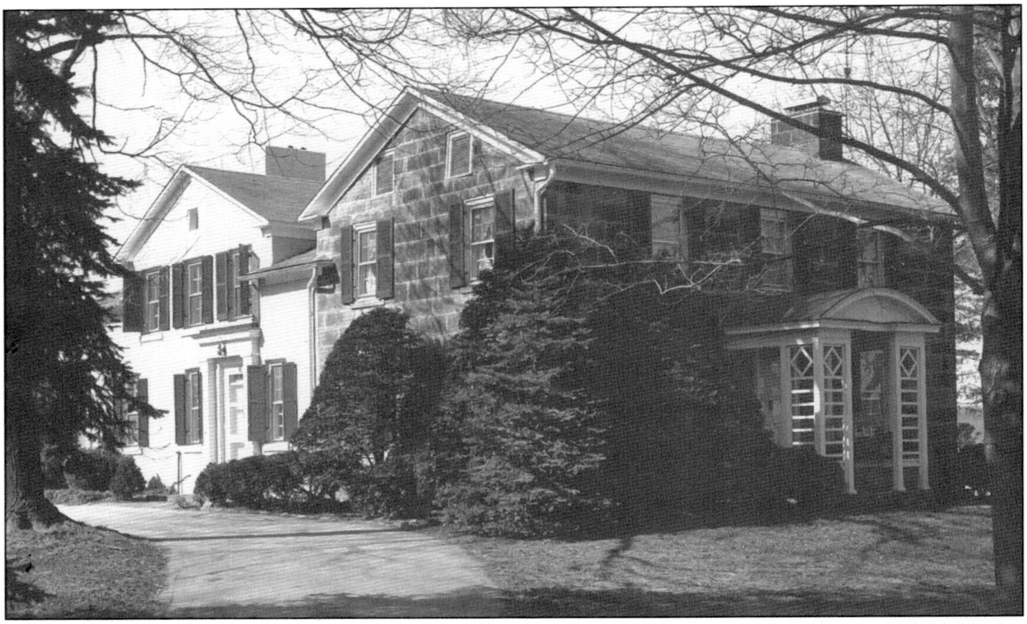

STROCK STONE HOUSE. In 1829, John Jordan bought 87 acres from George Wadsworth for $310.89. In 1830, Jordan sold it to William and Lydia Crum Strock. They hired William McClure, stone mason, to cut limestone blocks as large as 750 pounds from a South Turner quarry. Completed in 1831, the stone house had a large downstairs room with fireplace, two upstairs bedrooms, and a basement. Francis Henry bought the house in 1851 and sold it to David Anderson in 1862. In 1921, David's son Judge William Anderson added onto the house. Beginning in 1929, the MVSD chief engineer lived there. In 1992, the MVSD leased the house to Austintown Township. The Austintown Park Department maintains the exterior; the AHS furnishes and maintains the interior. It became a national historic landmark in 1976. (Above, courtesy J. P. Wilcox; below, courtesy Joyce Pogany.)

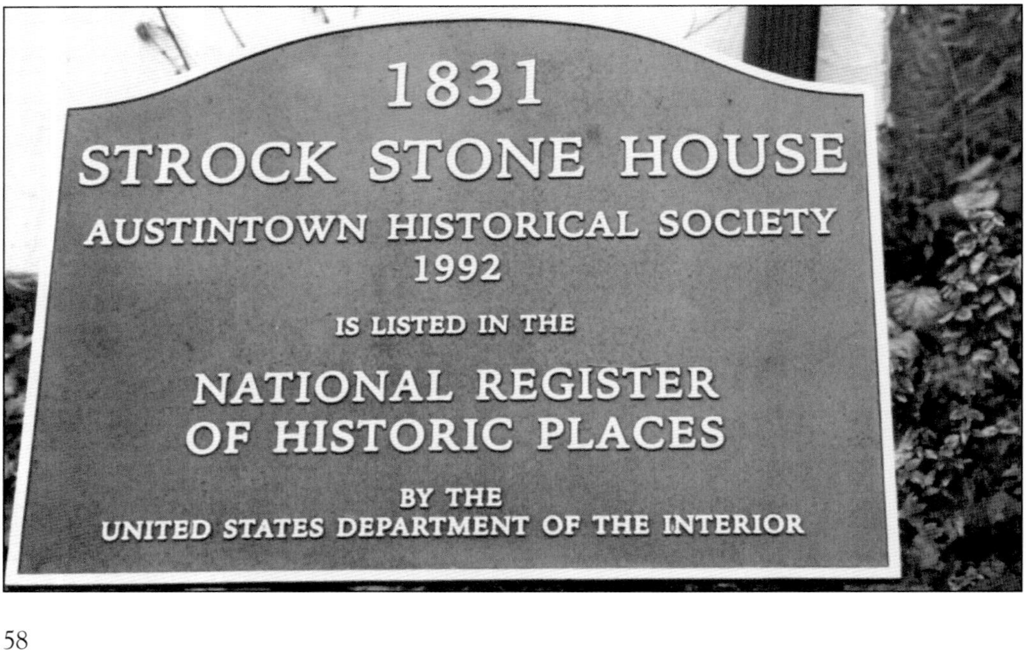

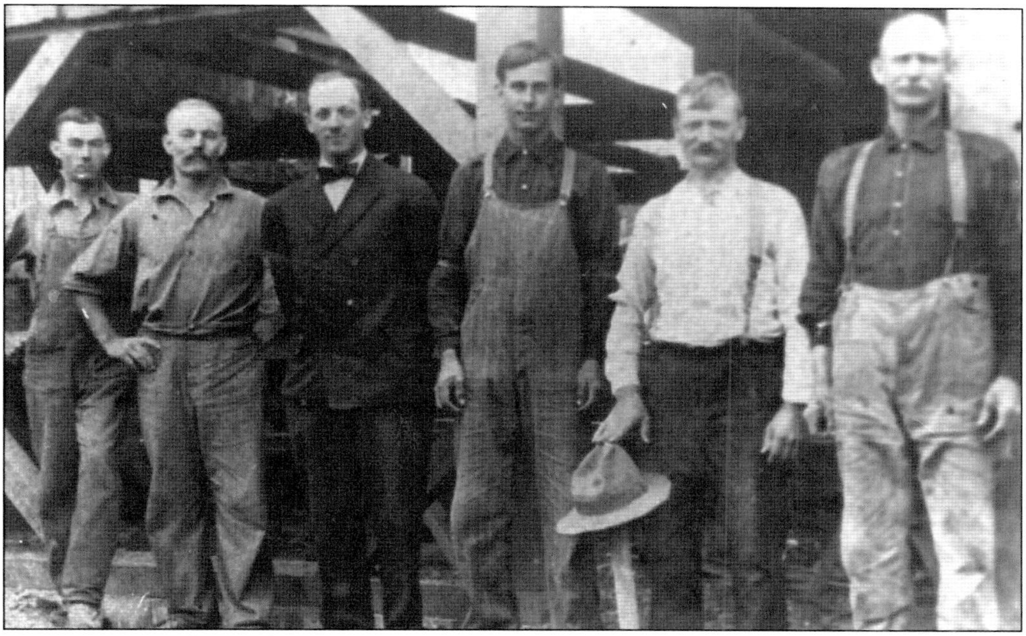

UNIDENTIFIED HIRED HELP ON ANDERSON FARM, 1900S. William Shaw Anderson inherited the Strock Stone House in 1890 from his father, David Anderson. William, an attorney and judge, and his wife Louise Shields Anderson raised four children—Blanche, William Noble, Randall, and Anna—on the 750-acre farm. The hired men helped with the farm, which included two houses; three barns; pump, log, milk, ice, tool, and poultry houses; a bull barn; a tool shop; and a corn crib. When William Shaw Anderson died in 1925, Randall and Blanche inherited the house. Randall, an Ohio state representative, wears a suit and tie here. The MVSD bought the house in 1929. (Courtesy AHS.)

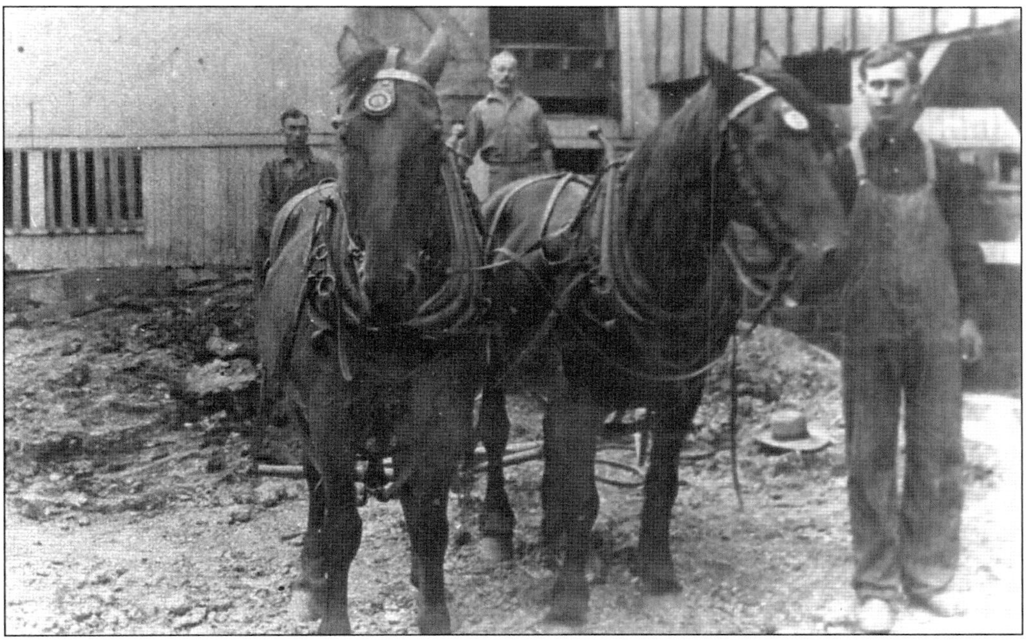

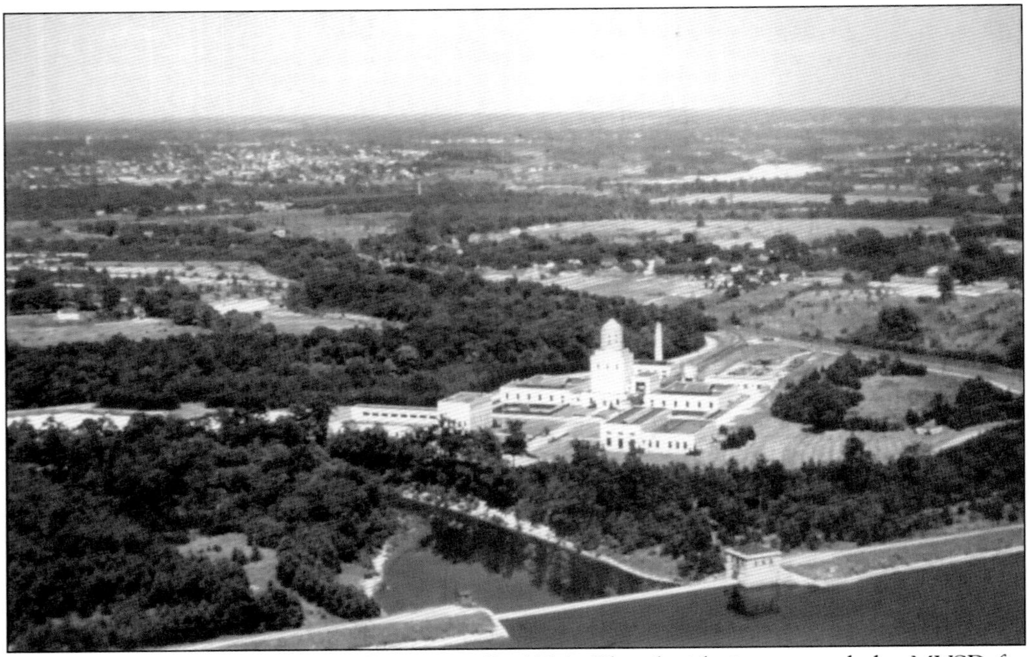

Mahoning Valley Sanitary District. In 1926, Ohio legislation created the MVSD for Youngstown and Niles, which had been getting drinking water from the contaminated Mahoning River. The administration, pumping, water treatment, and filtration buildings are located in the lower right. The Mineral Ridge Dam is in the lower center. (Courtesy MVSD.)

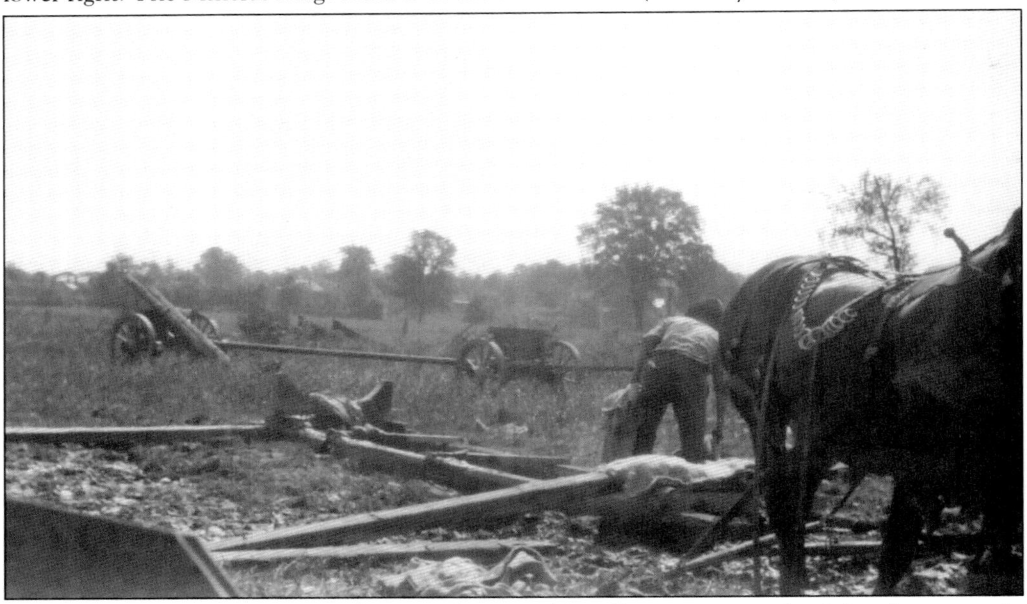

Clearing Meander Basin. The MVSD spent $2 million acquiring land for the reservoir. Many Ohltown residents filed lawsuits to stop them. Some residents stayed in their homes while workers demolished everything nearby; one was forcibly carried from her home. By April 1929, all families were removed from the basin area. One hundred workmen cleared the 2,010-acre, seven-mile-long and one-mile-wide basin by December 1929. (Courtesy MVSD.)

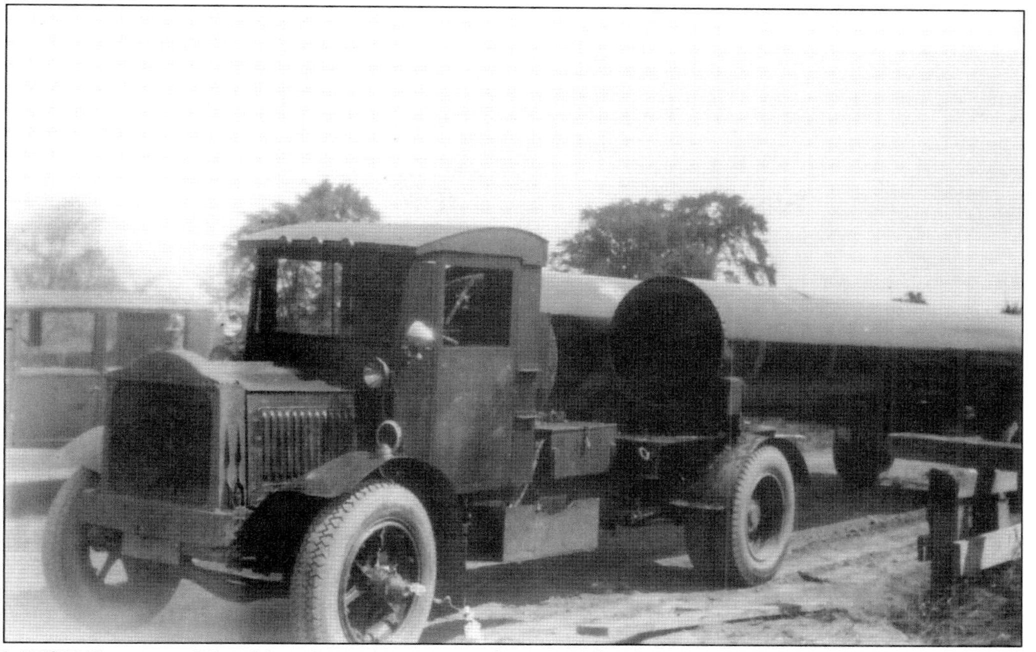

MVSD Pipeline. Two 36-inch steel mains, each 28,000 feet long, and one 48-inch concrete main, 14,500 feet long, were laid between the MVSD and the 30 million–gallon distributing reservoir in Youngstown. W. Dittoe was MVSD's first chief engineer from 1930 to 1939. Following him were L. Fawcett, D. Heffelfinger, John Tucker, David Tabak, and Tom Holloway. (Courtesy MVSD.)

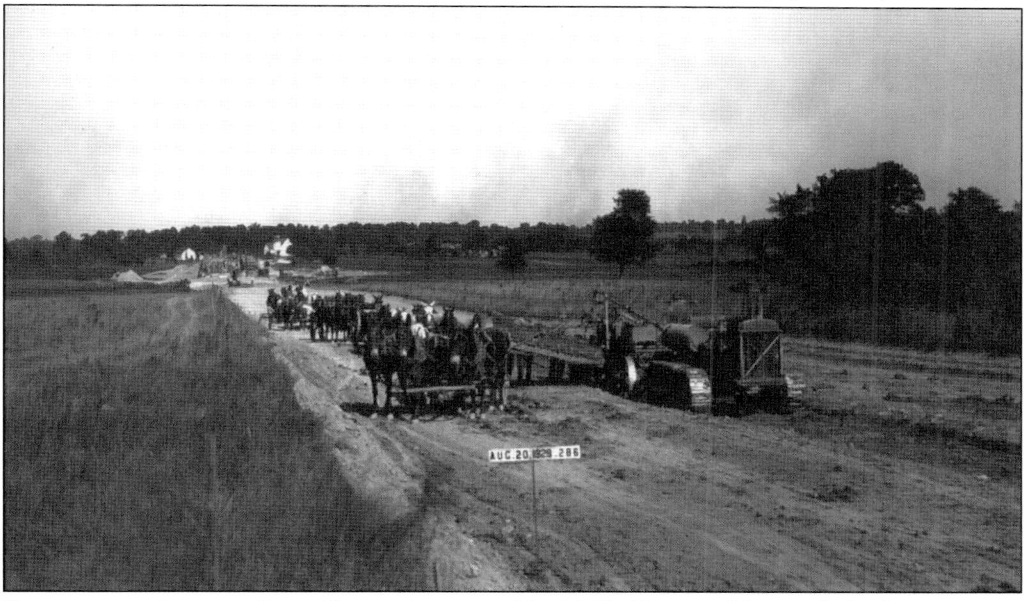

Rebuilding County Line Road, August 20, 1929. Teams of horses helped reconstruct County Line Road in Ohltown to accommodate Meander Reservoir. The Ohltown United Methodist Church is the large white building in the background on the right. The house on the left was destroyed. The entire MVSD is 5,807 acres, 4,109 acres in Mahoning County, 1,698 acres in Trumbull County. (Courtesy Tom Arne.)

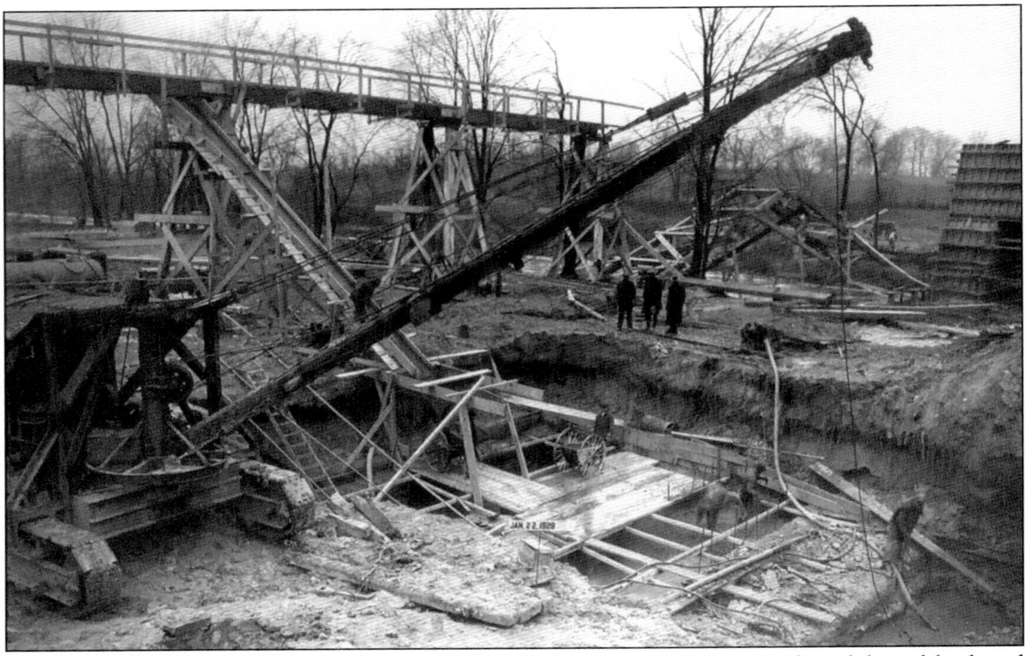

BUILDING MEANDER VIADUCT FOUNDATION, JANUARY 22, 1929. Workers labored by hand to construct the bridge foundation. They took concrete across the upper scaffolding, poured it down the central chute into wheelbarrows, and emptied them into the form. Workers in the hole finished the cement. The hose on the lower right pumped water from the construction site into Meander Creek in the background. (Courtesy Tom Arne.)

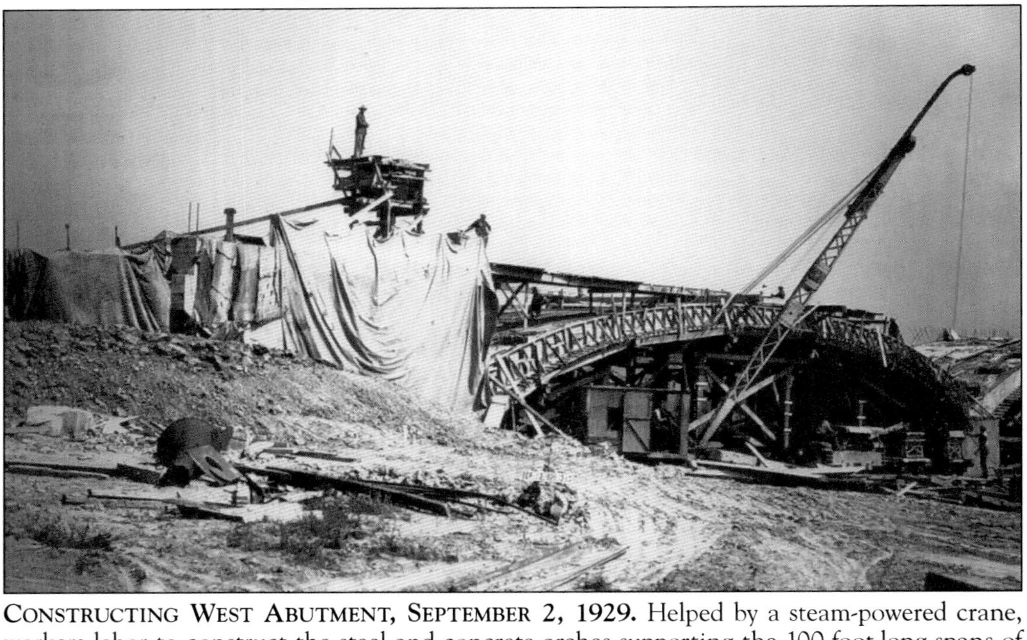

CONSTRUCTING WEST ABUTMENT, SEPTEMBER 2, 1929. Helped by a steam-powered crane, workers labor to construct the steel and concrete arches supporting the 100-foot-long spans of the viaduct. Workers were also building the 3,000-foot earthen and steel Mahoning Avenue causeway and bridge over Meander Reservoir. (Courtesy Tom Arne.)

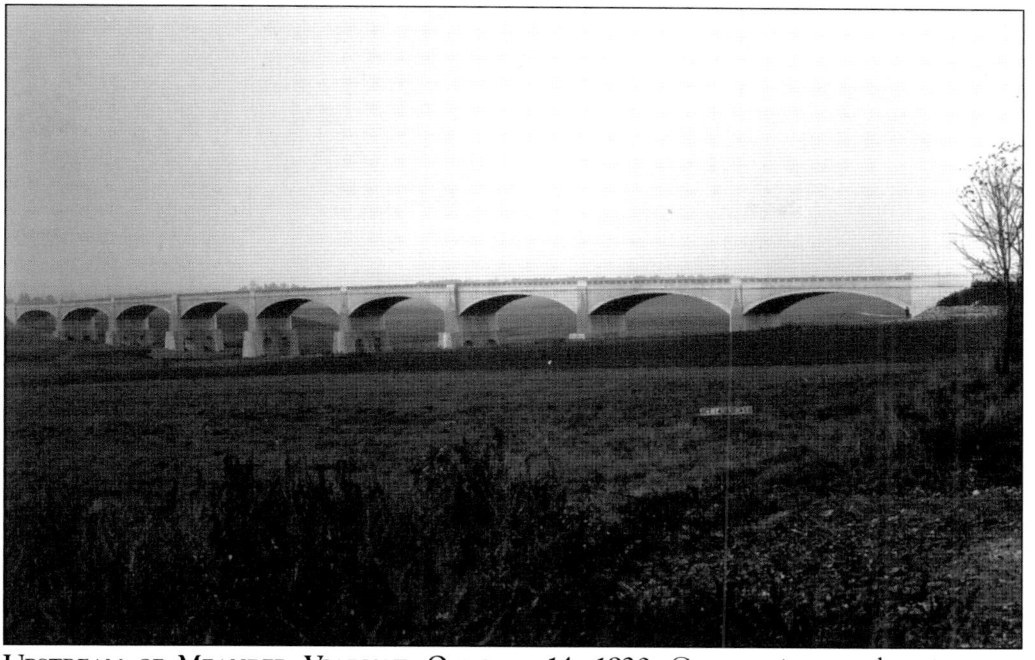

Upstream of Meander Viaduct, October 14, 1930. Construction on the nine-span concrete and steel viaduct began in October 1928 and was completed in July 1930. The $270,000 viaduct spanning Meander Reservoir at the Mahoning County line is shown before the reservoir was filled. The man on the far right is unidentified. (Courtesy Tom Arne.)

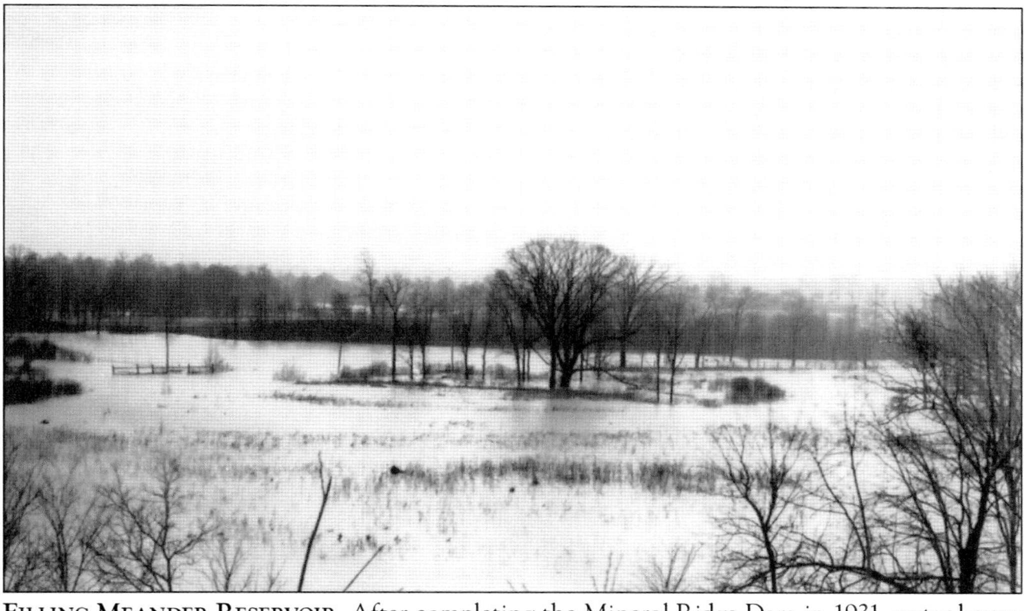

Filling Meander Reservoir. After completing the Mineral Ridge Dam in 1931, water began filling the 10 billion–gallon reservoir; it was full by January 1932 and provided water to Niles and Youngstown on July 9, 1932. The average reservoir depth is 17 feet, but ranges from 5 to 40 feet. The surrounding land was reforested with four million evergreens and is a fish and game refuge. (Courtesy MVSD.)

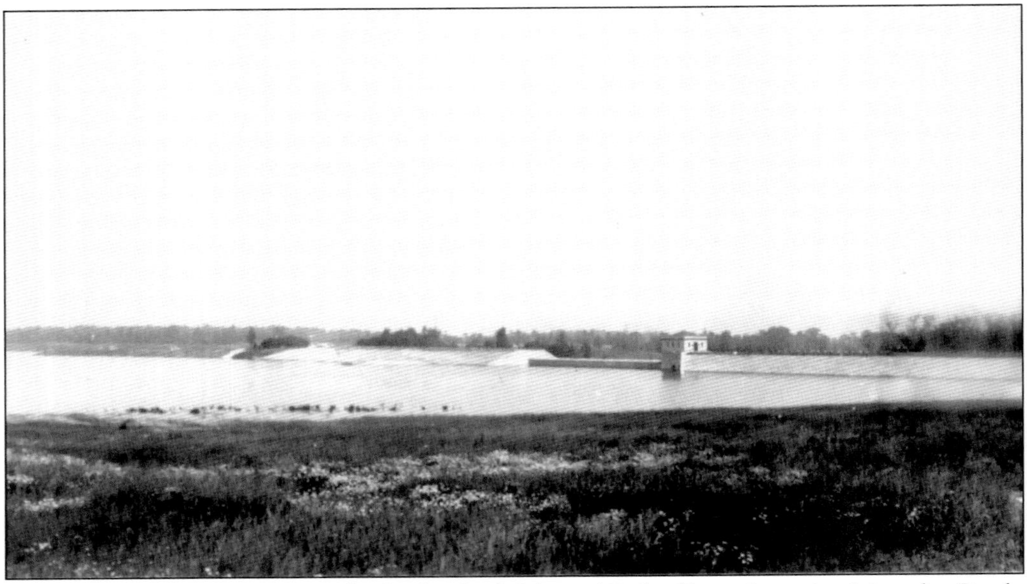

MINERAL RIDGE DAM, 1931. The 50-foot-high Mineral Ridge Dam, damming Meander Creek, is in Mineral Ridge. The $1.1 million, 3,550-foot-long dam has 260 feet of spillway. All but 300 feet of the dam is earth embankment. The reservoir has 40 miles of shoreline and supplies water to 300,000 people. (Courtesy MVSD.)

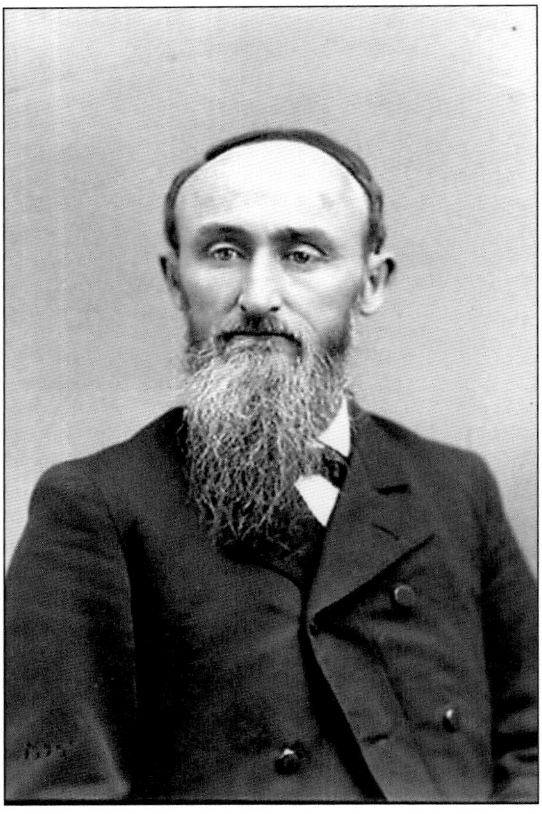

HENRY SOLOMON LEHR, FOUNDER OF OHIO NORTHERN UNIVERSITY. Henry Wehr, born in Ohltown on March 8, 1838, the 11th child of George Solomon and Salome Lessing Lehr, was raised in Wayne County and taught school in Alliance. He founded Ohio Northern University, then called the Northwest Ohio Normal School, in Ada in 1871 and served as the first president of Ohio Northern from 1871 to 1900. (Courtesy Ohio Northern University.)

Five

Other Areas of Austintown

In Austintown Township, many areas were named for people. Handworks Corner, at Kirk and Raccoon Roads, was named after John and "Polly" Handwork. Taylor's Corners, at Silica and North Turner Roads, was named for Andrew and Susan Taylor, whose carriage-building business employed 15 carpenters and made 125 carriages yearly. Smith Corners, at Kirk and Canfield-Niles Roads, named for Henry Smith's cooper (barrel manufacturing) business on the southeast corner, was sometimes called Brobst Corners or Sample. The Sample post office operated from 1888 to 1902. Riblets Corners, at North Meridian and Salt Springs Road, and Riblet Road were named for William and Terresa Bell Riblet. Watch Corners was at South Raccoon and Burgett Roads, by the Austin Log Cabin. Perkins Corners, at Mahoning Avenue and Meridian Road, had a post office from 1884 to 1903.

Peach Hill is the intersection of Kirk Road and Hamman Drive and was named for Frank and Elizabeth Hamman. Cornersburg, spelled Cornersburgh until 1893, is the corner of four townships—Austintown, Canfield, Boardman, and Youngstown. In 1880, 250 people lived in Cornersburgh, most in Youngstown Township.

Axe Factory Run, a creek originating west of Route 11 and winding through the Austintown schools complex and Wedgewood Park, is dammed near Meridian Road (on land owned by Ira McCollum in 1874), creating Meridian (Woodside) Lake. It flows into Mill Creek a half mile below Lanterman's Falls where John Ross operated an axe handle factory.

In 1924, Mahoning County built the five-building tuberculosis "TB" sanitarium, a specialized hospital for tuberculosis patients, on county land on Kirk Road near the present-day water tower. Tuberculosis was highly contagious and, in the days before antibiotics, often fatal. Needing high altitude and fresh air, patients were isolated and confined to the sanitarium for an average of 300 days. Staff lived there so they would not carry home the disease to their families. The sanitarium closed in 1974. Raymond Garea Associates bought it in 1978 for $100,000. Four buildings were demolished in 1982.

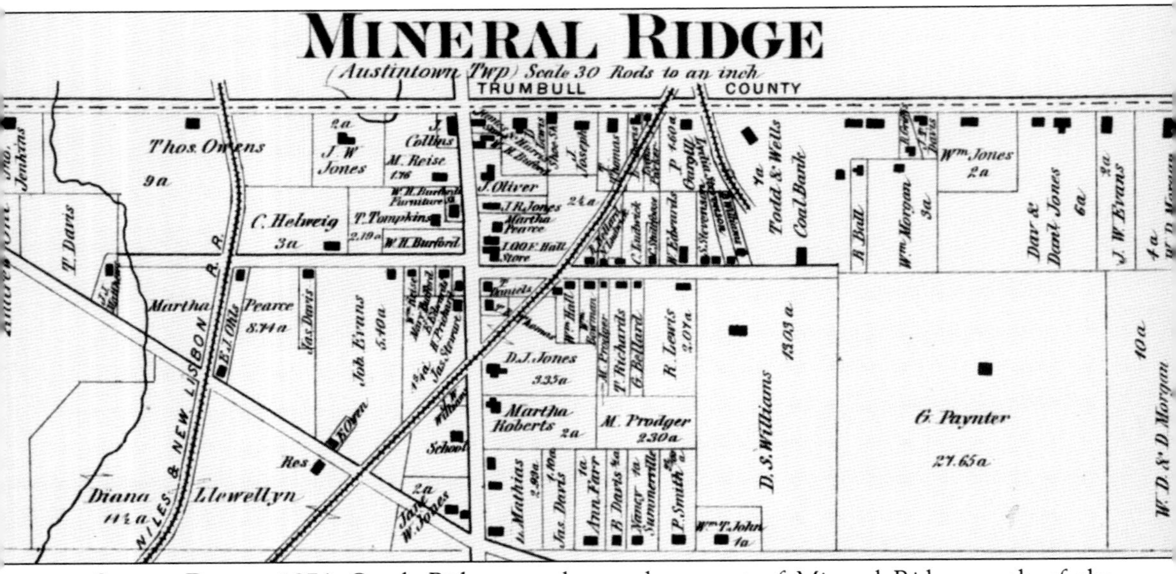

SOUTH RIDGE, 1874. South Ridge was the southern part of Mineral Ridge, south of the Trumbull County line, in Austintown Township. On the map, County Line Road runs from left to right across the top, Liberty Street runs from left to right near the center, Canfield-Niles Road runs from the center top to bottom, Webb Road runs diagonally across the left. Burford and Sons sold furniture, caskets, and undertaking goods at the site of the original Lane Funeral Home on Canfield-Niles Road. Andrew Ohl manufactured Taylor's Patent Buggy Wheel on Webb Road. The two-story Dutch Hill School was on the west side of Canfield-Niles Road just north of Webb Road. E. Ohl operated a general store on Webb Road between the railroads. Diana Llewellyn lived with her two bothers, Samuel and Edmond, who were engineers at the coal banks. (Courtesy AHS.)

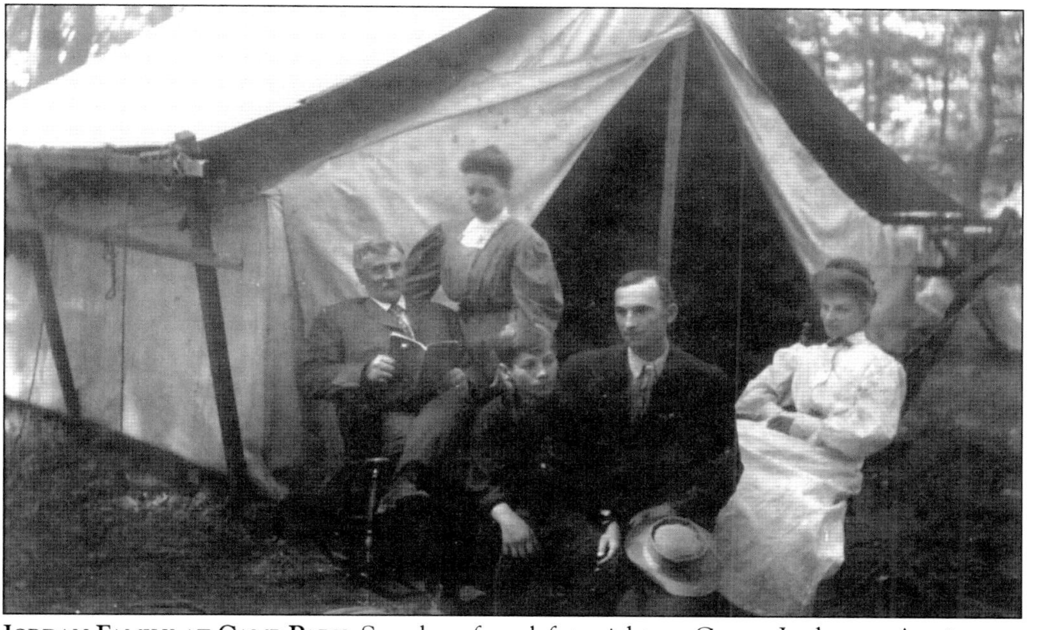

JORDAN FAMILY AT CAMP PARK. Seen here from left to right are George Jordan, an Austintown trustee in 1899 and 1902; Lizzie Clinker Jordan; Todd Scott Jordan; Peter Schrum; and Hazel Jordan. The Mexico one-room schoolhouse was located near Camp Park on the west side of South Turner Road, just north of the railroad crossing between Kirk and New Roads. (Courtesy West Austintown United Methodist Church.)

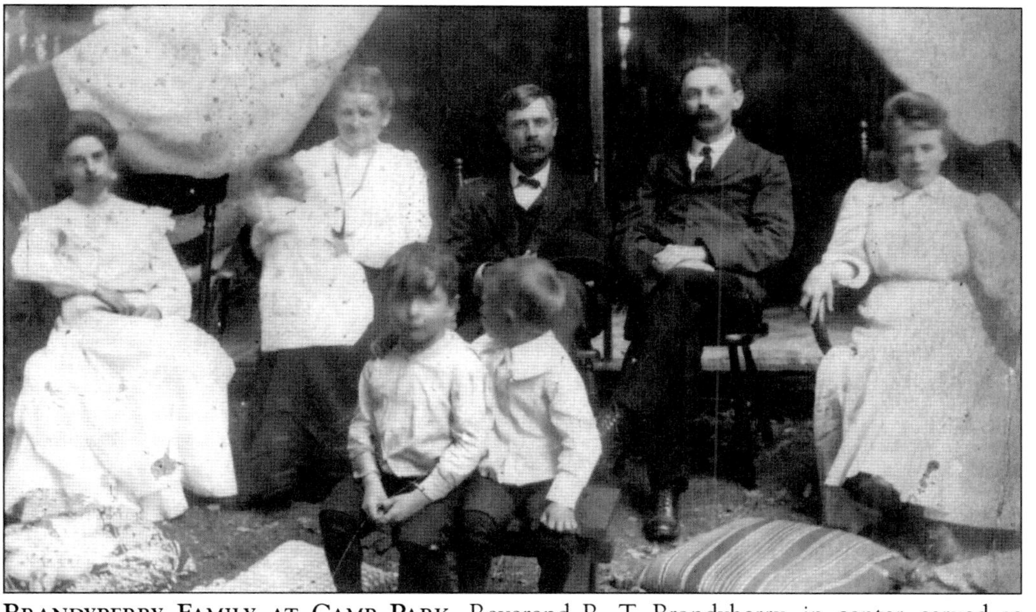

BRANDYBERRY FAMILY AT CAMP PARK. Reverend R. T. Brandyberry, in center, served as minister of the West Austintown Evangelical Church from 1903 to 1907. Traveling ministers held evangelical services at Camp Park, on the corner of Kirk and Turner Roads, from about 1820 to 1920. Large tents were erected for the services; families quartered in their own tents. (Courtesy West Austintown United Methodist Church.)

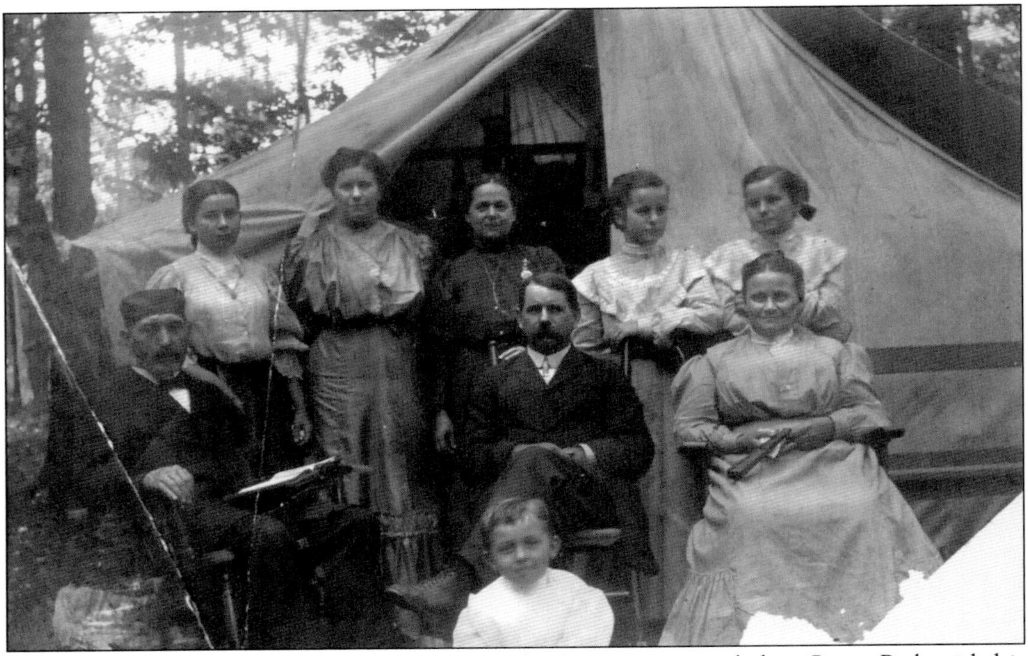

Butruff Family. Reverend Butruff, an evangelical minister, traveled to Camp Park with his family to provide services. Families came from miles around to Camp Park. Camp meetings were an important feature of religious life. (Courtesy West Austintown United Methodist Church.)

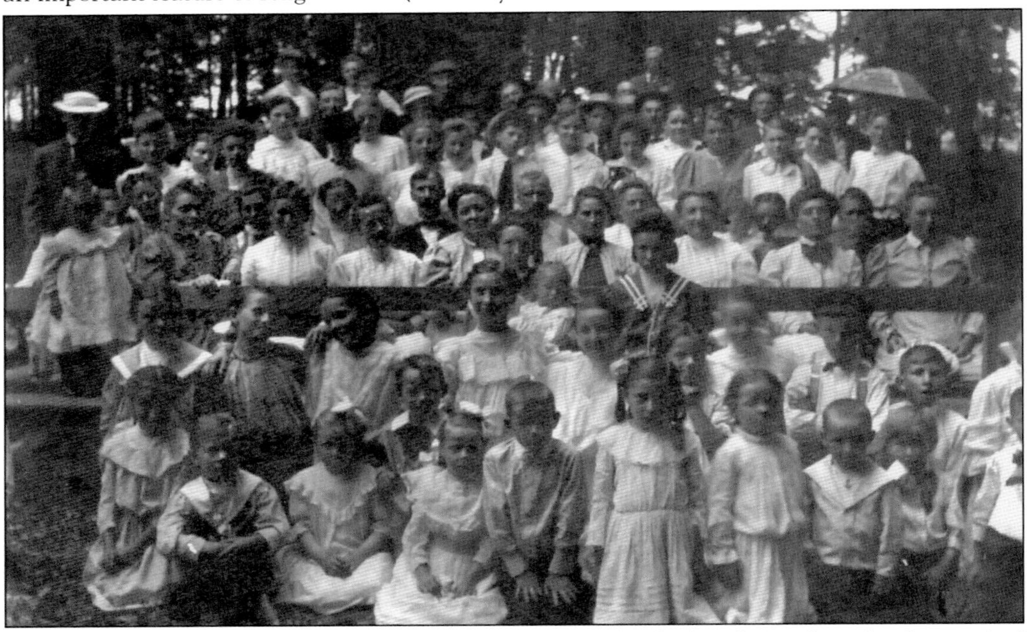

Sunday School Picnic. The West Austintown Evangelical Church Sunday school picnicked at Camp Park. Just east of Meander Creek, Camp Park was near the Ewing farm on the southwest corner of Kirk and Turner Roads. Archibald and Sarah Pauley Ewing settled on 110 acres of land in 1803. The land remained in the Ewing family until 1970. (Courtesy West Austintown United Methodist Church.)

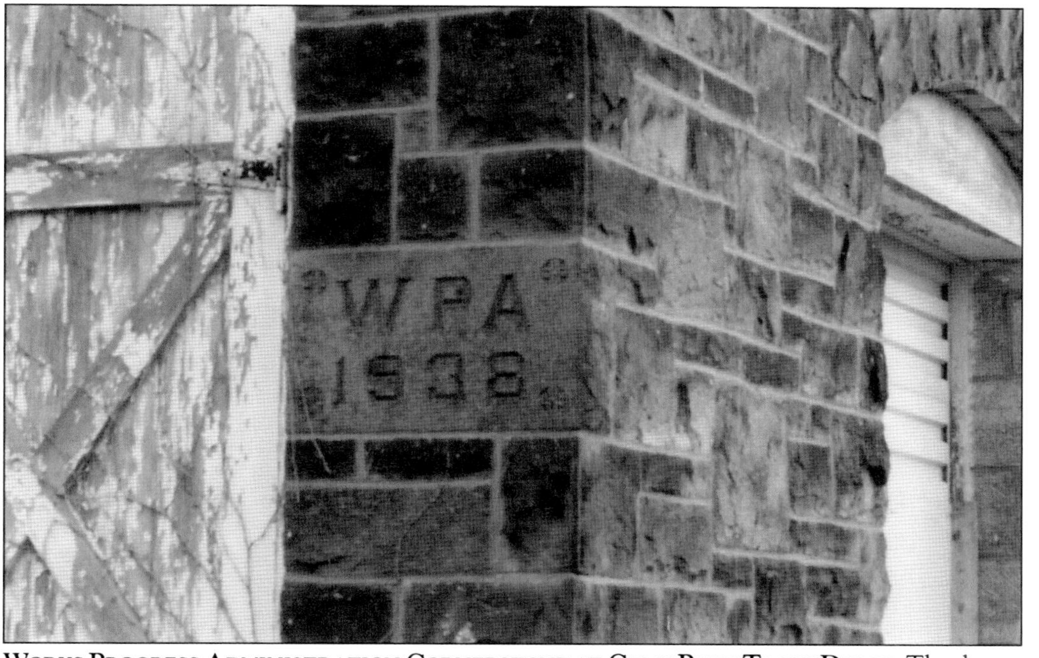

WORKS PROGRESS ADMINISTRATION CORNERSTONE AT CAMP PARK TRAIN DEPOT. The depot, constructed by the Works Progress Administration (WPA) in 1938, was a whistle stop on the Niles-New Lisbon Railroad; the train only stopped if there were passengers. Mill Creek Metro Parks Bike Trail converted the building for its trailhead in 2000. (Courtesy Joyce Pogany.)

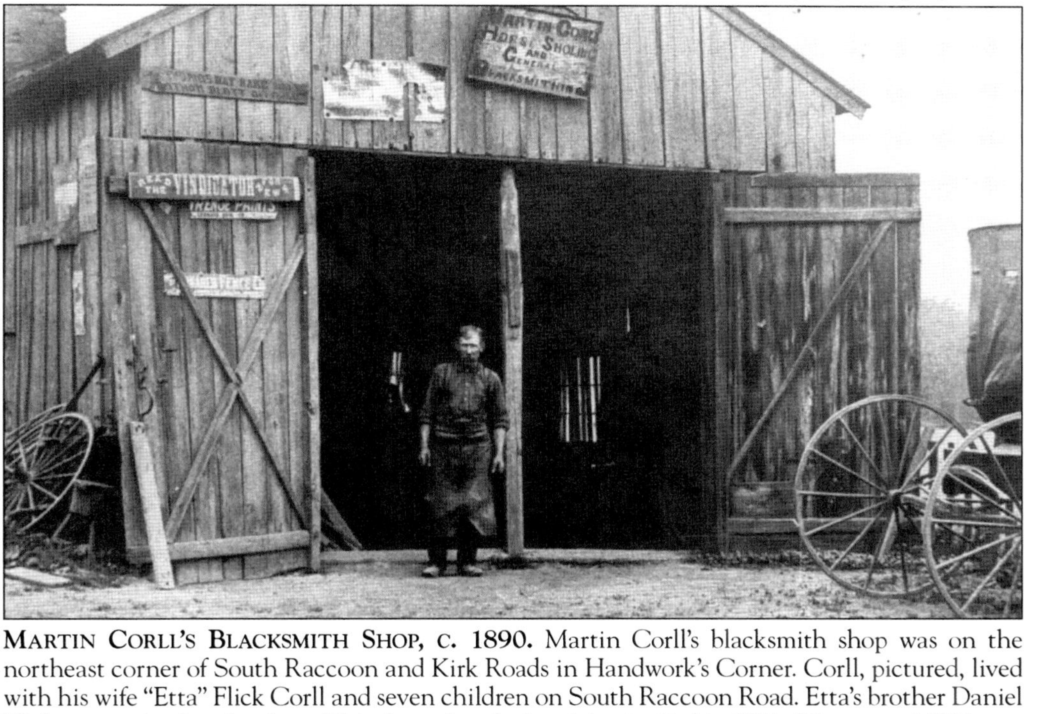

MARTIN CORLL'S BLACKSMITH SHOP, C. 1890. Martin Corll's blacksmith shop was on the northeast corner of South Raccoon and Kirk Roads in Handwork's Corner. Corll, pictured, lived with his wife "Etta" Flick Corll and seven children on South Raccoon Road. Etta's brother Daniel Flick apprenticed at the shop. This shop closed when Martin died in 1921. (Courtesy AHS.)

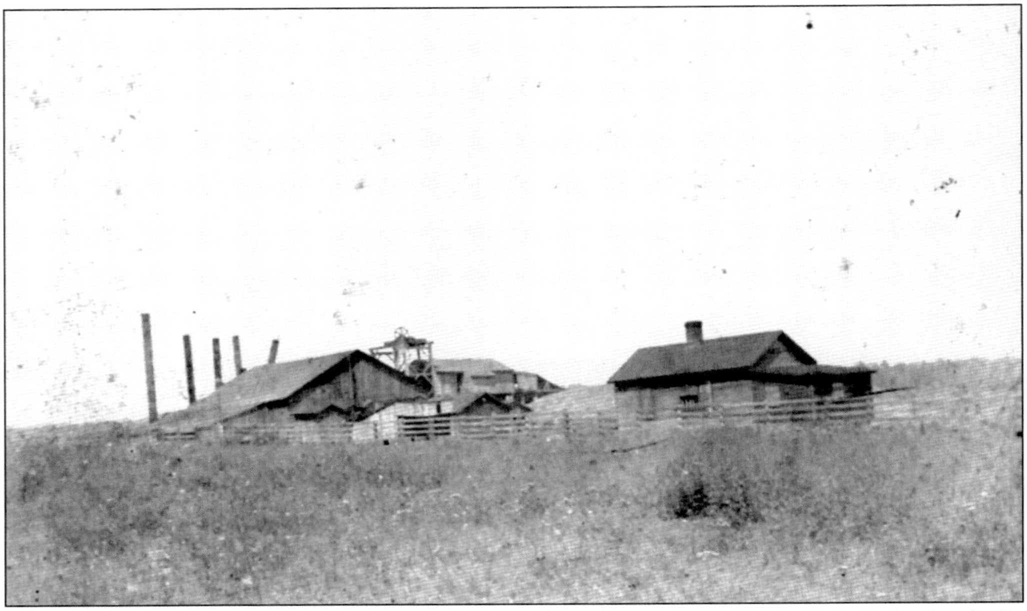

Leadville Lanterman Mine. In 1869, the Wick and Wells Company opened the Leadville Lanterman Mine located on the Lanterman farm near the north side of Wickliffe Circle. Due to an abundance of underground water, the 187-foot shaft cost $71,837 to sink. The mine suffered a large fire in August 1881. (Courtesy AHS.)

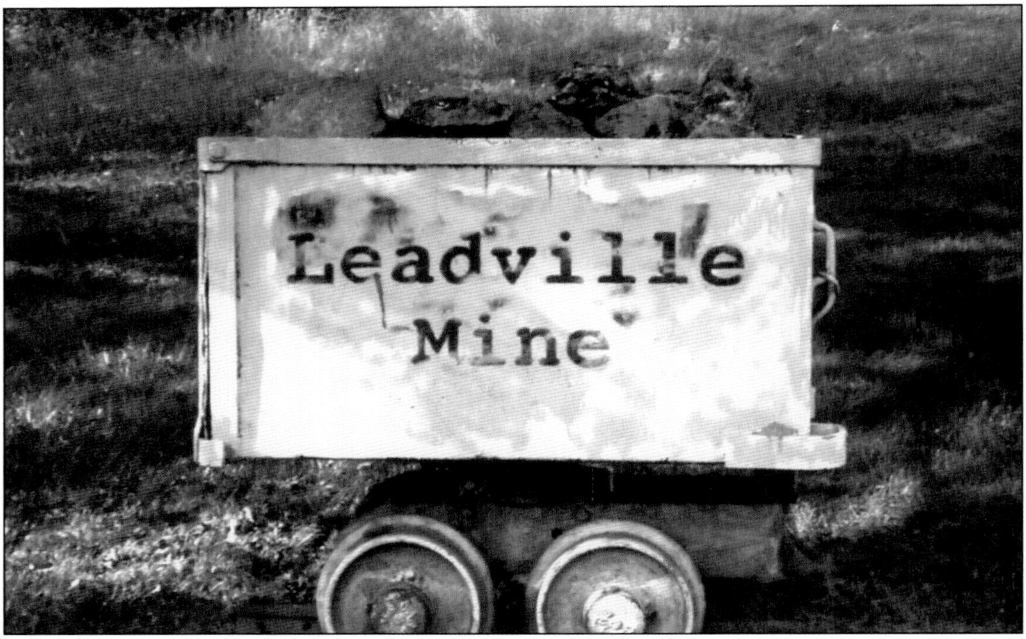

Leadville Mine Coal Car. The Leadville Lanterman mine coal seam was two-feet-six-inches to five-feet thick. In its heyday, the mine produced 200 tons of coal daily. The coal cars, like this one donated by Harold Wilson, were brought to the surface using steam-powered engines. The coal was transferred into railroad cars on the Youngstown-Austintown Railroad. (Courtesy Joyce Pogany.)

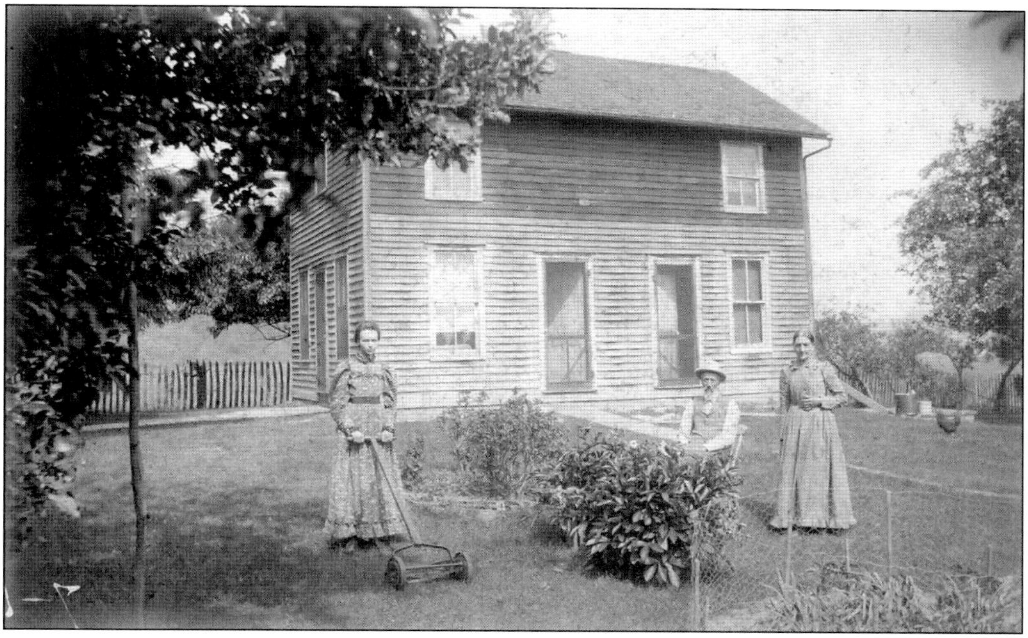

John Miller Home. Built in 1874 by John Miller, the house is located on Miller Lane, now known as Lanterman Road. In the 1896 photograph are John Miller (seated, 1835–1908) and his wife Mariah (born 1836), who lived 99 years. Cutting the grass with the hand-push mower is 19-year-old Clara "Pet." The photograph taken in 1960 shows the remodeled house on 4594 Lanterman Road. E. Vance Crum (1907–1970) and Alice Crum (1913–1972) and family lived there in the 1950s and 1960s. (Courtesy AHS.)

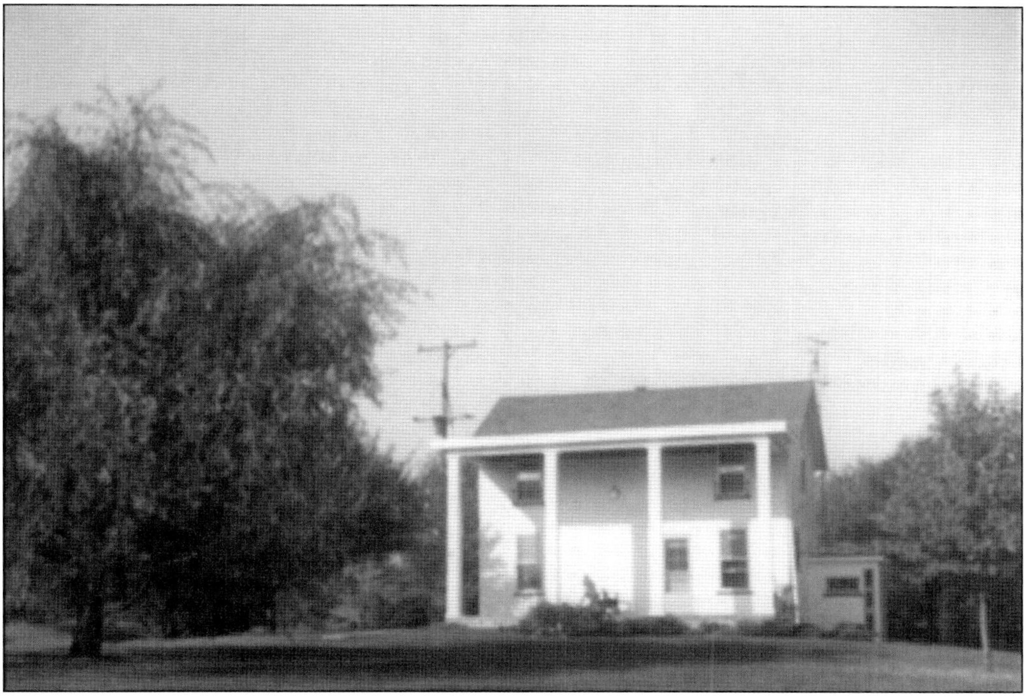

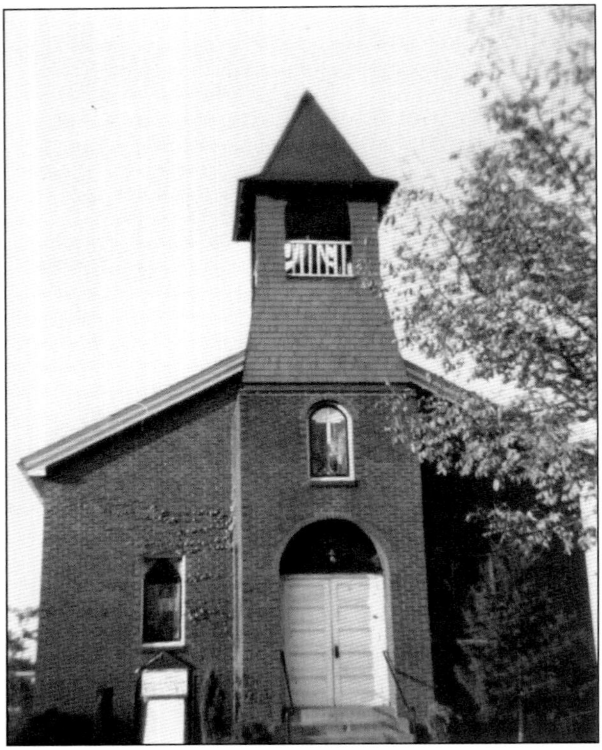

SMITH CORNERS CHURCH. The Smith Corners Evangelical United Brethren Church was built in 1861–1862. In 1925, church members raised and electrified the building and built a basement, bell tower, and front vestibule. In 1962, church members broke ground for the new church, located across the street on Canfield-Niles Road. (Courtesy AHS.)

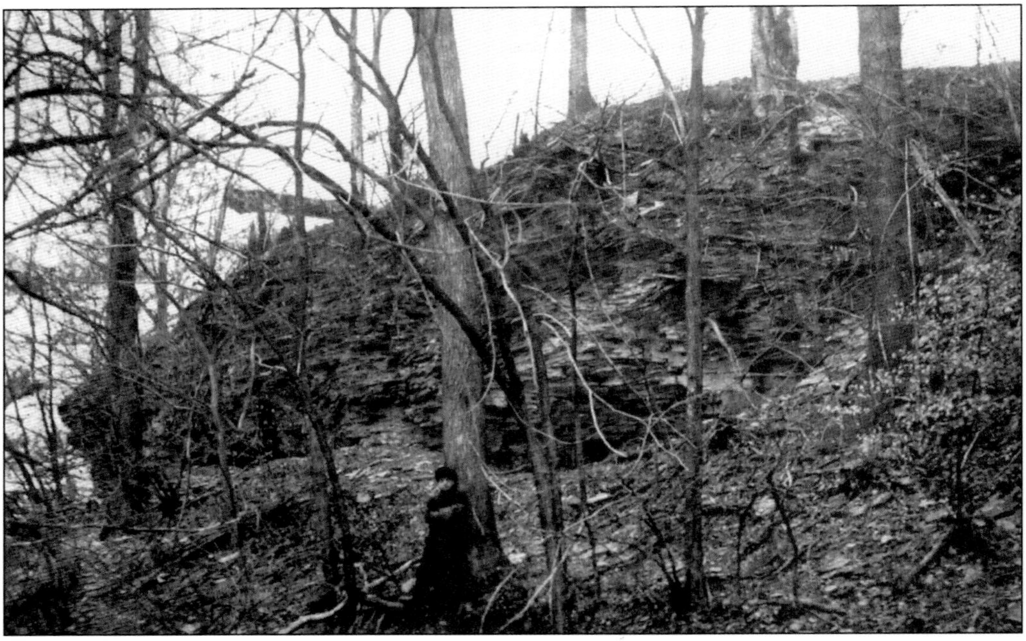

STONEY RIDGE. Located along the east side of South Turner Road, between Fairview and Kirk Roads, the stones from Stoney Ridge were used to construct the Strock Stone House and the Russell Stone House. The man in the photograph is unidentified. (Courtesy West Austintown United Methodist Church.)

Six

Austintown Schools

Schools provide a community with an identity. The earliest schools in Austintown, on Frederick Shively's and Jacob Parkhurst's farms, were subscription schools; parents paid $1.50 per child per term. In 1825, Ohio required taxpayer-supported public schools in each township.

In 1916, the eight operating one-room schoolhouses were consolidated into one building, the Austintown Centralized School, serving grades 1–9. In January 1922, the school added grades 10–12. In 1924, the school was renamed Austintown Fitch School. Additions in 1926, 1946, and 1954 included two gymnasiums, a boiler room, an auditorium, classrooms, and a band room.

Woodside Elementary School opened in 1949; Lloyd and John Davis Elementary Schools opened in 1954. Davis was named for Ohltown native John Davis, a Mahoning County probate judge from 1913 to 1925. Davis worked in West Austintown coal mines and taught in the Grove one-room schoolhouse to earn money for law school.

In 1954, a total of 2,725 students attended Austintown schools; in 1956, enrollment was 3,066. In 1957, six classrooms were added to Davis. In 1958, Lynn Kirk Elementary School, named after the Lynn Kirk plat, opened. Enrollment in Austintown schools reached 4,499 in 1959. Frank Ohl Junior High School opened on January 30, 1961, and was named for Frank Ohl, great-grandson of Michael Ohl. He was an Austintown Township trustee from 1932 to 1941 and drove a school bus for Austintown for 23 years. By 1962, a total of 6,022 students attended Austintown schools. Charles Watson Elementary School opened on January 2, 1962.

Kindergarten was offered in 1961 and 1962, but was cancelled after a levy failure. By 1965, there were 6,343 students enrolled. The new Fitch High School opened on September 9, 1968, with 2,400 students. The elementary schools were reconfigured to house grades K–4; Frank Ohl became a middle school housing grades 5–8, and the old Fitch building was rechristened Austintown Middle School (AMS) housing grades 5–8. In 1971, enrollment in Austintown schools peaked at 8,637.

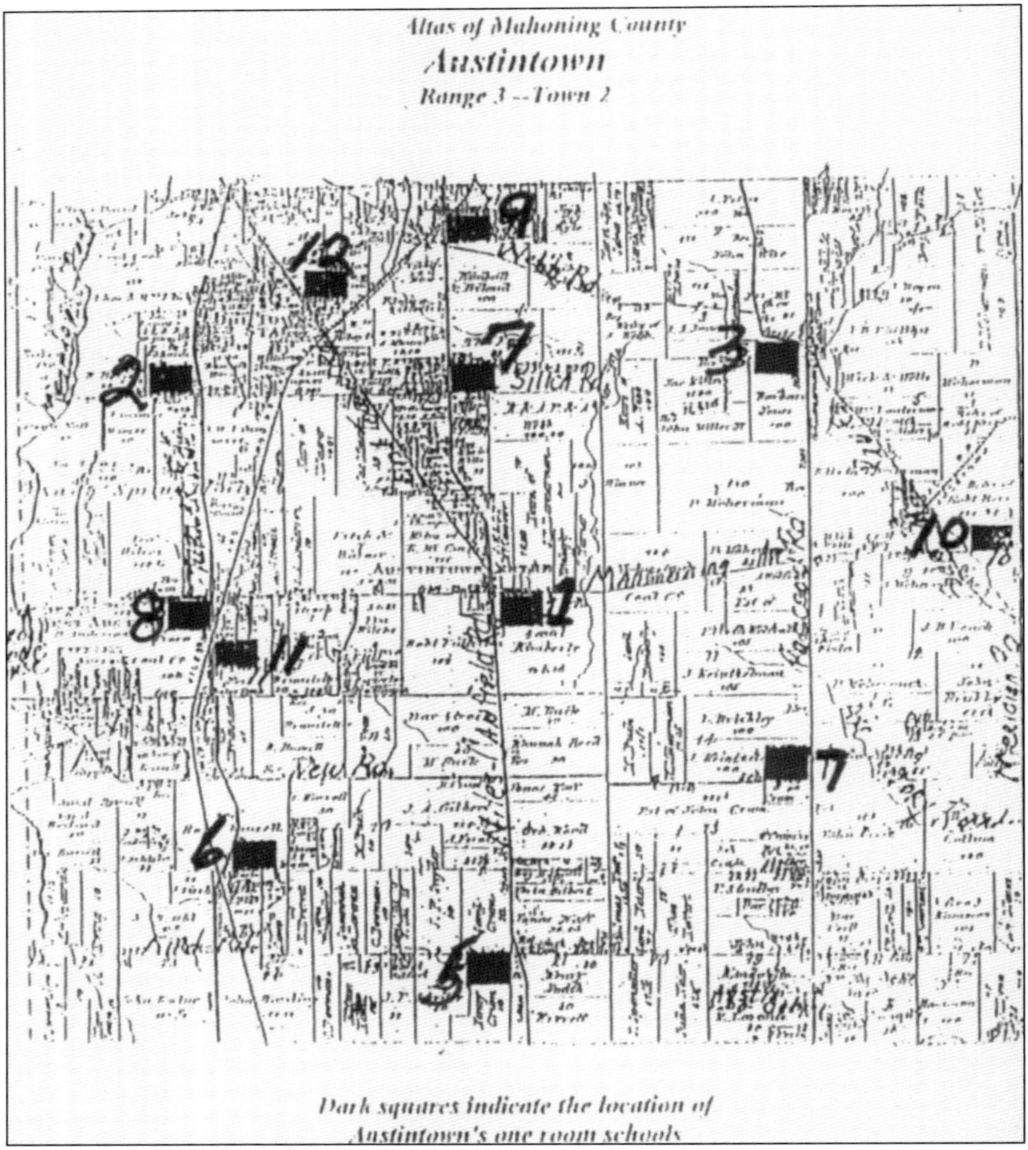

MAP OF ONE-ROOM SCHOOLHOUSES. Throughout the history of Austintown, there were 12 one-room schoolhouses. As the population shifted, new schoolhouses were built and old ones closed. Mahoning Avenue bisects the middle of the map, and from left to right were West Austintown (8), Austintown Center (1), and Perkins (10) Schools. On the far left, from top to bottom, is Turner Road where Taylor's Corners (2), Stoney Ridge (11), and Mexico (6) Schools were located. Canfield-Niles Road is in the center from top to bottom. Dutch Hill School (9) was west of Webb Road; Pleasant Hill School (7) was at Silica Road. Smith Corners School (5) was at the corner of Kirk Road. Ohltown Road runs diagonally off Canfield-Niles Road; Ohltown School (12) was near Dravis Street. Raccoon Road runs from top to bottom on the right. Four Mile Run School (3) was located on Four Mile Run near North Raccoon Road, and Grove School (4) was located near New and South Raccoon Roads. (Courtesy AHS.)

Sub-District No. 7,

Austintownship, Mahoning County, Ohio.

SCHOOL YEAR: August 31, 1891—May 19, 1892.

SCHOLARS.

ADDIE HERBERT,
ANNIE LEEK,
ALBERT BERGER,
ALBERT TIBBITS,
BIRDIE RUHF,
CARRIE SHIVELY,
CHARLOTTE WILLIAMS,
CLYDE MAURER,
CLOYS ASTRY,
DAVID WILLIAMS,
EMMA BERGER,
EVA DUNLAP,
ELLA JAMES,
EDWIN TIBBITS,
FREDERICK WELLS,
FRANK FEAR,
FORD TIBBITS,
GERTIE SHIVELY,
HENRY WILLIAMS,
HARRY FEAR
HERBERT MONEY,
JAMES FARR,
LEWIS SEAFORT,
MINNIE WELLS,
MINNIE DUNLAP,
MINNIE MONEY,
MINNIE SEAFORT,
MAGGIE WILLIAMS,
MARY FARR,
NETTIE BERGER,
NELLIE SHIVELY,
NELLIE FEAR,
PERRY BOWKER,
RICHARD FARR,
SINA LEEK,
SARAH JAMES,
SADIE FEAR,
THOMAS LEEK,
WALTON SHIVELY,
WILLIAM TIBBITS,
WILLIAM FARR.

JOB HERBERT,
JOHN SHIVELY, } DIRECTORS.

L. P. METZGER, Teacher.

PROGRAM FROM TAYLOR'S CORNERS SCHOOL, 1892. The Taylor's Corners one-room schoolhouse was located on Silica Road about one quarter mile west of North Turner Road. L. Metzger taught the 41 students in grades 1–8. One of the students, Walton J. Shively, served as Austintown trustee from 1926 to 1953. (Courtesy R. Walton and Genevieve Shively.)

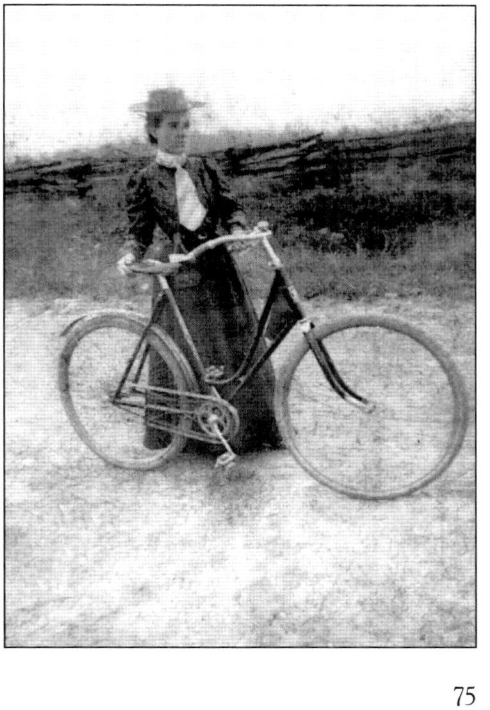

SARAH MILES, C. 1899. Sarah Miles, born in 1879, often rode her bike to the Taylor's Corners School where she taught children, stoked the stove, and cleaned the school building and outhouse. Miles earned $240 for eight months. Miles later married Walton J. Shively. (Courtesy Walt and Genevieve Shively.)

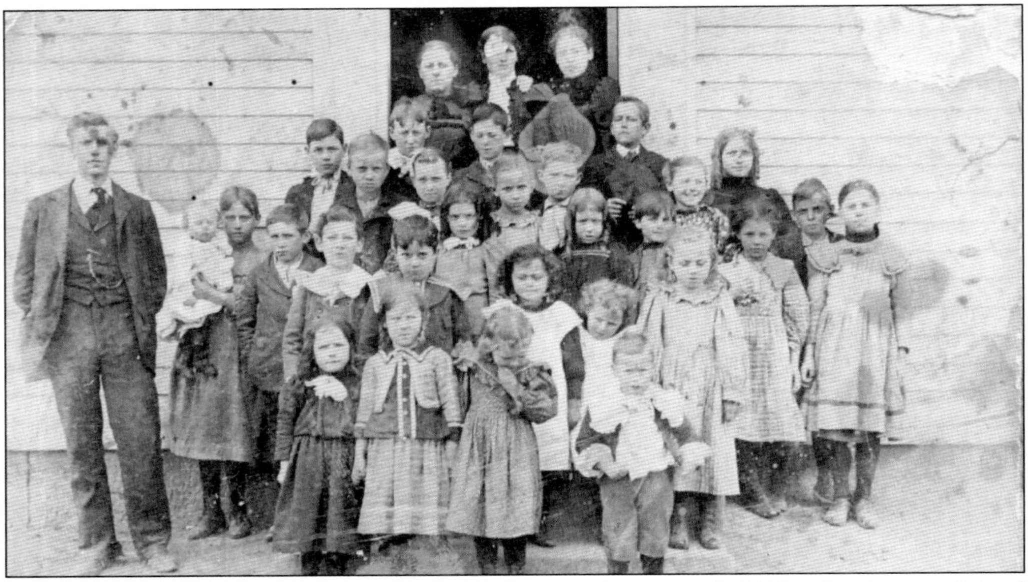

WEST AUSTINTOWN SCHOOL, C. 1898. Forty-three students attended West Austintown School on the southwest corner of Mahoning Avenue and Turner Road, September 13, 1897–April 28, 1898. Posing with their 20-year-old teacher Butler DeCamp are Estella, Annie, Ralph, Grace, Paul, and Ethel Wilcox; Lizzie, Minnie, Alice, Mary, and Willie Shaffer; Elva Fryfogle; Gertrude Anderson; Dottie and Toddie Jordan; Leoda, Ethel, Rudy, and Minnie DeVaux; Lillie and Grace Ebert; Dora, John, Roy, and Earl Bowman; Nellie and Frankie Ellis; Mayta, John, and Arazella Harris; John, Vernie, and Clarence Pennell; Glenn McMahan; Lillie Shifferstine; Eva and Alva Ripple; Gertie Lipkey; Nellie and Linna Brickley; Edna Boyd; John Grover; and Willie Randolph. (Courtesy AHS.)

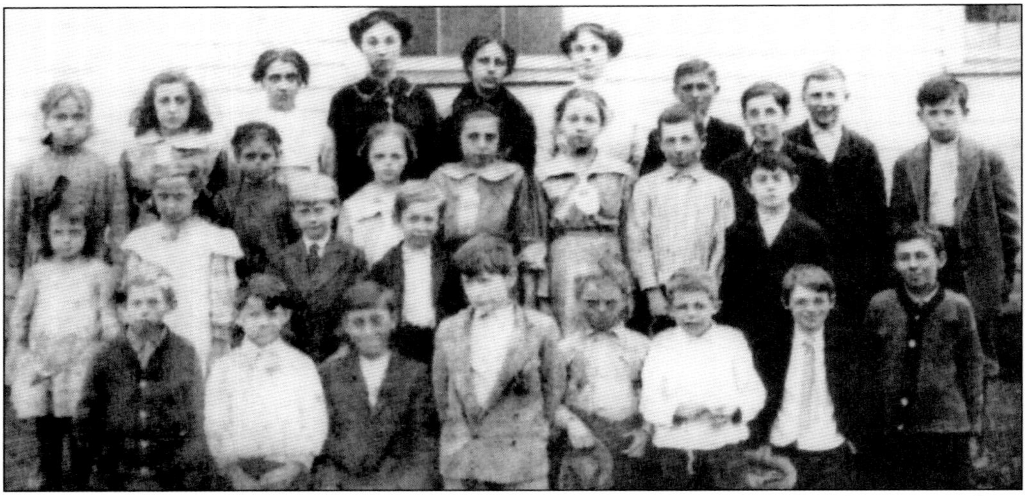

WEST AUSTINTOWN SCHOOL, 1912. Students attending included (first row) Harry Bishop, Harry Shoffner, Myron Ripple, Myron Bishop, and Raymond Flick; (second row) Evelyn and Hilda Fryfogle, Willis Bishop, Tod Flick, and Danny Ripple; (third row) Crea Ripple, Helen Bishop, Sadie Ripple, and Eva Donahue; (fourth row) Martha Shaffer, Myrtle Ripple, Edith Bishop, Effie Hake, teacher Lula Hake, Dewey Schisler, John Reed, and Emery Ripple. (Courtesy Lois Ripple Peterson.)

CORNERSTONE OF THE AUSTINTOWN CENTRALIZED SCHOOL. The Austintown School Board, J. H. Schnurrenberger (president), Frank Buchwalter, Henry Lanterman, Walton Shively, and clerk Ezra Houk, hired Miller and Son Architects to design the school patterned after the Huntsville-McArthur centralized school in Logan County with 10 standard classrooms, an auditorium with stage and non-fixed seating, a gymnasium, toilet facilities, and several basement rooms. (Courtesy Joyce Pogany.)

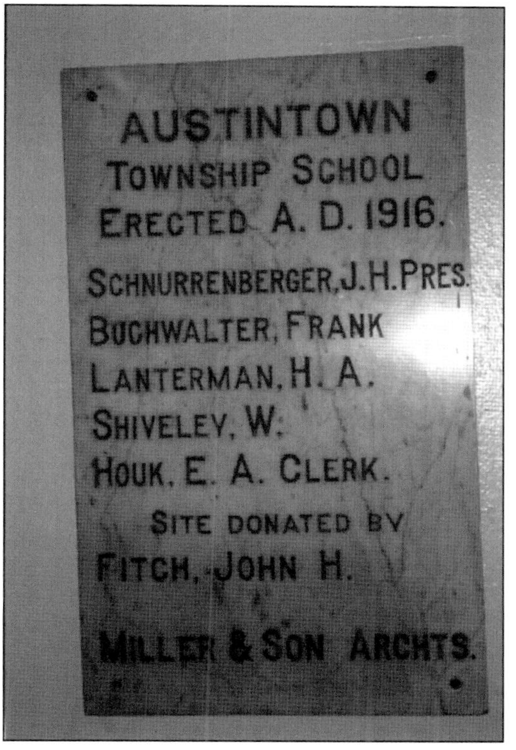

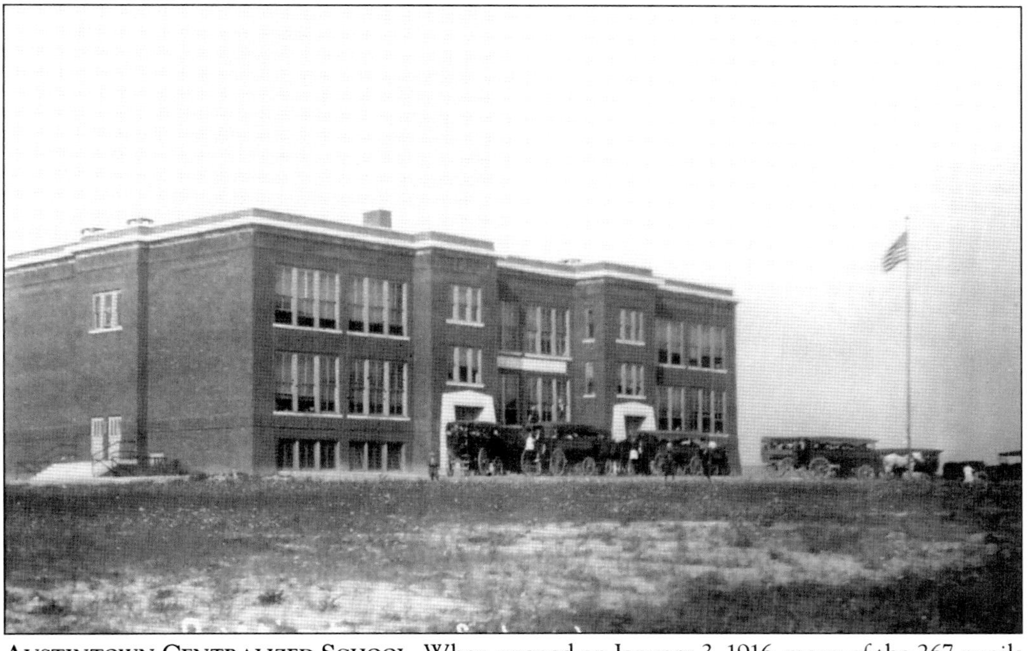

AUSTINTOWN CENTRALIZED SCHOOL. When opened on January 3, 1916, many of the 267 pupils in grades 1–9 encountered running water and electric lights for the first time. The high school consisted of 16 ninth graders. Students walked or were transported in one of eight horse-drawn "kid wagons." (Courtesy of West Austintown United Methodist Church.)

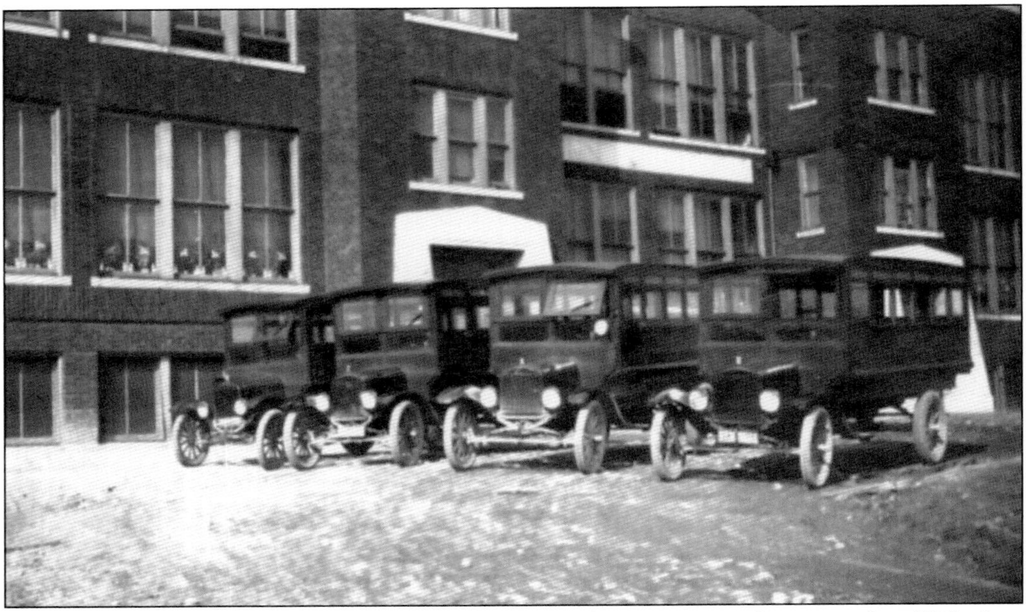

IMPROVING TRANSPORTATION AT AUSTINTOWN CENTRALIZED SCHOOL. In 1920, four motorized Model T buses (top photograph) replaced four horse-drawn kid wagons. In 1921, three more motorized buses were added. The seven motorized buses are pictured with children in the bottom photograph in 1923. In 1930, bus drivers Harry Hood, Robert Turner, Frank Ohl, Clarence Hopkinson, Paul Wilcox, and Bert Knight owned and operated their own buses The seven motorized independently owned buses have since been replaced by 50 yellow board of education–owned buses. (Courtesy AHS.)

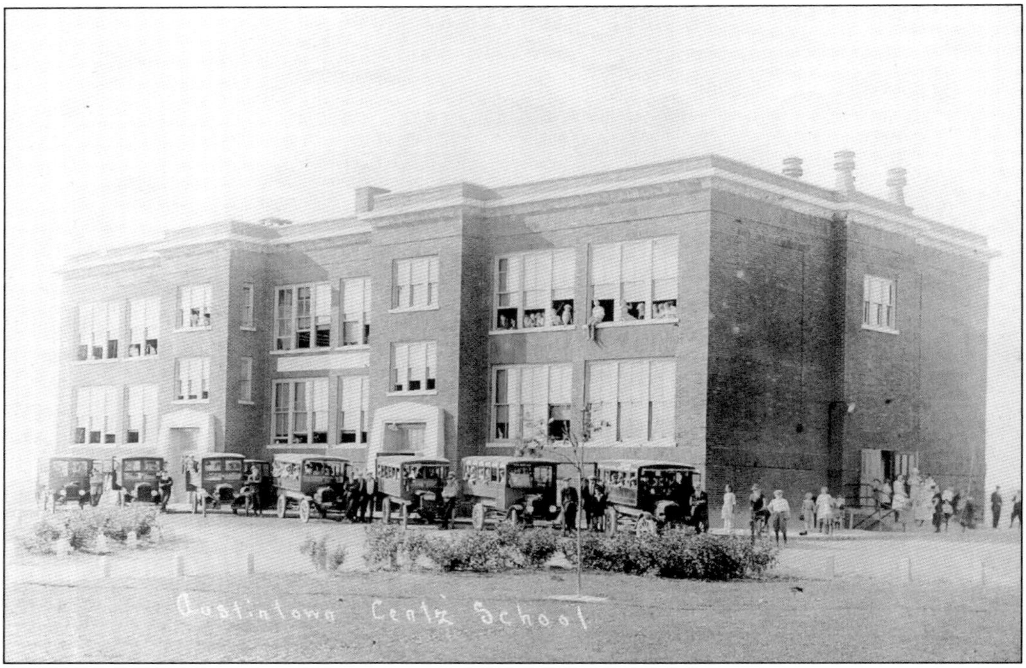

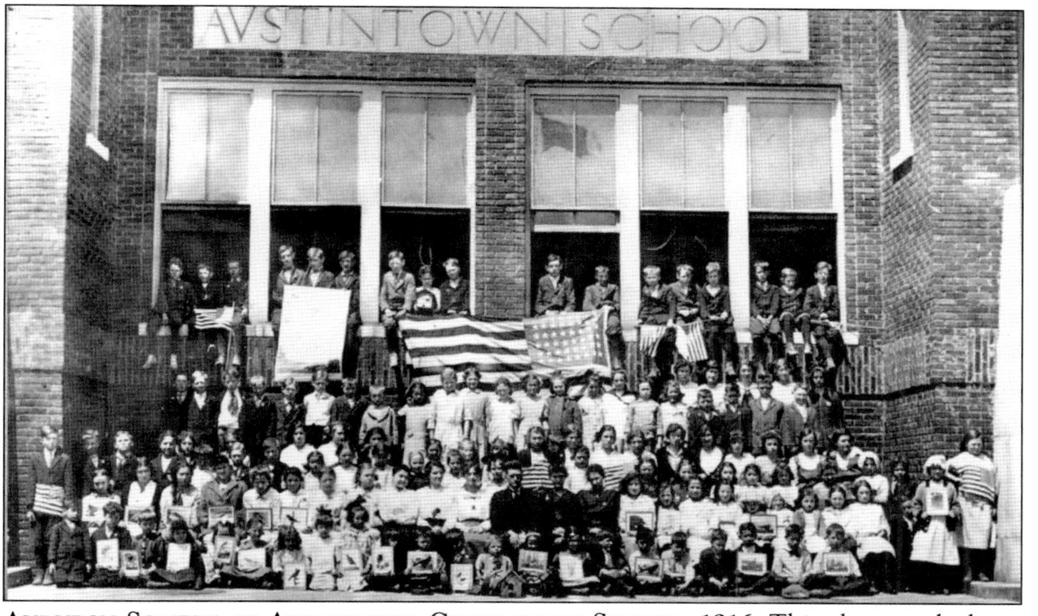

AUDUBON SOCIETY AT AUSTINTOWN CENTRALIZED SCHOOL, 1916. This photograph shows all teachers and students in grades 1–9. Notice the form of the letter *U* in Austintown. Other buildings in the area, including Stambaugh Auditorium, substituted the letter *V* for the letter *U*. (Courtesy AHS.)

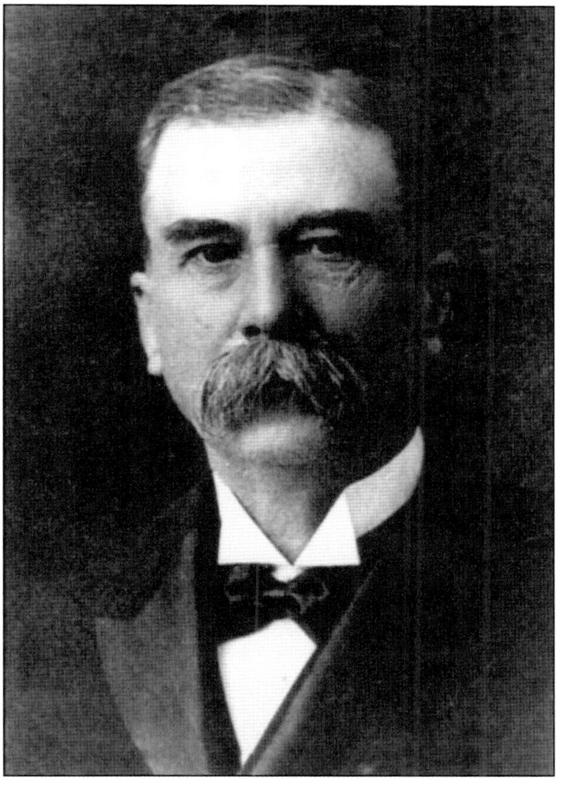

JOHN H. FITCH. Fitch was born to John C. and Elsa Brockway Fitch, west of Austintown Center, in 1843. In 1914, he donated eight of his 400 acres on Mahoning Avenue west of the center for a new school. After Fitch's death in 1919, Frank Ohl, Fitch's farm manager, circulated petitions to rename Austintown Centralized School to Austintown Fitch School. It was renamed on March 17, 1924. (Courtesy AHS.)

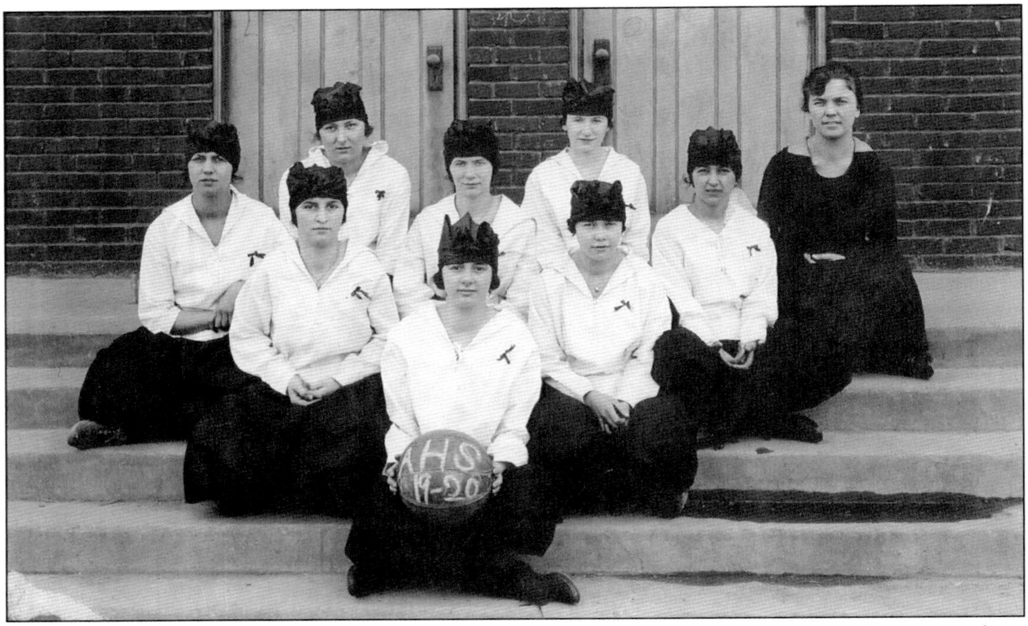

First Girls Basketball Team, Austintown High School, 1919–1920. Team members seen here from left to right include (first row) Helen Dunlap; (second row) Elsie Lucas and Florence Kling; (third row) Hilda Fryfogle, Mary Brickley, and Alice Buchwalter; (fourth row) Florence Leonhart, Greta Brickley, and coach Doris Cain. (Courtesy AHS.)

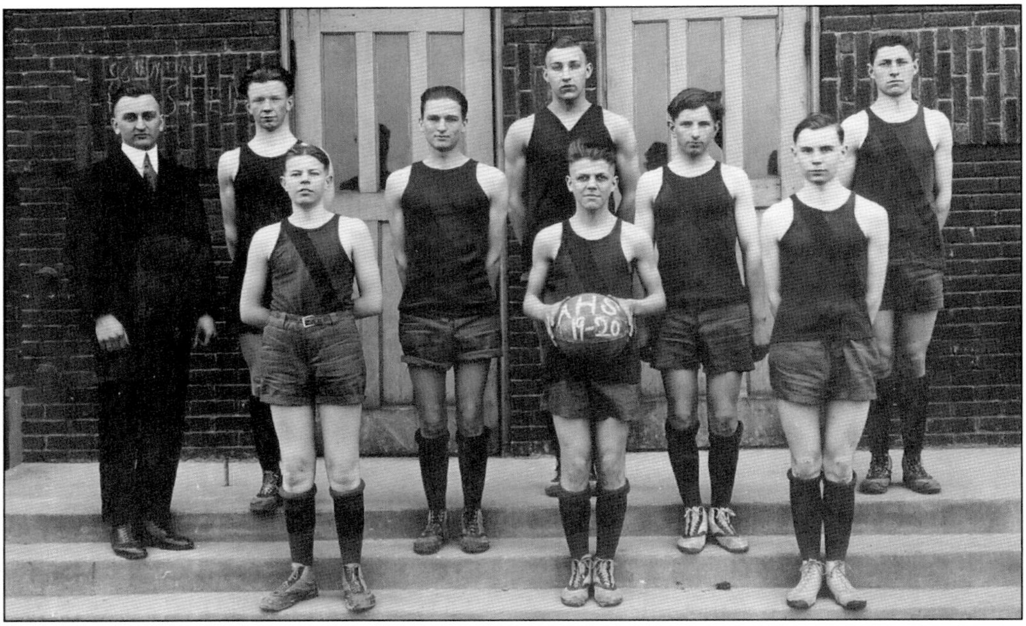

Austintown High School Boys Basketball Team, 1919–1920. This team was the first to participate in the Mahoning County basketball tournament. Members from left to right include (first row) Harold Brickley, Harold Ohl, and Noble Barnes; (second row) coach and principal John Eschleman, Thomas Kennedy, and John Creed; (third row) Louis Grove, Van Gruber, and Arthur Young. (Courtesy AHS.)

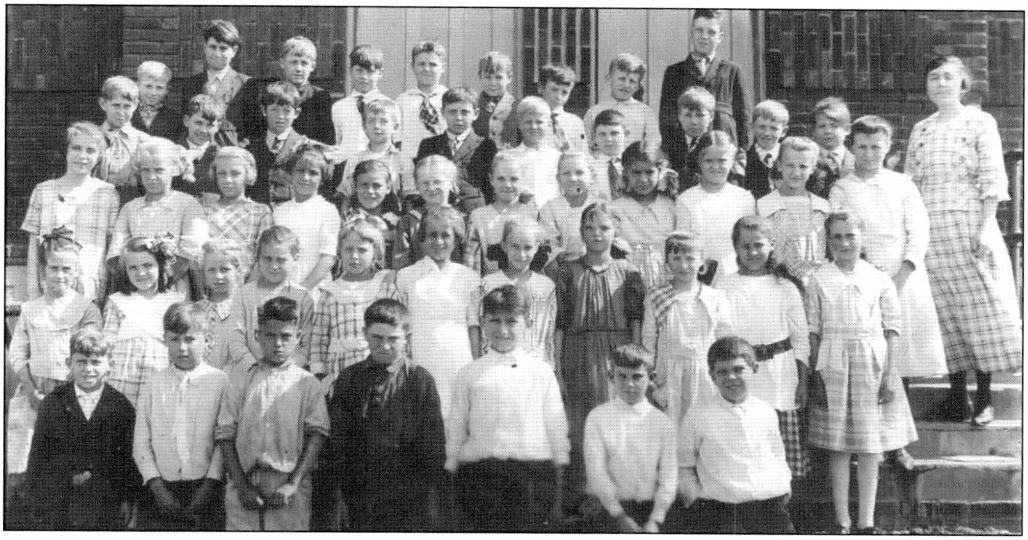

AUSTINTOWN CENTRALIZED SCHOOL, FOURTH-GRADE CLASS, 1920–1921. Martha Welsh's class includes (first row) Blaine Brandyberry, Howard Newport, George Misel, unidentified, Charles Klepins, Rath Bingham, and John Hoskinson; (second row) Ora Hood, Ethel Wilcox, Esther Dye, Jane Jerome, Velma Stark, Iola Krietzburg, Velma Yeager, Leota Klingerman, Gladys Lanterman, Helen Frederick, and Florence DeHoff; (third row) Myrna Darrol, Marion Moore, Ethel May, Mabel Wagner, Sarah Schuller, Catherine Roth, Emma Tessean, Katherine Felmet, Louise Thompson, Marion Leeworthy, Marie Goehring, and Florence Lanterman; (fourth row) John Mesmer, Edgar Hoffman, Herman Richel, Frank Schultz, Charles Richel, unidentified, George Stevenson, Frederick Pershing, Francis Bishop, and John Kerns; (fifth row) Venice Bortmas, William Goehring, Harold Duvall, Leroy Crum, Upson Bonser, Vincent ?, unidentified, and Homer Neff. (Courtesy Wilcox family.)

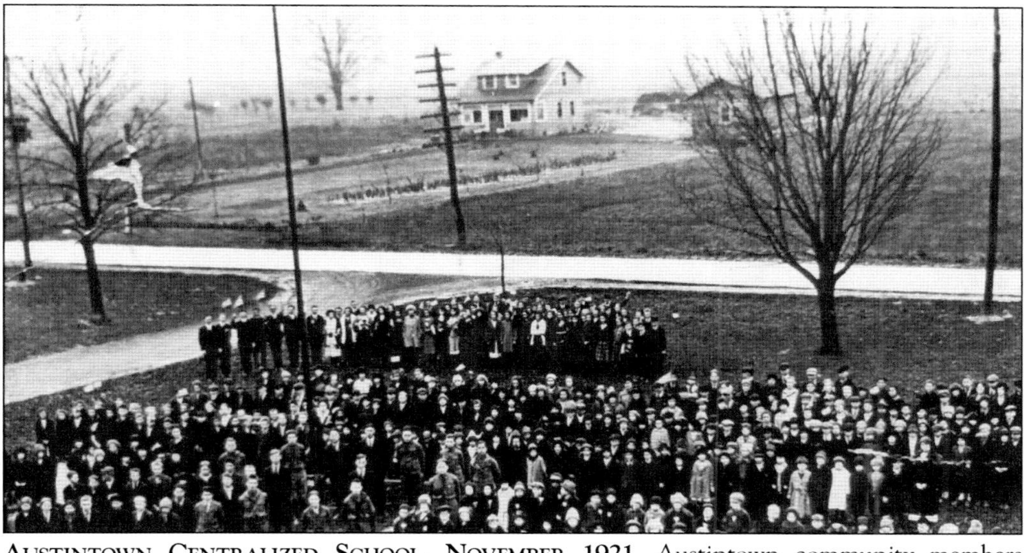

AUSTINTOWN CENTRALIZED SCHOOL, NOVEMBER 1921. Austintown community members celebrate Armistice Day in front of the school. The house across the street on Mahoning Avenue played an important role. The school had no telephone; the operator diverted calls for the school to this house. The woman who lived there raised a flag signaling a telephone call. (Courtesy AHS.)

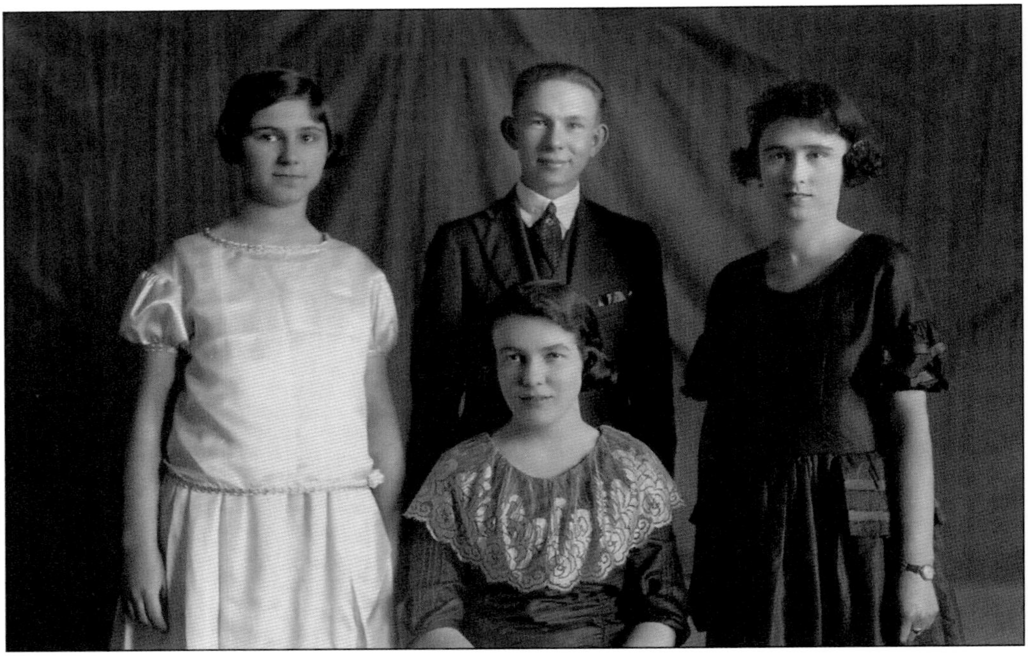

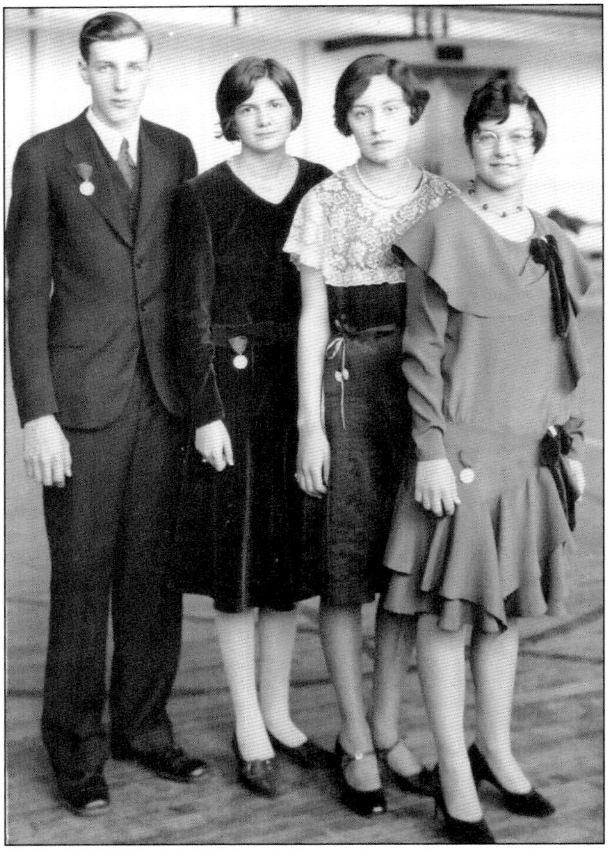

AUSTINTOWN SCHOOL, MAHONING COUNTY LITERARY CHAMPIONS. Even before being chartered as a four-year high school in 1922, the Austintown literary teams were Mahoning County Champions in 1921, 1923, 1924, 1925, and 1926, defeating established high schools Poland Seminary, Canfield, and Youngstown Rayen. The 1923 Mahoning County Literary Champions (above) from left to right include (first row) Marie Grimm, reading; (second row) Lillian Wagner, essay; Tod Flick, oratory; and Nellie Bickerstaff, short story. Literary champions in the undated lower photograph are, from left to right, Joe Roudebush, Ethel Maurer, Margaret Anderson, and Cornelia Kale. (Courtesy AHS.)

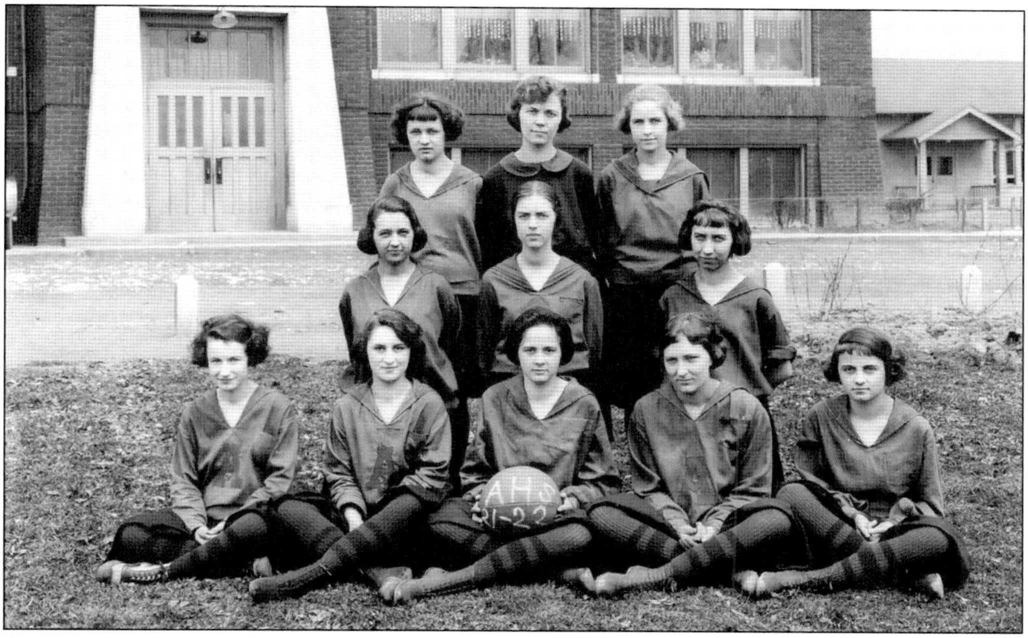

AUSTINTOWN HIGH GIRLS BASKETBALL TEAM, 1921–1922. This team includes (first row) Greta Brickley, Elsie Lucas, and Helen Dunlap; (second row) Alice Buchwalter, Ruby Bishop, and Inez Gates; (third row) Eve Fryfogle, coach Doris Cain, and Mildred Brandmiller. In the back right is the first addition to the school, eight classrooms, added in 1922 and costing $75,000. (Courtesy AHS.)

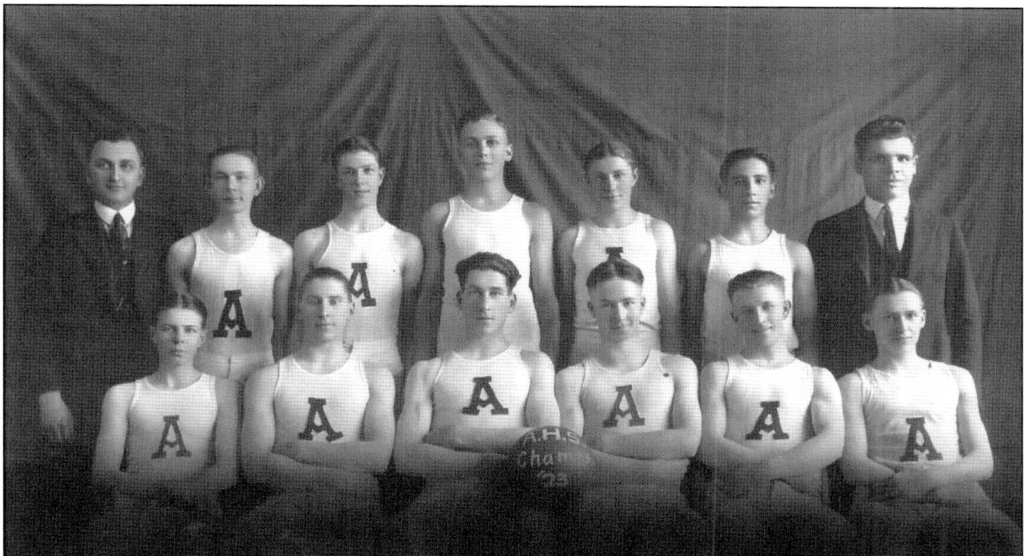

AUSTINTOWN HIGH BOYS MAHONING COUNTY CHAMPIONSHIP TEAM, 1923. The team seen here from left to right includes (first row) Harold Brickley, Clyde Helsel, Theodore Helsel, Howard Stitle, Mike Fasek, and Randall Kroeck; (second row) coach and principal John Eschleman, Tod Flick, Russell Hahn, Randall Ohl, Leroy Foster, Steve Summer, and assistant coach Wallace Clay. (Courtesy AHS.)

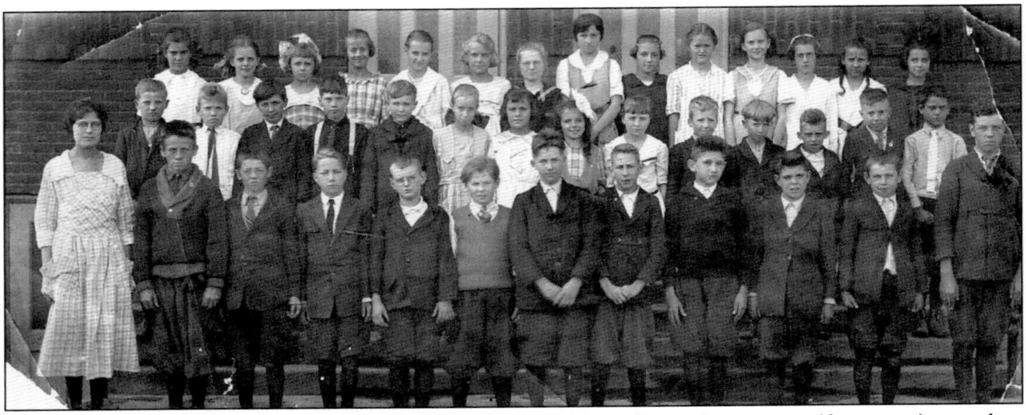

AUSTINTOWN SEVENTH-GRADE CLASS, 1923–1924. Seen here are (first row) teacher Miss Wagner, Leroy Fink, Herman Richel, Frederick Pershing, Edward Pelton, John Kerns, unidentified, John Mesmer, Charles Klepin, John Hoslonson, Donald Smith, and Homer Neff; (second row) William Hoover, Edgar Hoffman, Harold Duvall, Upson Bonser, Velma Yeager, Sarah Schuller, Ethel Wilcox, Gladys Lanterman, Maurice Marrow, Harmon Neff, Blaine Brandyberry, Howard Newport, and George Misel; (third row) Louise Thompson, Emma Tessean, Velma Stark, Iola Krietzburg, Marie Goehring, Marion Morre, Catherine Roth, Florence Lanterman, Ethel May, Marion Leeworthy, Dorothy Green, Florence DeHoff, Helen Frederick, and Florence Floor. (Courtesy Wilcox family.)

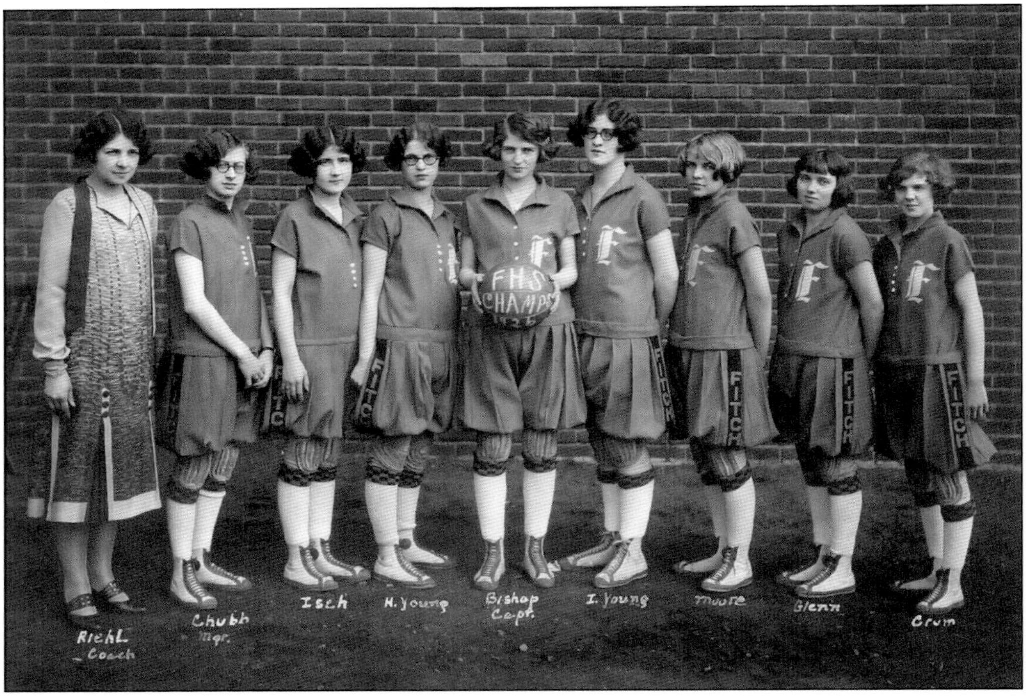

AUSTINTOWN FITCH GIRLS MAHONING COUNTY CHAMPIONS, 1926. With an 18-1 record, these team members include, left to right, coach Ina Riehl, manager Thora Chubb, Evelyn Isch, Helen Young, captain Isabel Bishop, Imogene Young, Marion Moore, Dorothy Glenn, and Alice Crum. Earning All County honors were Glenn and Bishop, first team; Chubb and Imogene Young, second team; Crum and Moore, honorable mention. (Courtesy AHS.)

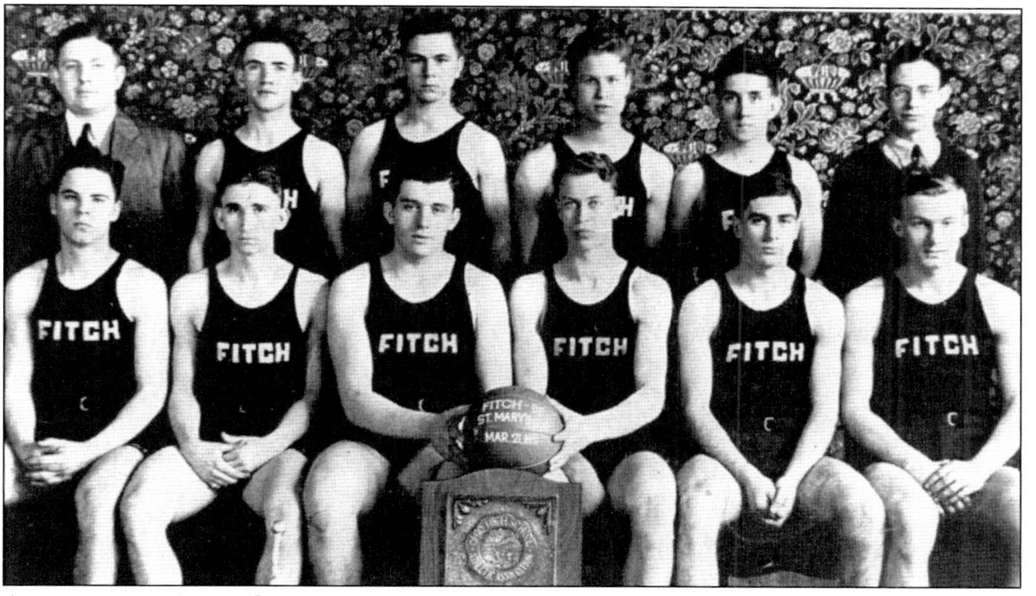

AUSTINTOWN FITCH OHIO BOYS CLASS B STATE CHAMPIONS, 1931. This team defeated Lancaster St. Mary's 26-24 in double overtime. From left to right they are (first row) William Beichler, Elmer Bokesch, Dominic Bertolini, captain Thomas Hood, Bernard Rullie, and Ed Kravec; (second row) coach Harold Rickert, Heston Bishop, Stewart Wagner, Paul Schmidt, Robert Isch, and manager Paul Zimmerman. (Courtesy AHS.)

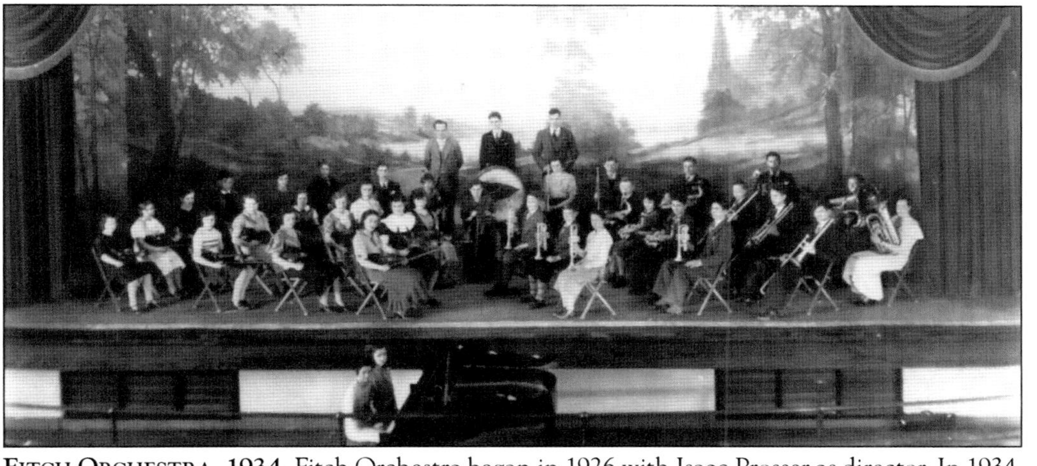

FITCH ORCHESTRA, 1934. Fitch Orchestra began in 1926 with Isaac Prosser as director. In 1934, Kenneth Evans directed the orchestra and band. The orchestra on Fitch High School's stage includes pianist Nancy Denham, assistant Rose Lutch; violins Anna Joseph, Dorothy Shook, Mary Markusich, Mary Kravec, Winifred Seigel, Betty Russell, Dorothy Pavlesic, Helen Fink, Violet Beck, Vasalie Popa, Thomas Ward, Evelyn Baker, Viola Leigh, and Martha Thompson; clarinets Howard Williams, Jack Sutton, Ada Creed, and Dorothy Wagner; trumpets Lenora Shears, Junior Wingert, Dwayne Snyder, and Guido Schiavone; trombones Sidney Stacey, Joseph Markusich, and Lee Powell; baritone Evelyn Chapman; saxophones Ralph Boyer, Doris Wagner, Martin Eberth, and Frank Gorgie; alto horn George Unger; bass horn Thelma Foster; cello Genevieve Schnurrenberger; and drums Henry Marshman and Arnold Bokesch. (Courtesy Joseph Pelligrini.)

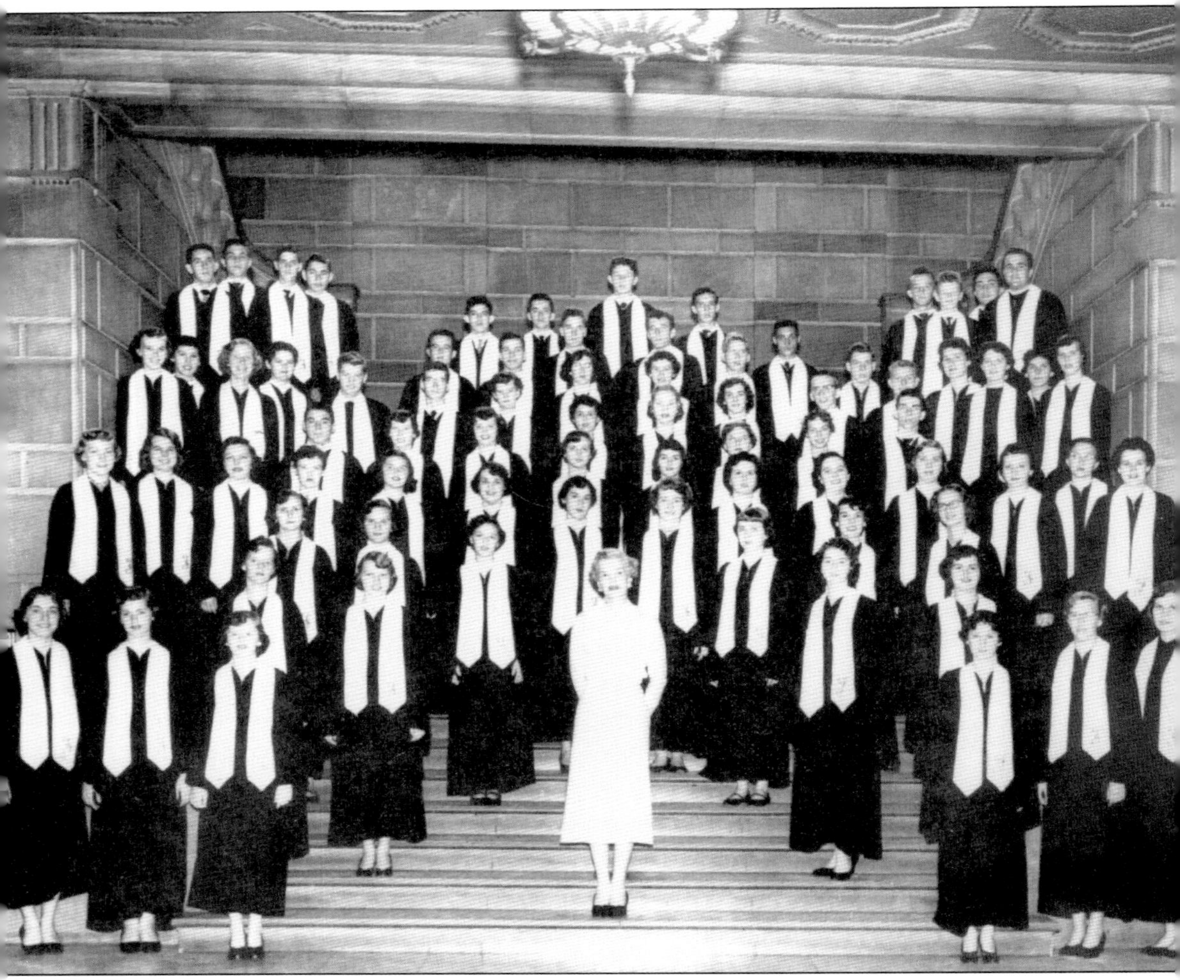

FITCH CHOIR AT STAMBAUGH AUDITORIUM, 1954. Appearing in concerts, at the baccalaureate service, and on television, choir members from left to right are (first row) Maureen Erb, Peggy Glodde, Barbara Terlecki, Carol Gonaware, Joan Weaver, and Sandra Schmidt; (second row) Helen Rothrock, Janice Vinion, director Jean Rothwell, Nanette Peters, and Carol Brandmiller; (third row) Nancy Waller, Irene Strayer, Aurora Pavone, Marjorie Brown, Barbara Priore, and Marilyn Davis; (fourth row) Sally Nelson, Lestia Clegg, Barbara Deemer, Millicent Hogarth, Connie Morris, Lois Does, Margaret Cottrell, Nancy Pasha, Theresa Pinter, Faye Rowe, Sally Davis, Thelma Kimmel, Sally Waller, and Donna Finley; (fifth row) Rick Thorp, Roberta Wood, Jacqueline Rees, Clare White, Rae DeGregory, Joan Susko, Arlene Kirby, and Jerry Stark; (sixth row) Commilla Hern, Judith Brott, Susan Allen, Mary Louise Creed, Robert Hollowell, James Griffiths, Elaine Samuels, Rosalie Dorman, Jacqueline Kolesar, Diane Cline, Thomas Proverbs, Robert McNeil, Frank Lombardo, Elaine Juhasz, Joan Victor, Diane Bruno, and Joyce Sleighter; (seventh row) Bruce Kirkland, James Wilhide, Donna Vanasdale, Dianne Yogie, Donald Davidson, and Alfred Mound; (eighth row) Thomas Roth, Thomas Clegg, Eugene Higgins, Robert Haydu, Donald Brothers, David Kimmel, Michael Liposchak, Robert Marsch, Paul Vath, Thomas Glassford, Angelo Italiano, and James D'Eramo. (Courtesy AHS.)

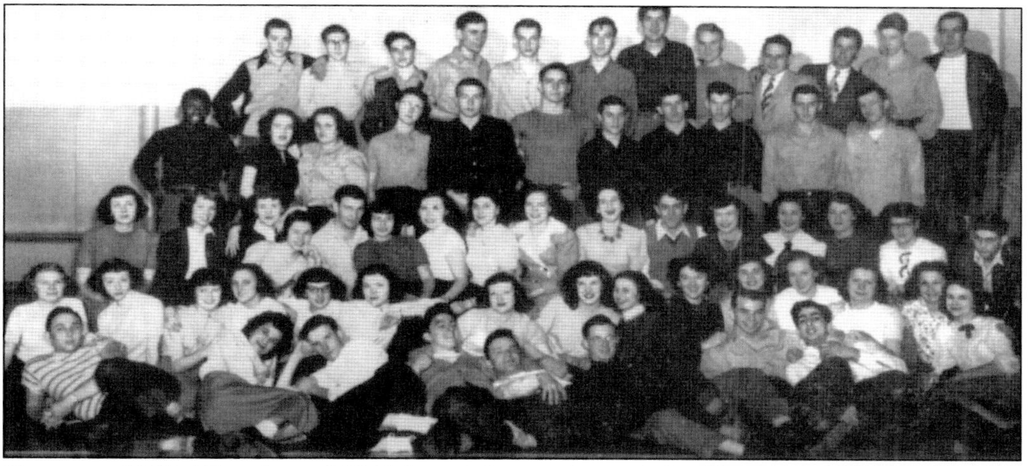

CLASS OF 1949. The class of 1949 from left to right includes (first row) Rich Martin, Jean Amendol, Charles Chappell, Bud Tocco, Bill McClain, Ralph Ryhal, Andy Scotchie, and John Mousie; (second row) Peggy Lee, Tudie Brenner, Sally Higgins, Rose Bieltz, Ann Herschel, Sally McMahon, Delores Barger, Ruth Brickley, Natasha Blair, Dot Tavener, Bunny Boyer, Janet Pohl, Jean Renninger, Nancy Kramer, and Helen Brenner; (third row) Delores Gross, Consetta Bruno, Bev Johnson, Connie Leepard, Dick Mills, Rita Mozzy, Pauline Ekoniak, Naomi Upole, Mildred Tautkus, Betty Lingenfelter, Jim Barton, Kate Hogarth, Mary Ann Savino, Edith Schrum, Harriet Stephenson, and Frank McCormick; (fourth row) Irvin Padgett, Shirley Buchwalter, Joyce Kroeck, Mary Lou Trimlin, Ed McPhillamy, Bob Husic, Nick Julian, Jerry Medland, Jack Adams, Bill McCormick, and Bill Krause; (fifth row) Tom Miller, Bob Roth, Bob Sullivan, Roland Lehman, Eugene Smith, Howard Waite, Russ Young, Bob Conger, Fred Ciarniello, Leslie Terwillinger, Don Mitchell, and Bob Raidel. (Courtesy AHS.)

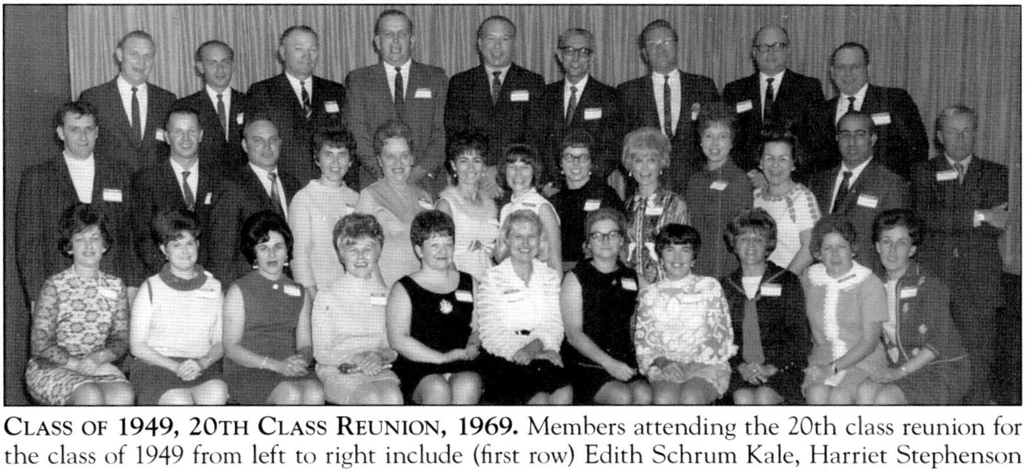

CLASS OF 1949, 20TH CLASS REUNION, 1969. Members attending the 20th class reunion for the class of 1949 from left to right include (first row) Edith Schrum Kale, Harriet Stephenson Roth, Helen Brenner Blackburn, Peggy Lee Corbett, Delores Barger Walker, Betty Brown Conger, Dorothy Tavener Kunde, Ann Herschel Mika, Rose Bieltz Carradine, Sally Higgins Schocchera, and Shirley Buchwalter Snyder; (second row) Bill McCormick, Leslie Terwilliger, Bob Sullivan, Lillian Boyer Divelbiss, class advisor Iscah Boyer, Mary Ann Savino, Natasha Blair Pacic, Connie Leepard Hitchcock, Catherine Hogarth Hoffman, Janet Ohl Wigton, Nancy Schwarten Schwartz, John Mousie, and Bob Krause; (third row) Bob Conger, Nick Julian, class advisor Art Steiskal, Bob Raidel, Ed McPhillamy, Jim Barton, Bob Roth, Ralph Ryhal, and Fred Ciarniello. (Courtesy AHS.)

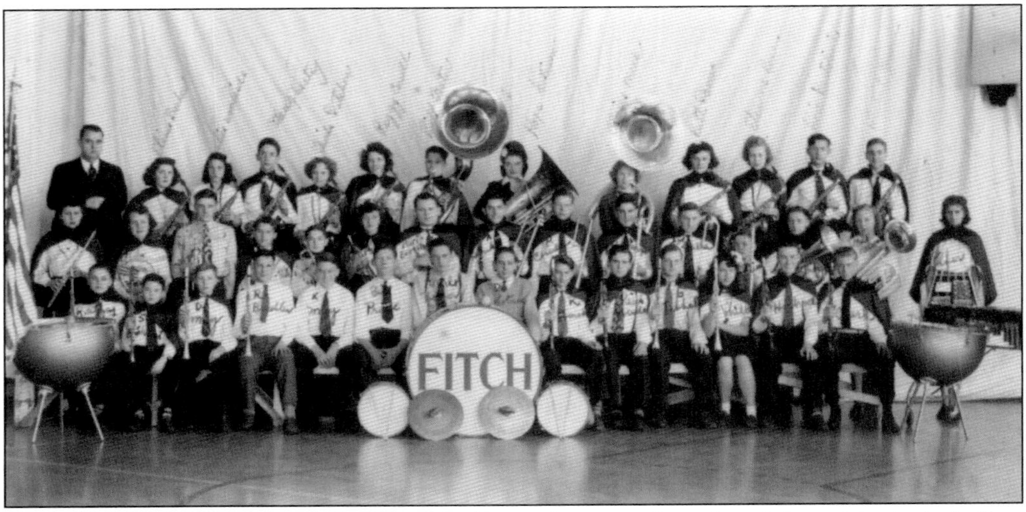

FITCH BAND, 1944. Directed by Glenn Snell, members seen here from left to right include (first row) Richard Athey, S. Short, Dale May, Richard Buechler, Ken May, Bill Price, Merle Boyer, D. Kotouc, Ray Houk, Richard Hendel, G. Tibbits, ? Wilber, ? Holbrook, and Robert Clarke; (second row) Mildred Grubiss, Eileen Crum, Dick Detchon, P. Schmidt, Bill Delaney, Fay Wagner, Mario Bertolini, Armand Houk, Paul Cerull, Lawrence DeCamp, Joe Balla, Paul Cline, Harry Bishop, Mae Nelson, and Marjorie Pifer; (third row) Glenn Snell, Elaine Barber, Alice Woodside, ? Daugherty, Twila Detchon, Peggy Cerull, Bill Foster, Hope Gettmann, Clare Meek, Ruth Davies, Eleanore Rose, Livio Bertolini, and Herbert Greene. (Courtesy Lawrence Snell.)

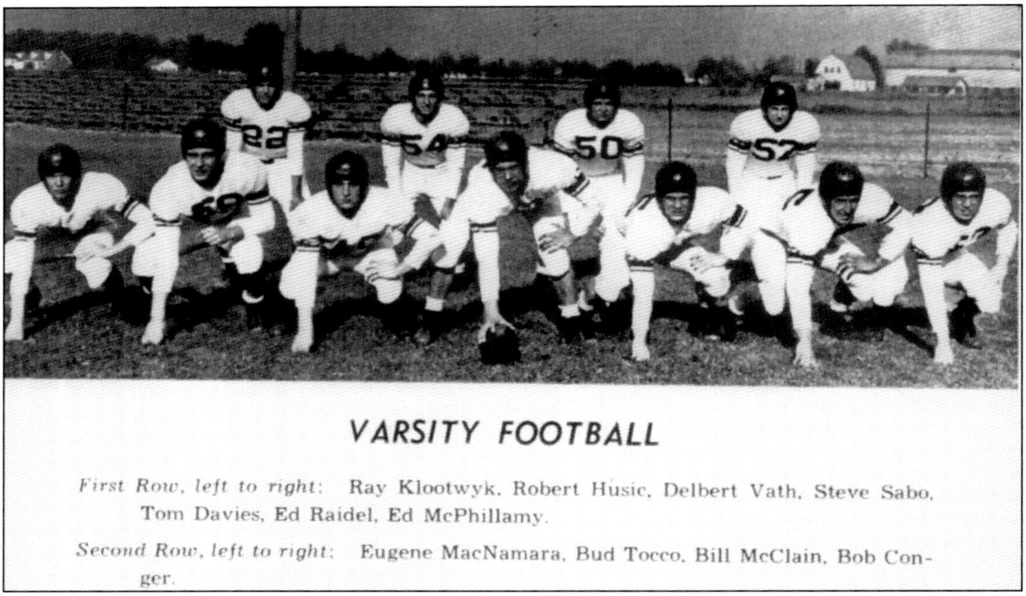

FITCH VARSITY FOOTBALL TEAM, 1949. Before the football stadium on Mahoning Avenue opened on October 14, 1933, the Fitch team played on a farmer's field on Canfield-Niles Road. Opponents called them the Fitch Farmers because, as evident here, there were farms nearby. The first football game played at the new Fitch sports complex on Falcon Drive was in 1969. (Courtesy AHS.)

JACK MORRISON, FITCH CLASS OF 1955. Jack Morrison, who scored 473 points in a single year averaging 21 points per game over three years, scored 52 points in one game against Hubbard on February 19, 1955, setting school, Steel Valley Conference, and state records for his performance. Fitch won the game 55-54. Morrison is still listed in Ohio Boy's Basketball Individual Scoring records. (Courtesy AHS.)

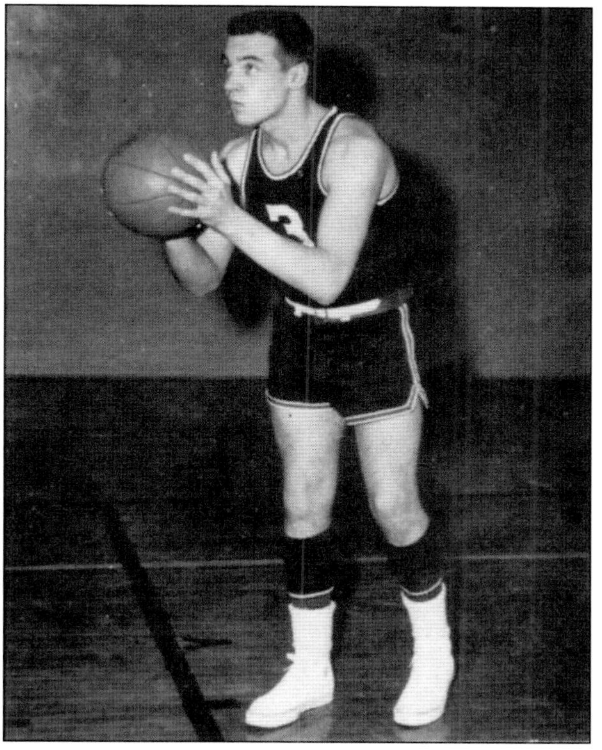

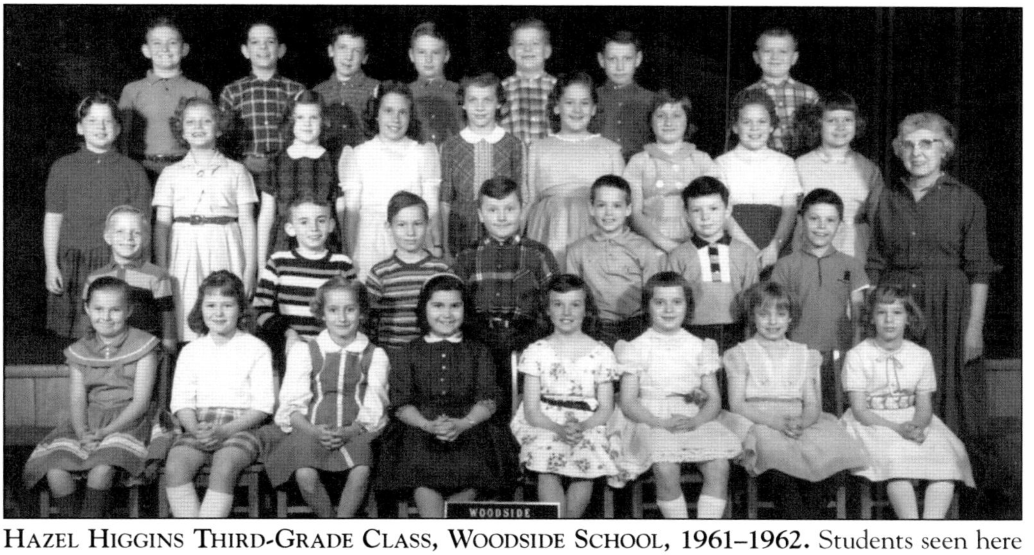

HAZEL HIGGINS THIRD-GRADE CLASS, WOODSIDE SCHOOL, 1961–1962. Students seen here from left to right include (first row) Becky Grist, Janet Lamia, Doris McGirr, Marlene Puskas, Cathy Sturm, Carol Sesko, Judith Nyers, and Sylvia Forquati; (second row) Danny Salsgiver, Michael Case, Richard Patoray, Jack Whitehouse, Jeffrey Poppke, Gregory Pennett, Richard Massie, and Mrs. Higgins; (third row) Marsha Clarke, Cosette Gearhart, Paula Davis, Sharon Ray, Mary Neptune, Marsha Jewell, Sallie Serbati, Patty Wallace, and Karen Bruno; (fourth row) Michael Gray, Robert Morris, John Russell, Donald Conroy, Norman Ditman, Gregg Watterson, and Donald Bodnar. (Courtesy AHS.)

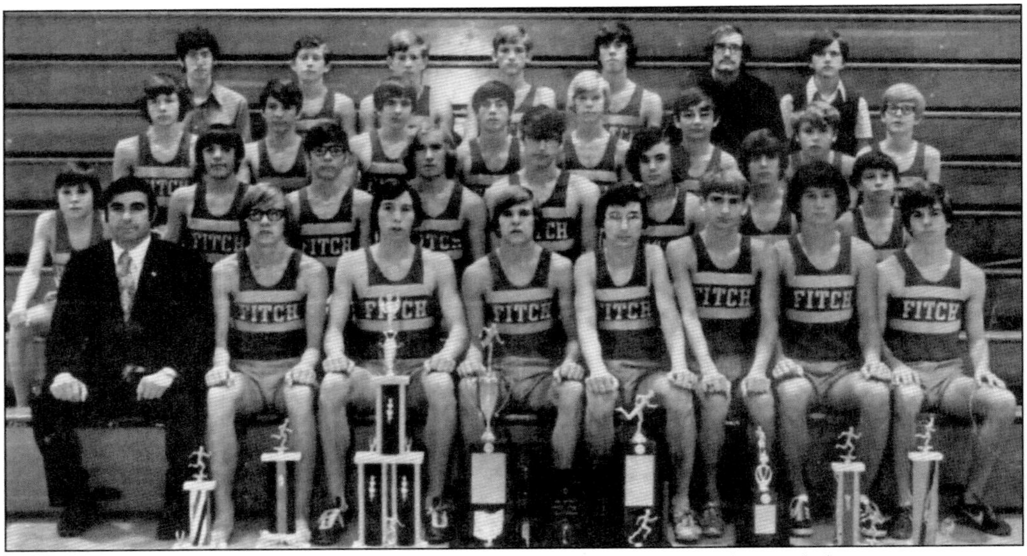

Ohio Cross-Country Champs, 1972. In 1971, 1972, and 1975, the Fitch boys cross-country teams won the state cross-country championships. The team was runner-up in 1970 and 1974. In 30 seasons, Coach Mike Garcia's cross-country teams won 490 meets, 101 major championships, and were 42 major championship runners-up. Members of the 1972 team from left to right include (first row) Coach Garcia, Eldon Jones, Rich Kempe, Bob Lunn (state champion in 1973), Paul Giba, Jeff Kunkle, Steve Fedyna, and Dalvin Baehler; (second row) Tom Corbett, Jeff Fabian, Rob McEaneney, Alex Shaffo, Jim Rider, Ken Erdner, Rick Parker, and Kevin Kempe; (third row) Chuck Foster, Keith Bigley, Steve Bernard, Jim Little, Rich Hamaker, Ken Giba, Jeff Durn, and Steve Mariash; (fourth row) statistician Bryan Ostroff, Paul Stevens, Jeff Walter, Tony Bayer, Chris Davis, manager Dave Mentges, and statistician Bill Padisak. (Courtesy Mike Garcia.)

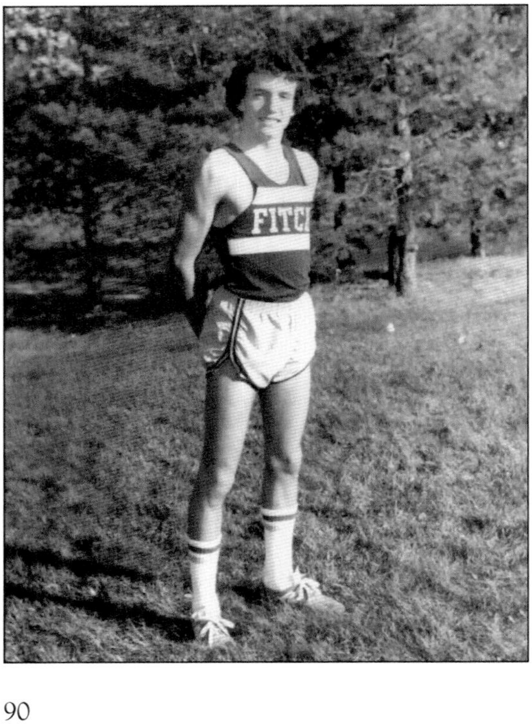

Alan Scharsu, 1975 Ohio State Cross-Country Champion 1975, 1976, 1977. Scharsu was the first Ohio state champion three consecutive years. An Ohio High School All-American, Scharsu set a national record for 14–16 year olds in the two mile in 1977 with a time of 8:45.8 and is still listed sixth on "All-time US High School Boys 2 Milers" with a time of 8:44.03. (Courtesy Mike Garcia.)

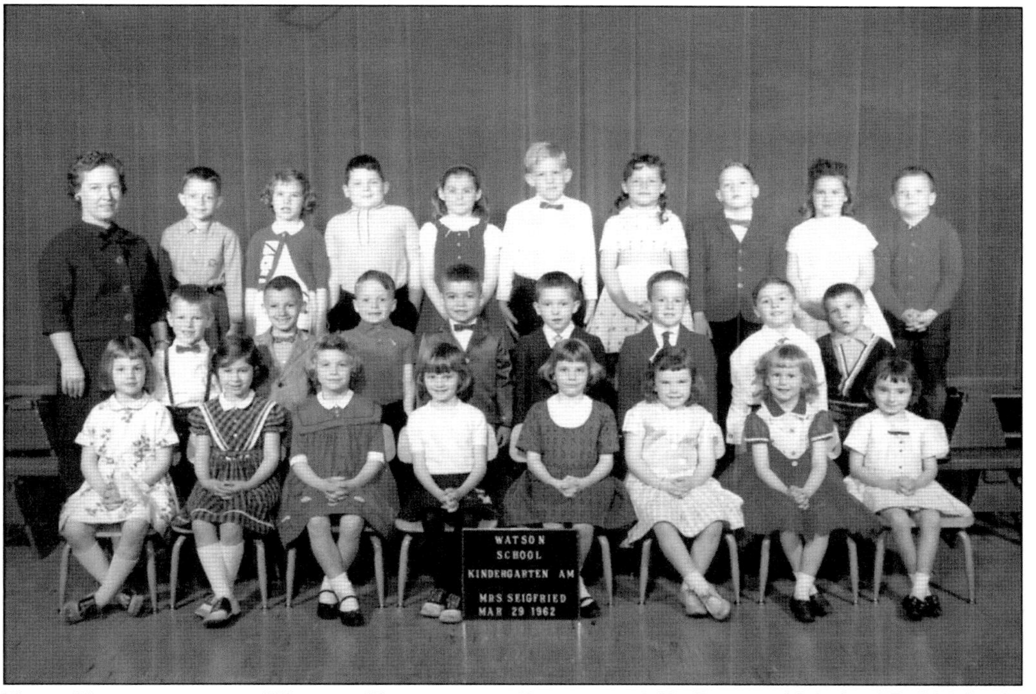

FIRST KINDERGARTEN, WATSON ELEMENTARY SCHOOL, 1962. Principal Merlin "Bo" Valot Jr. opened Watson Elementary on January 2, 1962. Watson was named for Charles Gamble Watson, Austintown resident and president of Youngstown Welding and Engineering, 1937–1958. When some of the kindergarten students were high school seniors in 1974, they scaled the stadium fence one night and painted their class numbers on the bleacher seats. (Courtesy Joyce Pogany.)

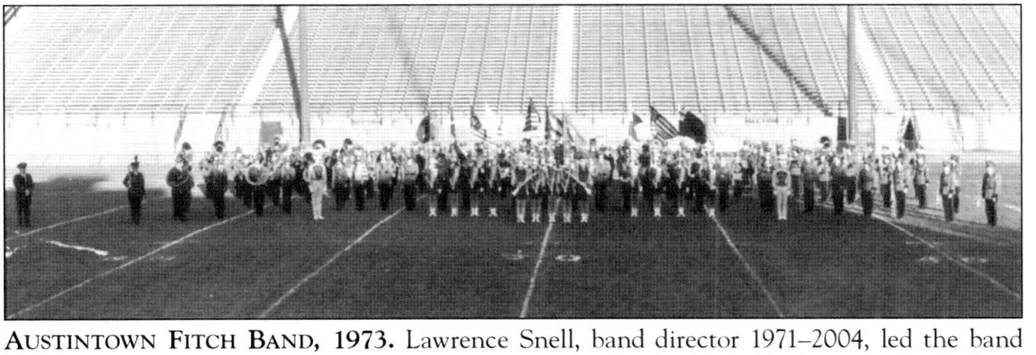

AUSTINTOWN FITCH BAND, 1973. Lawrence Snell, band director 1971–2004, led the band to 24 consecutive superior ratings at state competition. In the Fitch Stadium are Snell, drum major Paul Rohrbaugh, assistant drum major Rick Whitten, and 154 band members. Notice no numbers are on the stadium seats, these were painted in 1974 by the class of 1974. School personnel began painting the numbers in the 1980s. (Courtesy Lawrence Snell.)

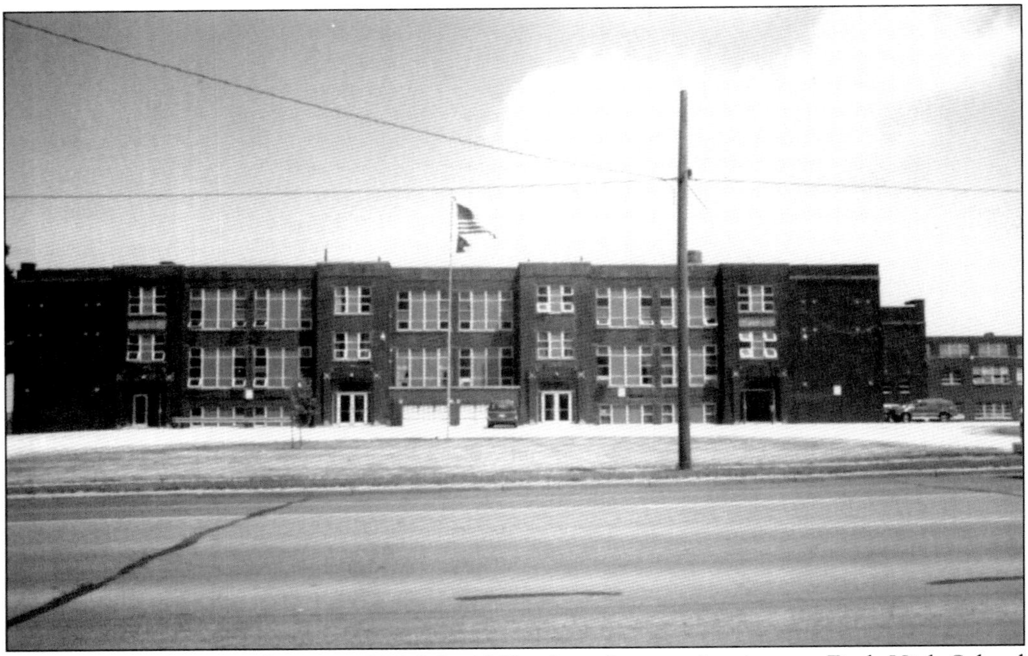

AUSTINTOWN MIDDLE SCHOOL, 2006. In 1968, when the new Austintown Fitch High School opened, this building was rechristened the Austintown Middle School (AMS), housing 1,600 pupils in grades 5–8. The red-and-gold Trojan served as the school mascot until 1998. The school is to be demolished in 2007. (Courtesy Joyce Pogany.)

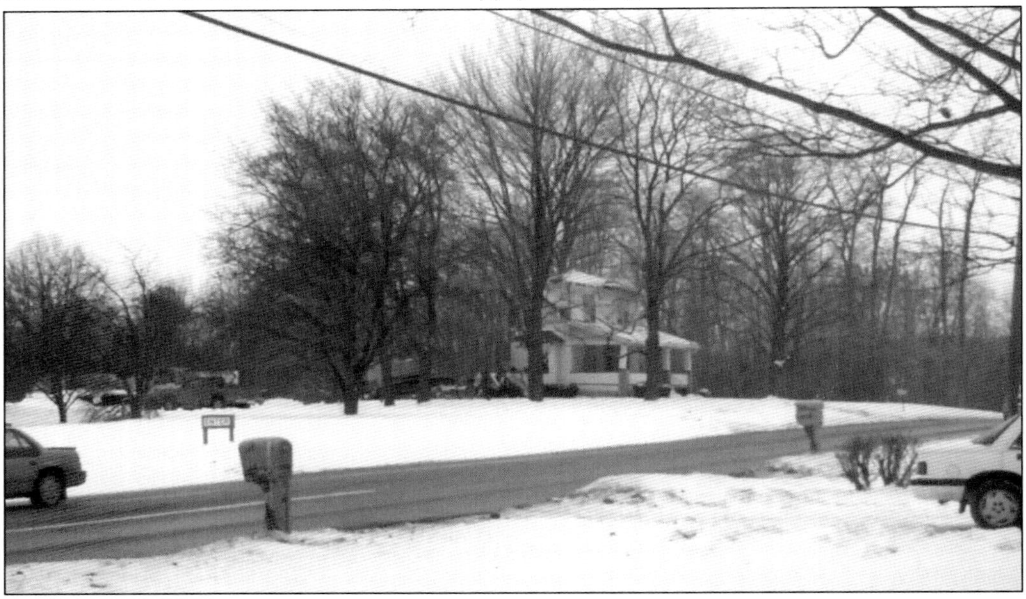

LOCATION OF NEW AUSTINTOWN MIDDLE SCHOOL. In February 2004, the Joseph and Julia Laskey farmhouse on South Raccoon Road was razed to make way for the new Austintown Middle School. The school, constructed with funds from a bond issue passed by taxpayers, will house approximately 1,200 students in grades 6–8 and is slated to open in September 2007. (Courtesy Joyce Pogany.)

Seven

Social Life and Recreation in Austintown

Most early settlers socialized with other residents at church, weddings, and funerals. In 1874, John McCaughtery held monthly dances at the Indian Queen Hotel in Austintown Center. Many saloons were in West Austintown's Anderson Block. Miners frequented Mickey McCartney's saloon, on the east side of South Turner Road, south of the Fairview Road intersection. In the 1900s, some of Austintown's restaurants and taverns included Green Acres, Whippoorwill, Golden Pheasant, 7 Mile Inn, Ice House Inn, R Villa, Paul's Steak House, and Little Man's jazz bar on Lanterman Road. John Eschleman started the annual fall school fair where students displayed their schoolwork and homegrown produce. In 1926, when August Kroeck and Sons brought a radio to the school fair and tuned it to the Dempsey-Tunney fight, some Austintown residents heard a radio for the first time. In 1941, Fitch School began showing weekly movies intended "to educate but also create a friendlier feeling in the community." The first movie was Mickey Rooney's *The Hoosier Schoolboy*. Austintown and Youngstown residents enjoyed the annual circus under the big tops on North Meridian Road. Roller skaters enjoyed daily skates and Friday night dances at the Rollerena on Oakwood Avenue. From the mid-1950s to the 1980s, residents enjoyed the Austintown Drive-in Theater on Mahoning Avenue across from Wilcox Road. The Russell Avenue YMCA provided recreational activities. Little Leaguers developed their skills at the many baseball fields. Community members continue to gather together at Fitch High School to pay their respects at the Memorial Day parade and Veteran's Day ceremony.

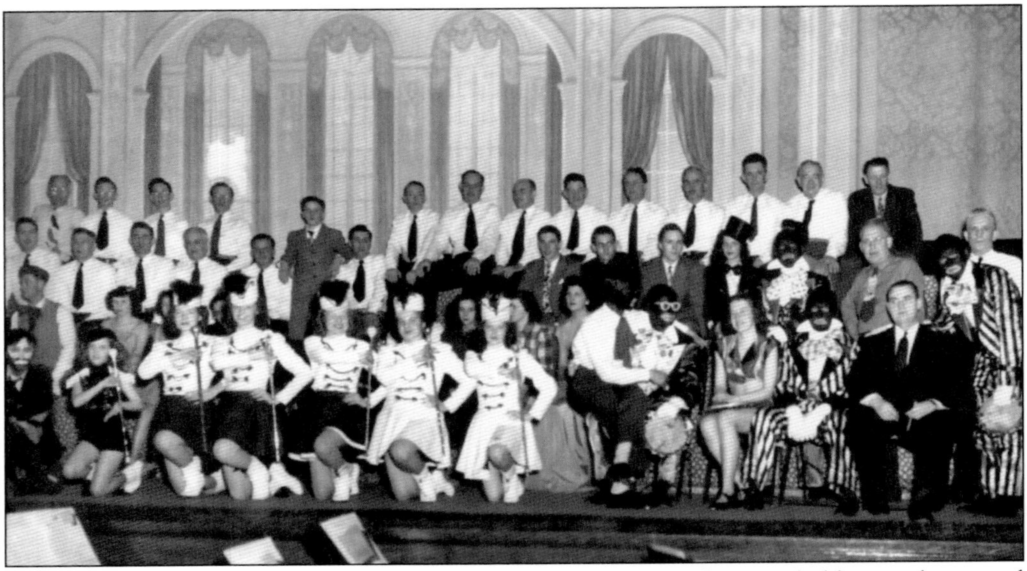

AUSTINTOWN COMMUNITY MINSTREL SHOW, 1950. Fitch Productions held annual minstrel shows in the spring of 1940 through 2000. The shows featured a variety of performers including Fitch majorettes and a chorus (in back rows wearing ties). Glenn Snell (seated on far right) directed the show band. Fitch Productions also performed many benefit shows. (Courtesy Bernice Boyer.)

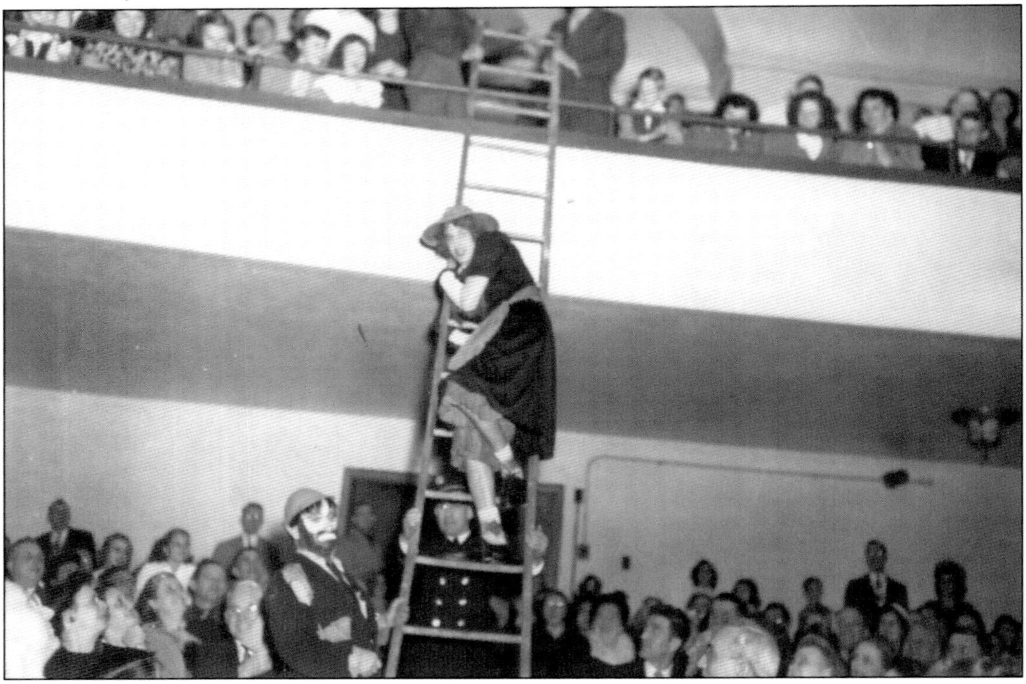

GENE BOYER, AUSTINTOWN COMMUNITY MINSTREL SHOW, 1950. "Lady" Boyer climbs to the balcony of the Fitch School Auditorium (on Mahoning Avenue). Proceeds from the shows were donated to the community including the Fitch High Band, George Shinker Fund, and Champ McGhagan Fund. (Courtesy Bernice Boyer.)

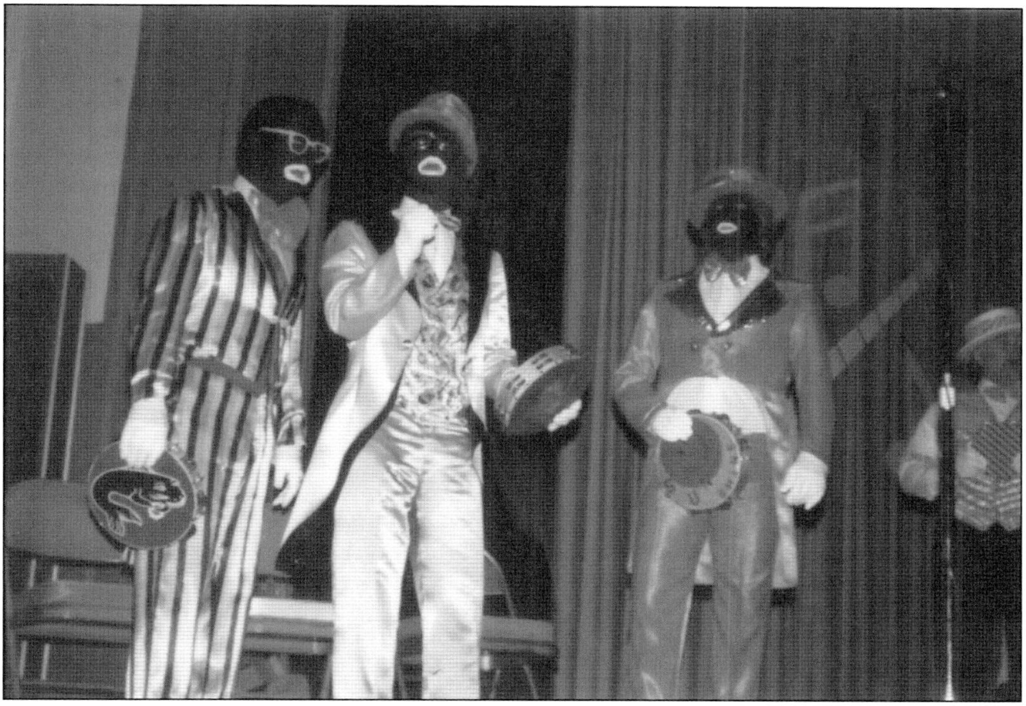

END MEN, 1981. Performers in blackface were a tradition at minstrel shows. The End Men from left to right are Bill "Catfish" Curley, Bill "Gumdrop" Wayland, Sam "Sunshine" Stambaugh, and Bill Streiner. In the 1990s, Fitch Productions received approval from the local NAACP to use blackface. (Courtesy Sam Stambaugh.)

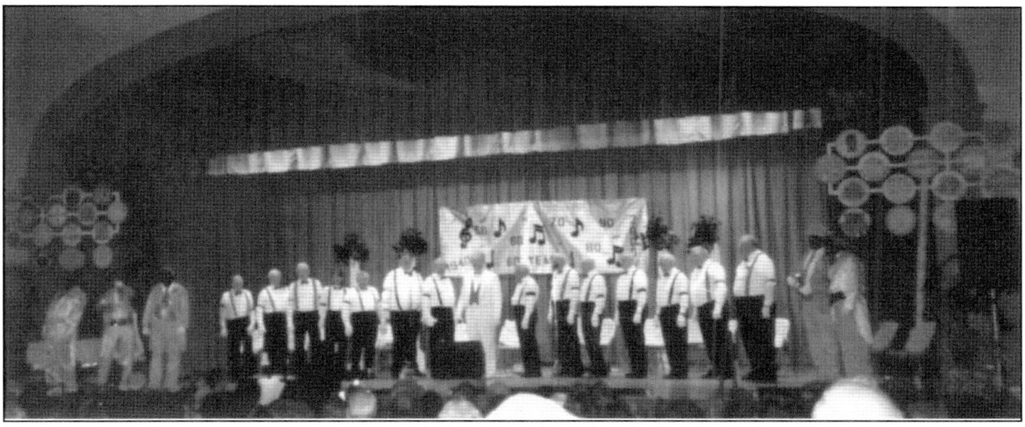

LAST SHOW, 2000. Seen here at Austintown Middle School from left to right are Dave "Punkin" Prosser; "Gumdrop" Wayland; "Sunshine" Stambaugh; Steve Marrie; Orin Carr; unidentified; Jimmi Weed; Don Batisky; Bob Ridel; Walt Labozan; Tom Hathhorn, interlocutor, in white tuxedo; Larry Ortz Sr.; Elmer Grischow; unidentified; Bob Liposchak; unidentified; George Smolko; Ron Neff; Don "Legs" Lemke; and Mike "Sweet Lips" Liposchak. Chorus members not pictured include George and Mike Diamond, Ray Hevener, David Mullane, and Tom Petrenick. (Courtesy Mike Liposchak.)

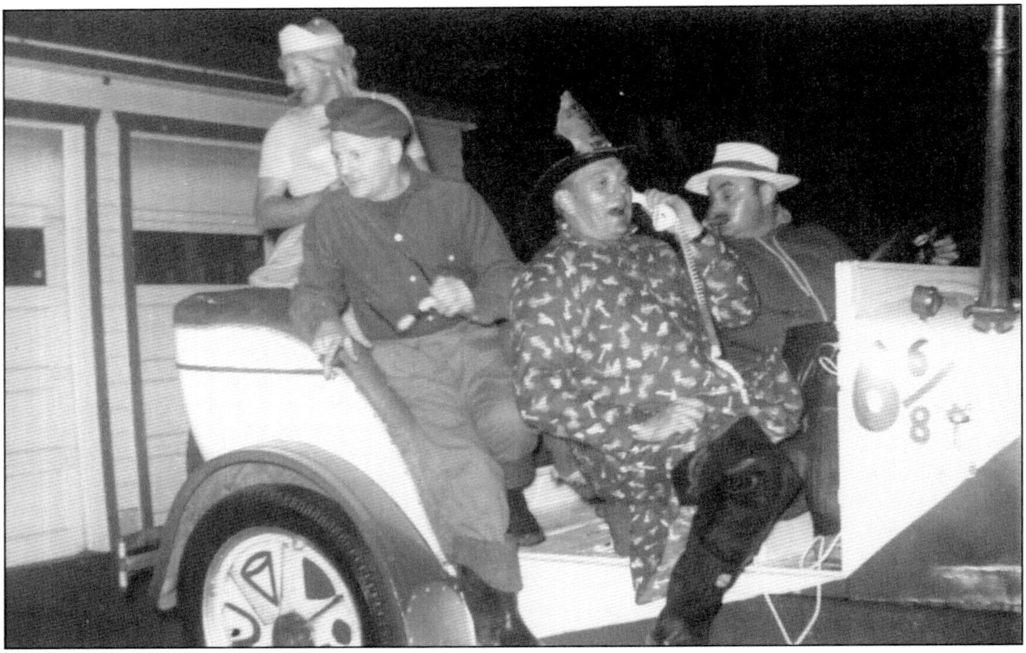

AUSTINTOWN FIREMEN'S CLUB CRAZY CAR. A popular entry in the Austintown Firemen's parade, and other parades, this "crazy car" was named because its different-sized wheels rocked the car from side to side. Pictured from left to right are an unidentified fireman, Jim Shepard, Lucius McIntyre, and Paul Planton (driver). (Courtesy AHS.)

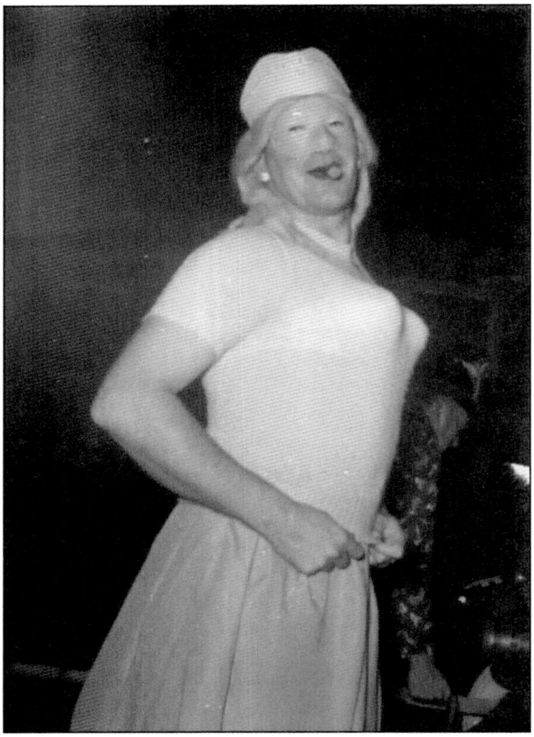

FIREMEN'S PARADE PARTICIPANT. In 1940, the Austintown's Firemen's Club raised money for equipment by holding an ice-cream social at Austintown Community Church; it moved to Fitch School and eventually included a parade on Mahoning Avenue from Woodside School to Fitch. The parade, discontinued in the late 1970s, included over 100 fire trucks from nearby departments. (Courtesy AHS.)

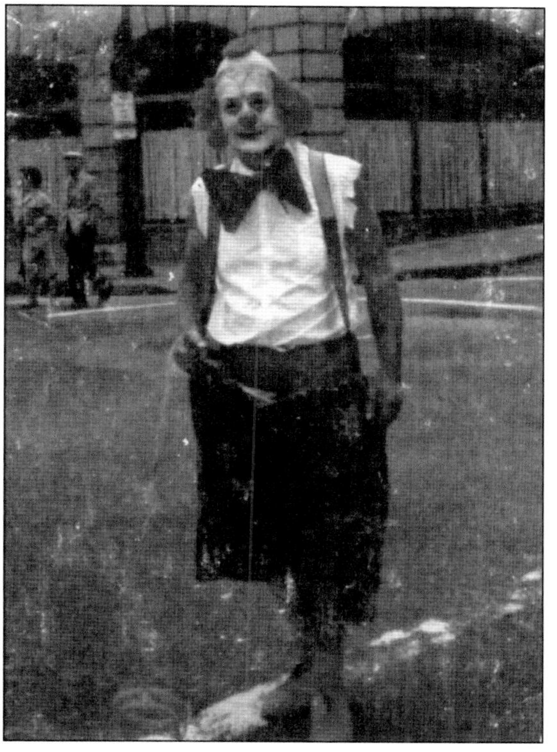

CAPT. ROBERT RICKER WALKING INVISIBLE DOG. Capt. Robert Ricker is dressed as a clown for the firemen's parade, which kicks off a three day ice-cream social at Fitch School every July. This high point of Austintown's summer social life includes ice cream, cakes made by the firemen's wives, games, and carnival rides. (Courtesy Robert Ricker.)

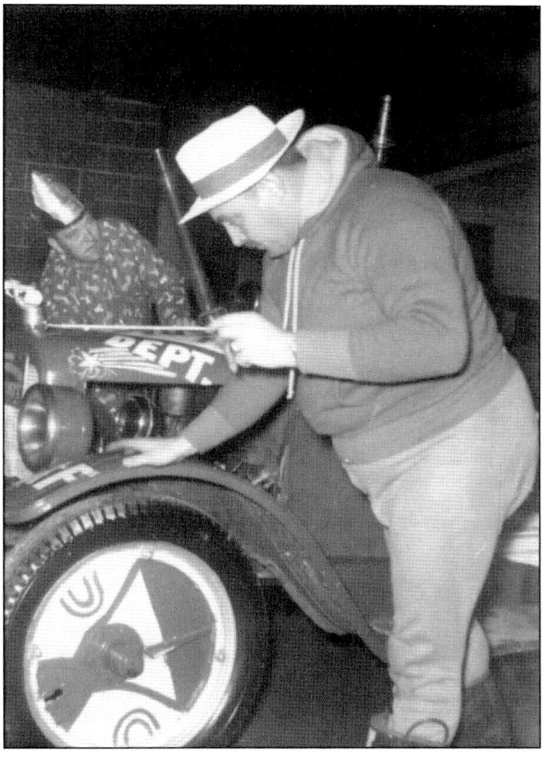

PREPPING THE CRAZY CAR. Firemen Paul Planton, in the foreground, and Lucius McIntyre, in the parade costume in the background, prepare the crazy car for the annual firemen's parade. The crazy car appears in an average of 10 parades per year. The firemen's parade also includes the Fitch Band, scout groups, and local dignitaries. (Courtesy AHS.)

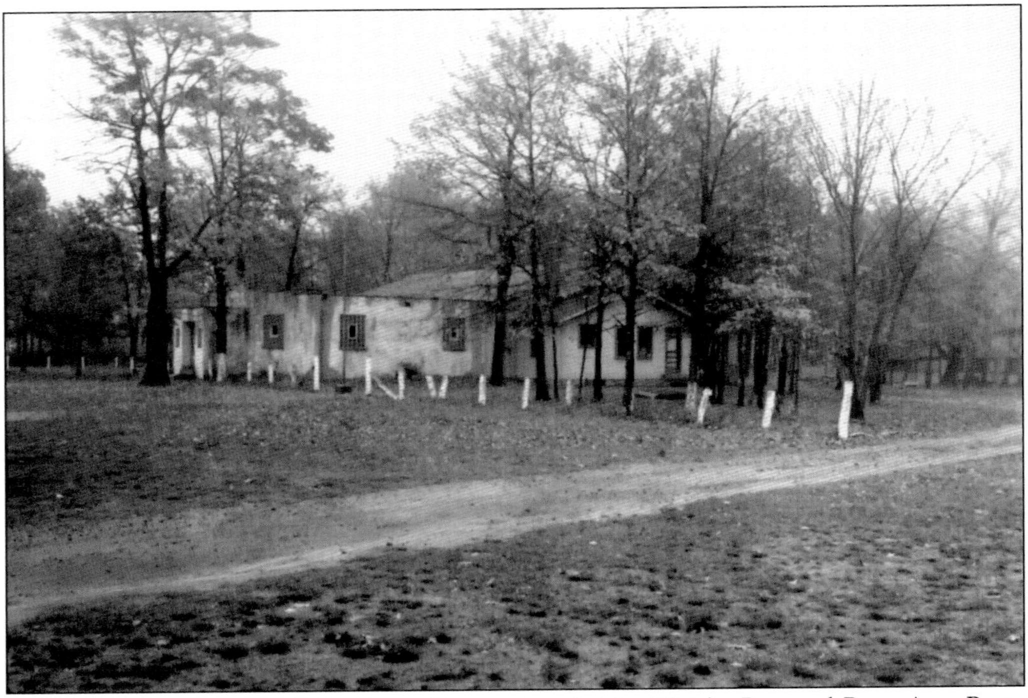

WHIPPOORWILL GROVE, 3931 CRUM ROAD. Founded in 1934 by Ben and Rose Ann Barta Yuhasz, the Whippoorwill included a bar; dance hall; picnic grounds; and outdoor dance floor, cooking area, refreshment stands, and playground. The Croatians, Serbians, Electrical League, Isaly's, and others rented the Whippoorwill. Over 2,000 attended the Hungarian Day picnic in 1938. Many local bands performed there. The picnic grounds closed in the 1960s after Ben Yuhasz's death. Rose continued operating the bar and dance hall, helped by her daughter, Elaine, and son, Bob. Rose died in the 1970s. Bob and Elaine remodeled the dance hall, turning it into a banquet hall. (Courtesy Bob Glasser.)

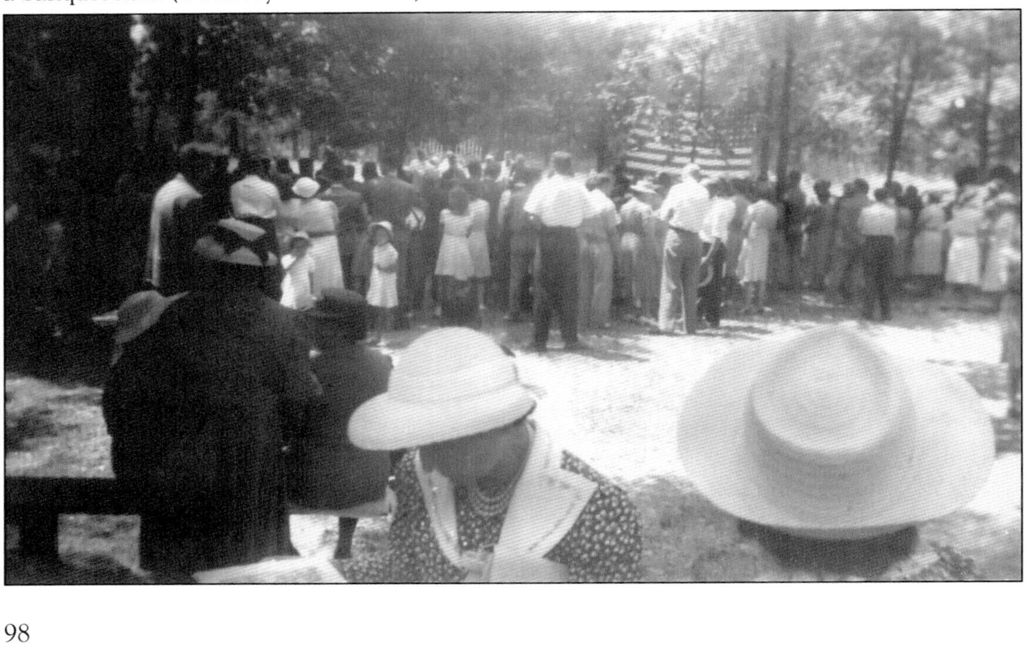

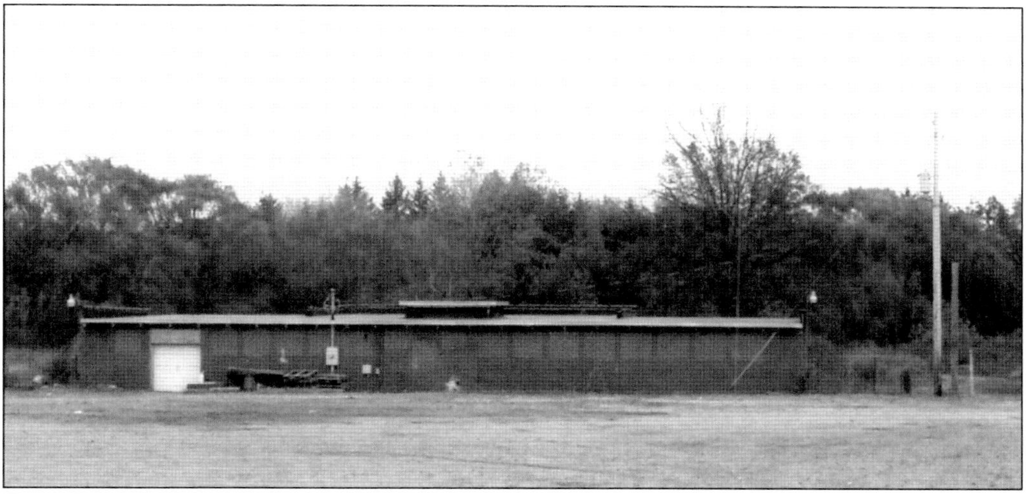

Rose Lake Bathhouse and Earl Bailey's House. In the 1930s, Rose Lake, a natural spring-fed lake located on 33 acres on the northeast corner of South Raccoon and Kirk Roads, opened to the public. Earl Bailey operated this popular summer spot, which also included a sand beach, bathhouse, and diving boards. Bailey developed Evelyn Road and (Rose) Lake Road. He sold Rose Lake in 1960 to St. Anne's Ukrainian Catholic Church. When the church and school opened in 1966, Bailey's house on Kirk Road became a convent for the nuns of St Anne's. St. Anne's operated Rose Lake for approximately three years before closing it. (Courtesy Joyce Pogany.)

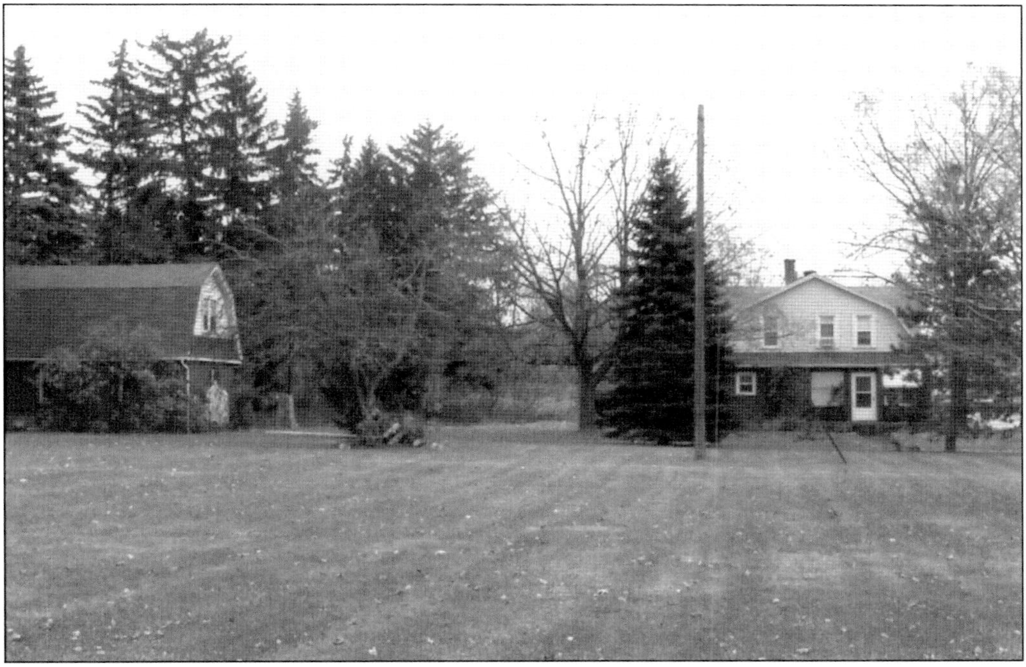

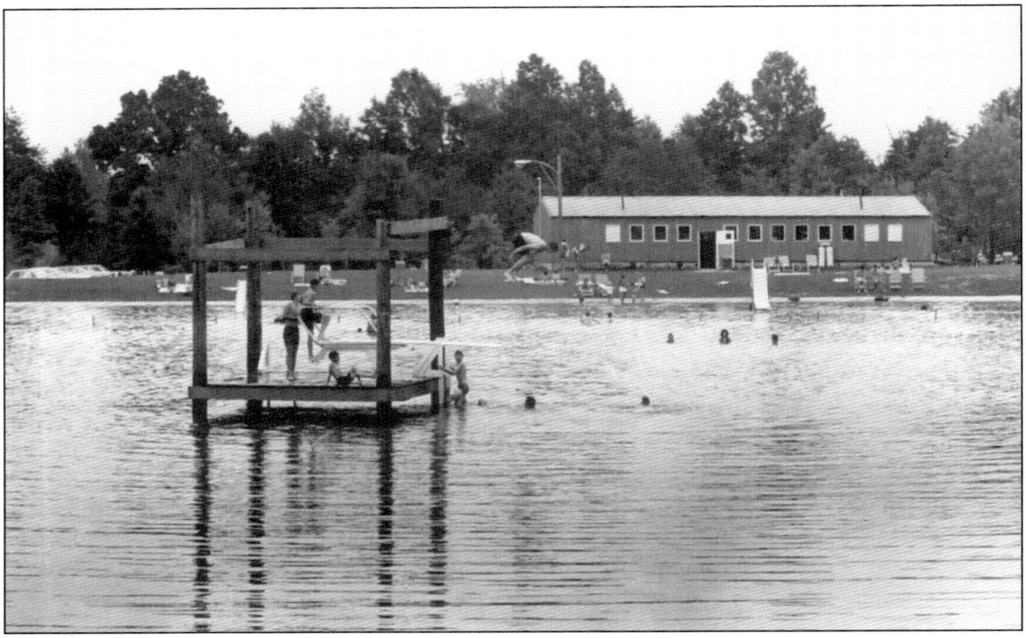

JAN-ED LAKE PARK. Edward Carl and Janet Dalton Keich purchased 45 acres off Fairview Road from the Kovach family. They poured 10,000 square feet of concrete to cover part of the bottom of the 2.75-acre spring-fed lake; part of the lake had a sandy bottom. Opened in 1968, the park featured an Olympic-size diving board, several fiberglass sliding boards, a 15-acre picnic area, a five-acre horse show ring, an 18-hole miniature golf course, swimming and scuba diving lessons, and a 20-by-64-foot bathhouse including showers, dressing rooms, and a concession stand. Janet serves, from left to right, an unknown boy, Bill Keich, and Judy Keich Mechling. (Courtesy Janet Dalton Keich McHenry.)

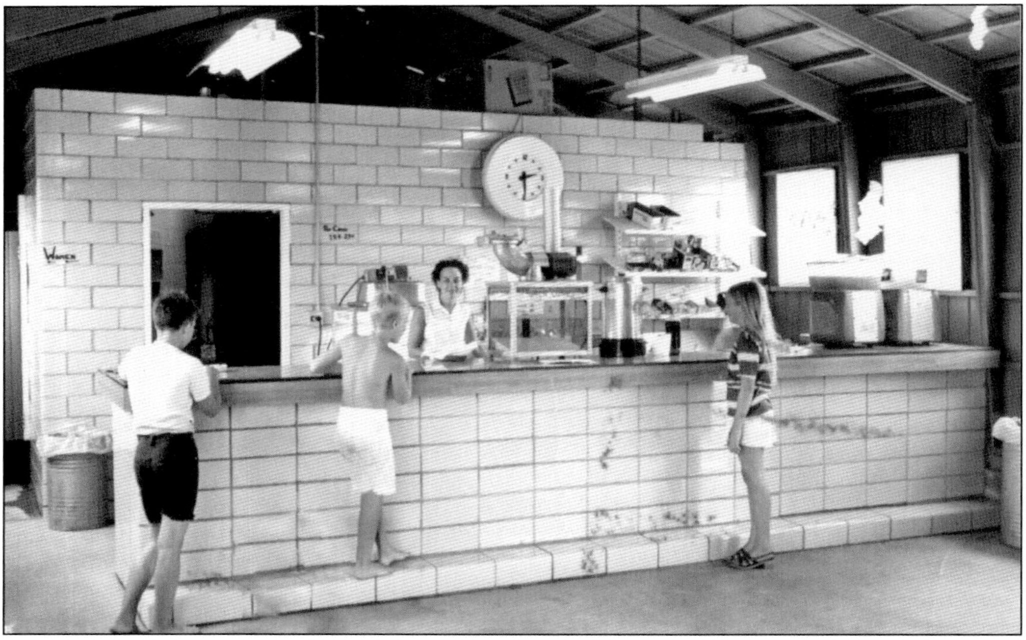

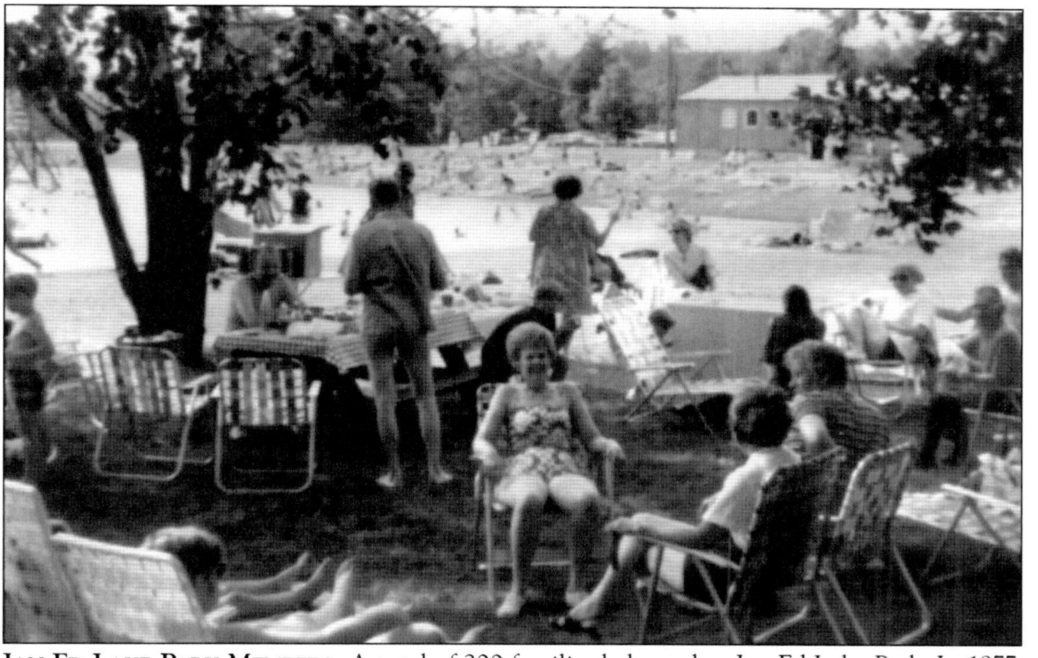

Jan-Ed Lake Park Members. A total of 200 families belonged to Jan-Ed Lake Park. In 1977, family membership for a season cost $50, married couples cost $35, and single memberships cost $20. The park closed in 1979. In 1981, Joe Koch bought it and developed Fairview Estates there. (Courtesy Janet Dalton Keich McHenry.)

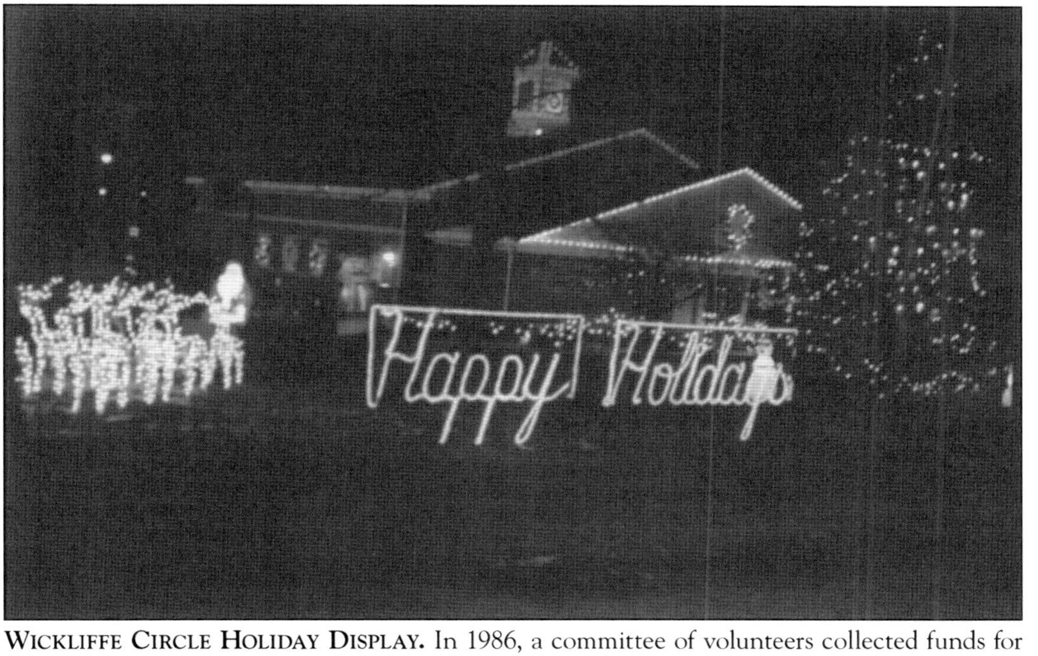

Wickliffe Circle Holiday Display. In 1986, a committee of volunteers collected funds for a holiday display on South Wickliffe Circle, Mahoning Avenue. The seasonal display expands each year. The annual event includes the tree lighting, Santa's arrival on a fire truck, and a free reception for approximately 600 people at Wickliffe Fire Station. (Courtesy Joyce Pogany.)

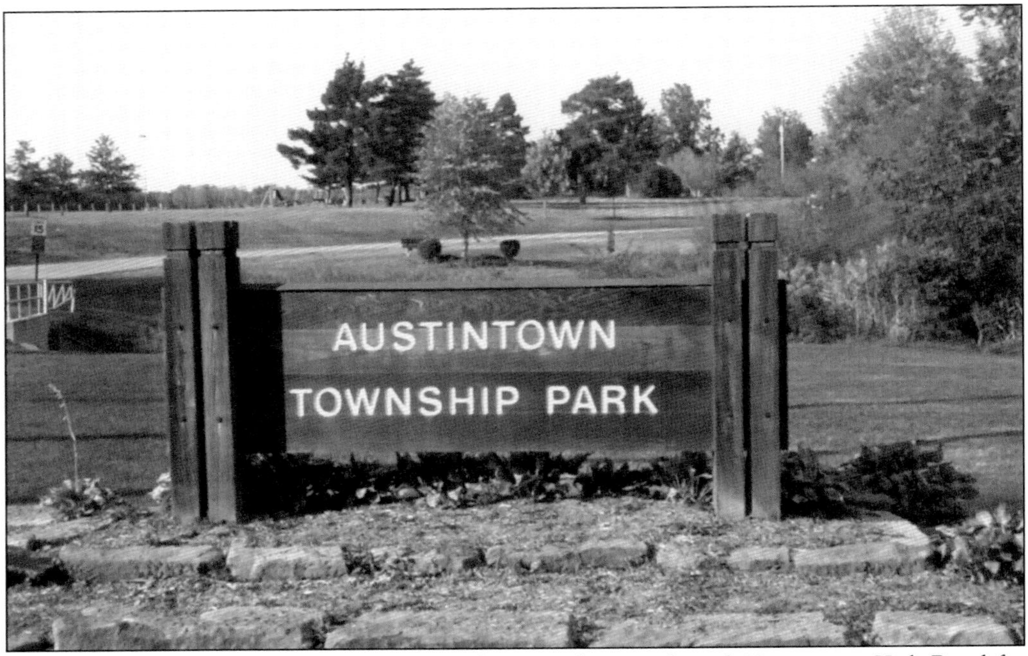

AUSTINTOWN TOWNSHIP PARK. In 1960, the township purchased 98 acres on Kirk Road for $40,000 from Francis Corll, creating Austintown Township Park. The park system now totals 200 acres with 156 acres at Austintown Township Park, 17 acres in Wedgewood, and acreage in other areas. (Courtesy Joyce Pogany.)

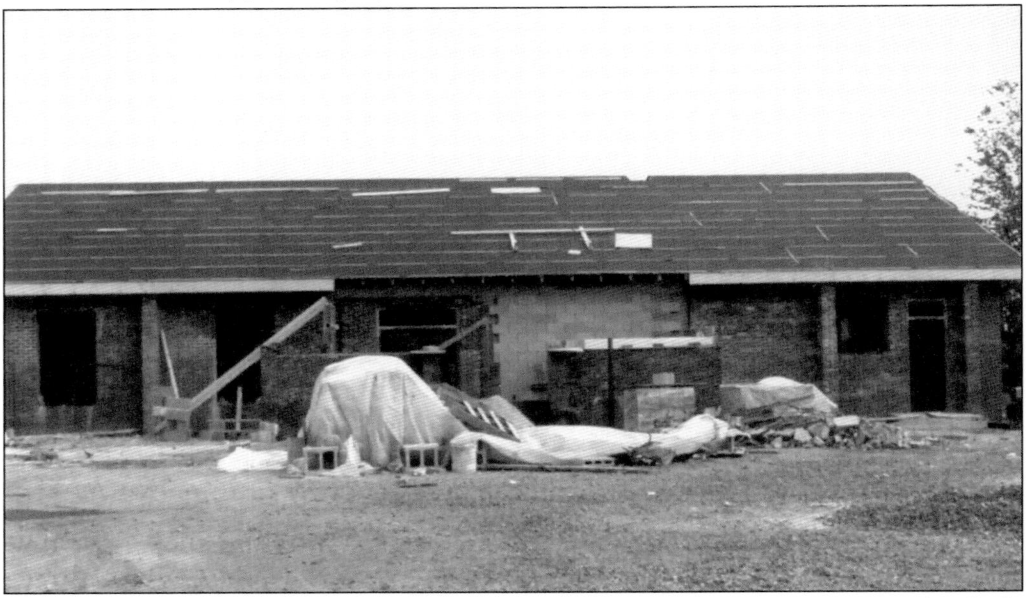

STACEY PAVILION, 1984. In 1961, Austintown Township built, in Austintown Township Park, the $30,000 heated Stacey Pavilion, which included a kitchen, restrooms, and a fireplace. It was named for Sydney Stacey, a park board member instrumental in acquiring the land and developing the park. The pavilion is photographed during the $177,186 renovation. (Courtesy Joyce Pogany.)

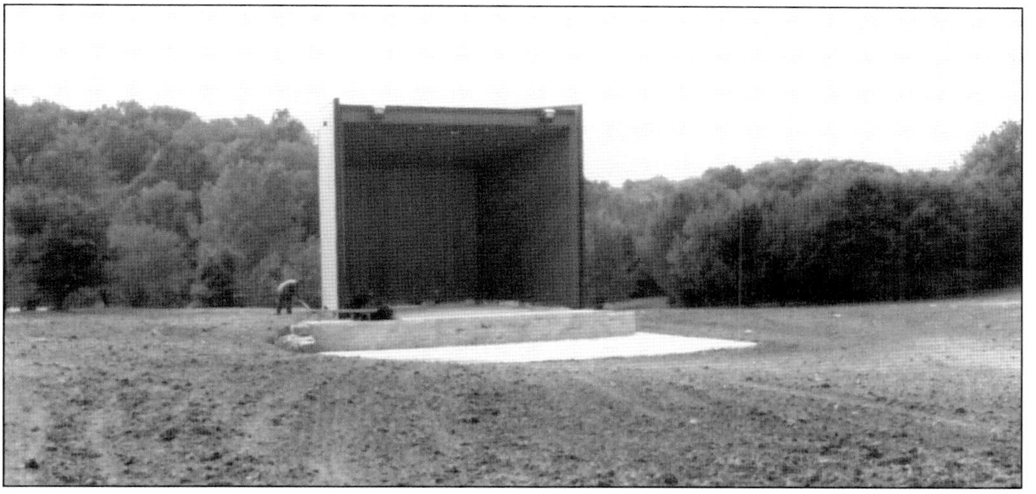

ROTARY BAND SHELL CONSTRUCTION, AUSTINTOWN TOWNSHIP PARK, 1983–1984. In the early 1980s, citizens and organizations lobbied the park board to provide a place for concerts in the park. The Austintown Rotary Club spearheaded the fund-raising for the $30,000 band shell, which is home to the free concerts in the park held every Tuesday in the summer since 1984. (Courtesy Joyce Pogany.)

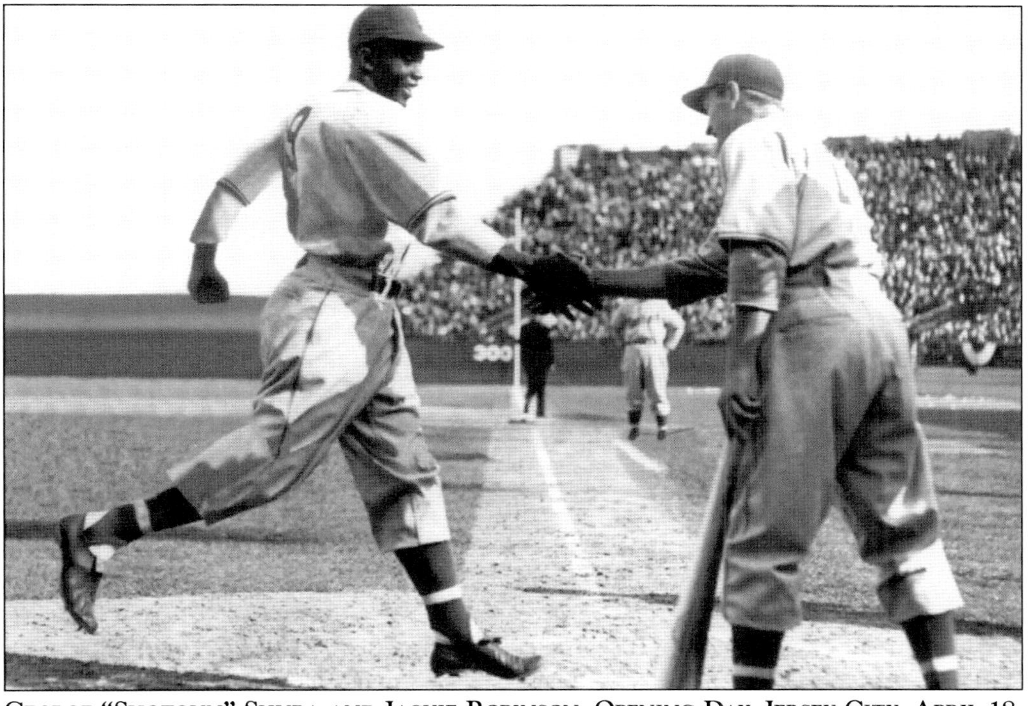

GEORGE "SHOTGUN" SHUBA AND JACKIE ROBINSON, OPENING DAY, JERSEY CITY, APRIL 18, 1946. Austintown resident George "Shotgun" Shuba shakes Jackie Robinson's hand, a teammate on the Montreal Royals Brooklyn Dodgers farm club. This was "the first interracial handshake" in baseball. Shuba, who played for the Dodgers from 1948 to 1955, delivered a pinch-hit homer in the 1953 World Series opener. Shuba occasionally appears with other "boys of summer." (Courtesy George and Mike Shuba.)

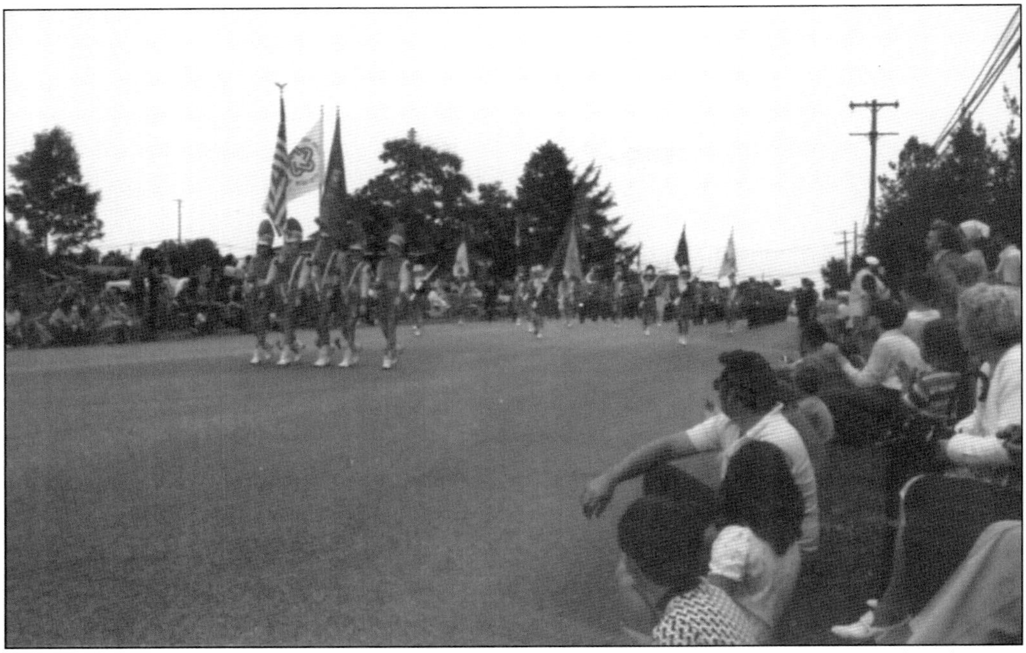

AUSTINTOWN FITCH COLOR GUARD, JULY 4, 1976. From left to right, Capt. Sheryl Lynn Rossler, Betty Barton carrying the American flag, Cindy Thompson carrying the American bicentennial flag, Patty Daubenspeck carrying the Austintown township flag, and Patty Lawson marched in the first Fourth of July parade on South Raccoon Road beginning at Fitch High School and ending at the Austin Log Cabin. (Courtesy Joyce Pogany.)

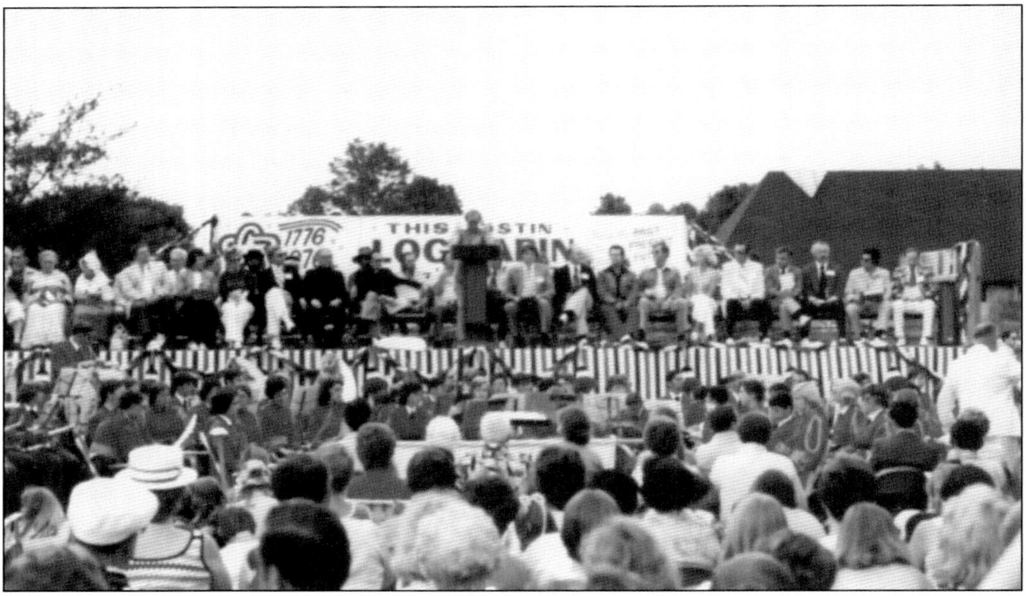

DEDICATING THE AUSTIN LOG CABIN, JULY 4TH, 1976. Since 1976, Austintown, a "Bicentennial Community," has annually celebrated Independence Day with an ecumenical service at the Austin Log Cabin, parade on South Raccoon Road from Kirk Road to Falcon Drive, and fireworks at Fitch High School stadium. (Courtesy Joyce Pogany.)

Eight

Government of Austintown

In 1804, the Ohio legislature required all townships to elect three trustees, a clerk, two overseers of the poor, a "sufficient number" of highway supervisors, a justice of the peace, and as many constables as necessary. Several years later, townships were also required to have a treasurer and tax assessor. Regrettably, few records exist of who held these early offices in Austintown. Early justices of the peace include James Russell, John Carlton, William Truesdale, Jacob Dustman, J. Leach, James Ross, John Moore, and Davis Randolph. Today three elected trustees and a fiscal officer govern the township.

Militias originally protected the township. During the War of 1812, many Austintown men served in Col. William Rayen's 1st Regiment, 3rd Brigade, 4th Division in the Battle of the Peninsula and Kelly's Island. During the Civil War, many Austintown men fought in Company H of the 20th Ohio Volunteer Infantry and in Company B of the 19th Volunteer Infantry. Austintown residents have served in all military conflicts thereafter.

The township was policed by part-time constables who worked on a commission and received a percentage of the fines and court costs imposed by the justice of the peace. The first full-time constable, Jack Bishop, was hired in 1951 at a salary of $425 per month. The full-time police department was formed in 1963; James Hazlett was chief, and John Statler was assistant.

The volunteer fire department was chartered by George Rose Jr., Kenneth Yeager, G. Schnurrenberger, J. Schnurrenberger, George Henry, and Paul Schrum in May 1938 with Glenn Evans as chief. The first fire truck was a converted beverage truck. The first fire department call was on August 1, 1939, for a car fire at Schiavone's grocery store in Wickliffe.

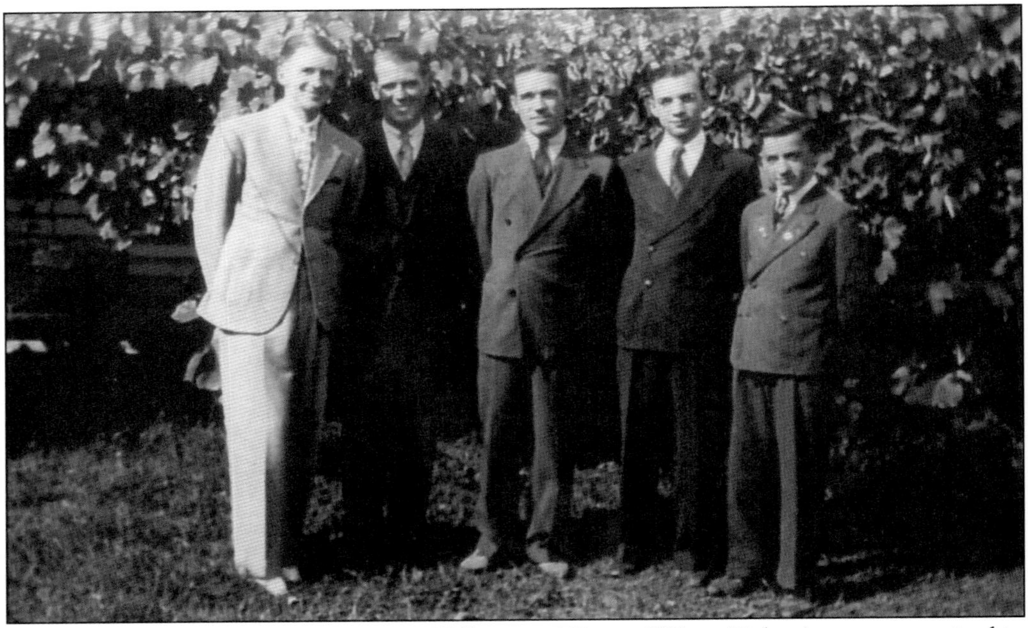

BISHOP BROTHERS, SEPTEMBER 1940. William and Emma Wilson Bishop's sons were raised in West Austintown and all served in World War II, from left to right they are Kenneth, 23, U.S. Navy; Floyd, 22, U.S. Army; Jack, 20, U.S. Army; Bob, 19, U.S. Navy; and Harold, 16, U.S. Army. Despite injuries, all returned home safely. Bob survived the Japanese attack on Pearl Harbor on December 7, 1941, and attended the 65th anniversary in 2006. (Courtesy Bob Bishop.)

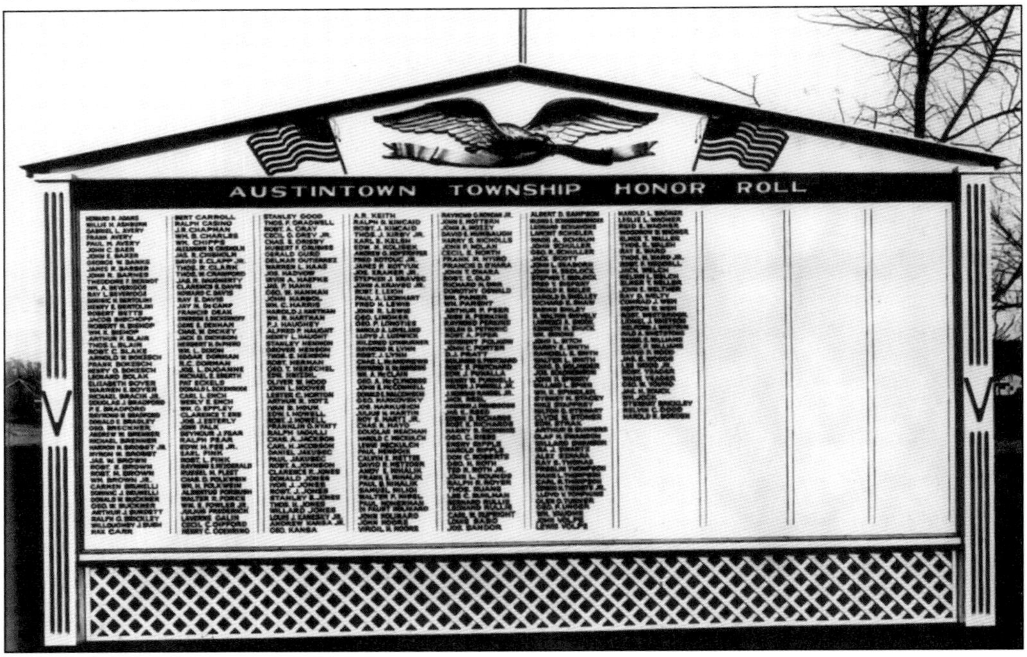

AUSTINTOWN TOWNSHIP HONOR ROLL. In 1942, this list of the Austintown men and women serving in World War II was erected on South Wickliffe Circle, now known as Memorial Park. This sign was removed sometime after World War II. (Courtesy Walt and Genevieve Shively.)

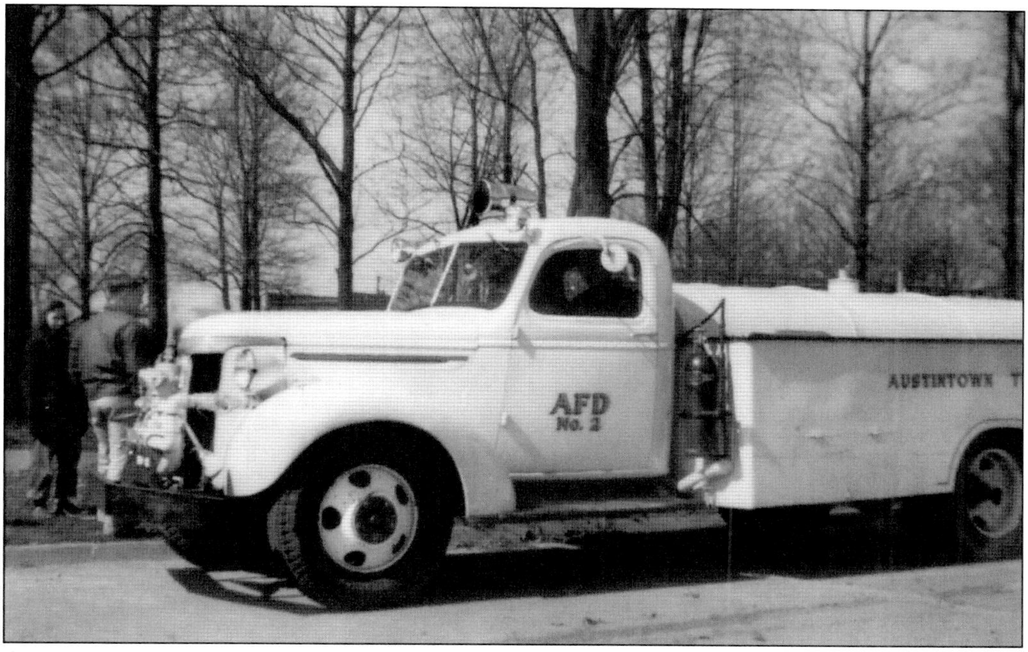

AUSTINTOWN FIRE TRUCK NO. 2. In 1930, Austintown's only fire hydrants were on Mahoning Avenue from Wickliffe to West Austintown. Purchased in June 1939, this Seagrave pumper, the fire department's first new truck, pumped 600 gallons per minute, had 1,400 feet of hose, and cost $8,040. (Courtesy West Austintown United Methodist Church.)

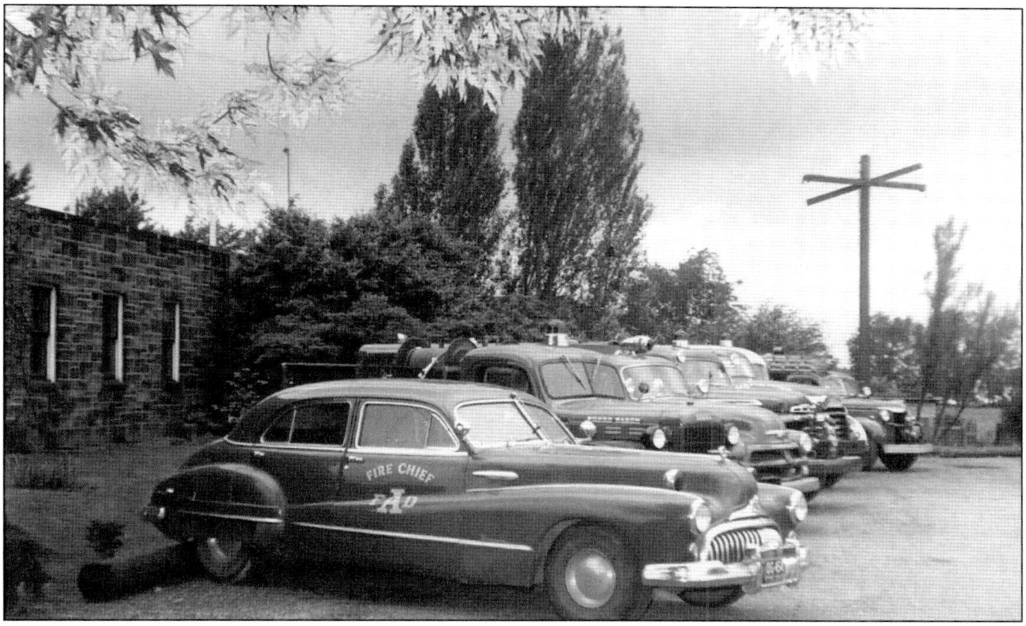

AUSTINTOWN FIRE DEPARTMENT VEHICLES. In 1954, the Austintown Fire Department had one chief's car and five trucks. The only paid firefighter in Austintown was the fire chief; all other volunteers were paid $1 per year. Before 1938, the Youngstown Fire Department responded to fire calls in Austintown. (Courtesy AHS.)

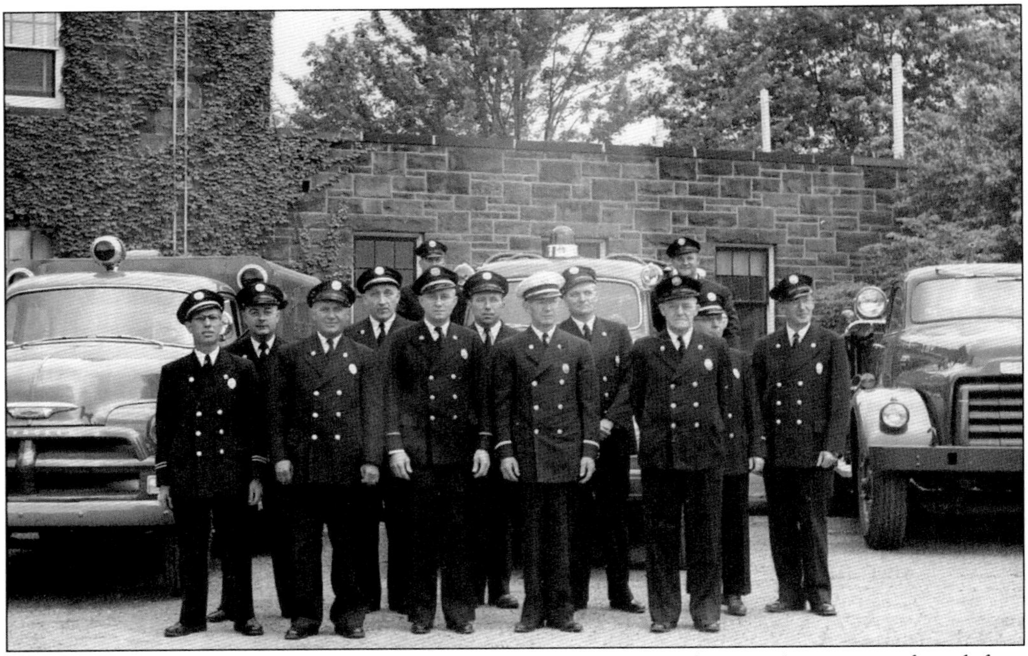

AUSTINTOWN FIREFIGHTERS, 1954. At Fire Station No. 1 on Mahoning Avenue are, from left to right, Jack ?; Bob Ricker; unidentified; Lloyd Gruver; Ken Yeager; Ed Renz; Chief Leroy Halstead (in white hat); Lucius McIntire; unidentified; Reverend Swinehard, fire department chaplain; and unidentified. The two firefighters in the back row are unidentified. (Courtesy AHS.)

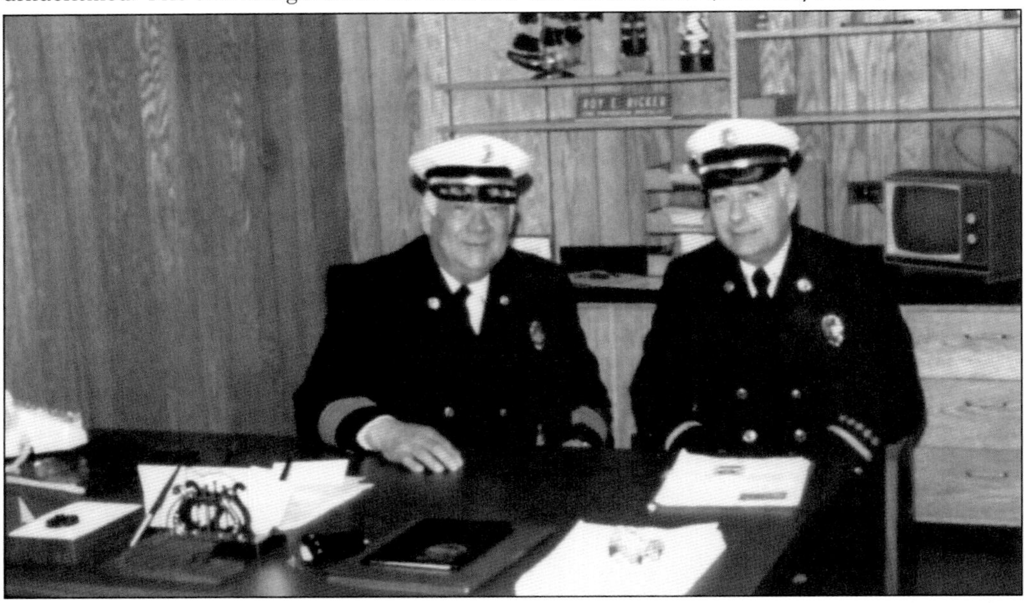

CHIEF ROY RICKER AND BROTHER, CAPT. ROBERT RICKER, 1979. Roy Ricker (left) served as fire chief from 1952 to 1954 and from 1979 to 1989 and as assistant fire marshal from 1954 to 1963. When Ricker was appointed chief in 1952, he and his family lived upstairs at Fire Station No. 1 on Mahoning Avenue. Since 1948, a member of the Ricker family has served in the Austintown Fire Department. (Courtesy Robert Ricker.)

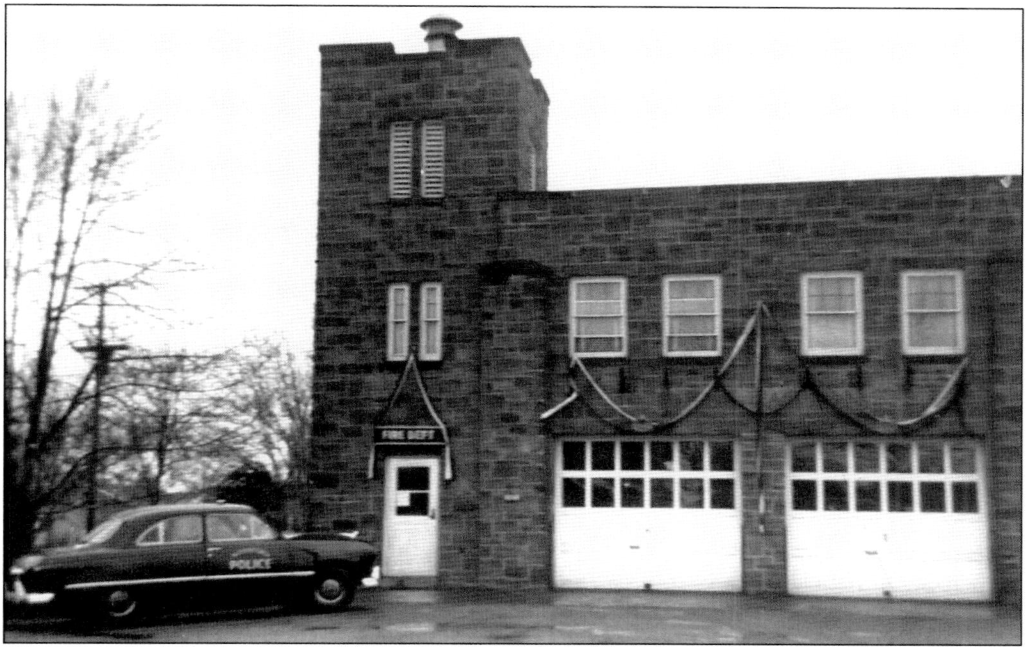

FIRE STATION NO. 1, 5340 MAHONING AVENUE. This building, built by the WPA in 1938 at a cost of $60,000, was sold to a private citizen in 1992. At one time, trustees and the police, road, and zoning departments occupied the second floor. (Courtesy AHS.)

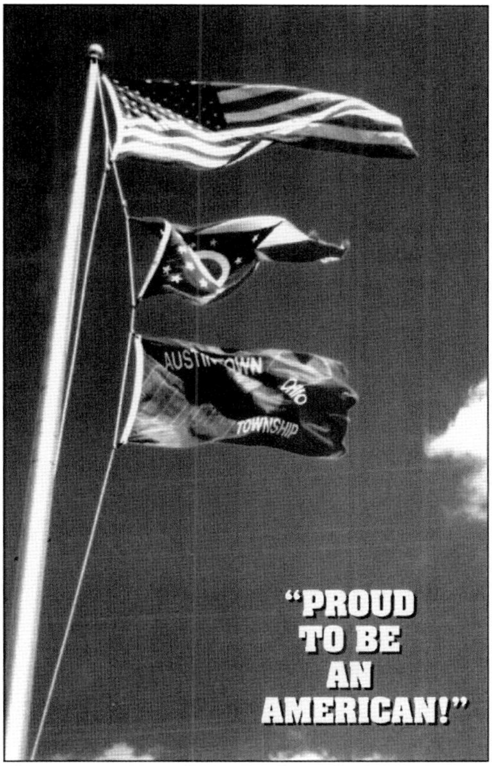

UNITED STATES, OHIO, AND AUSTINTOWN TOWNSHIP FLAGS. The Austintown Township flag, designed by Fitch High School junior Scott Morrison, was first flown at the 125th Canfield Fair in 1973. Emil Bertolini, Austintown Township trustee and Mahoning County Trustees' Association president, coordinated the fair flag display. (Courtesy Paul Pogany.)

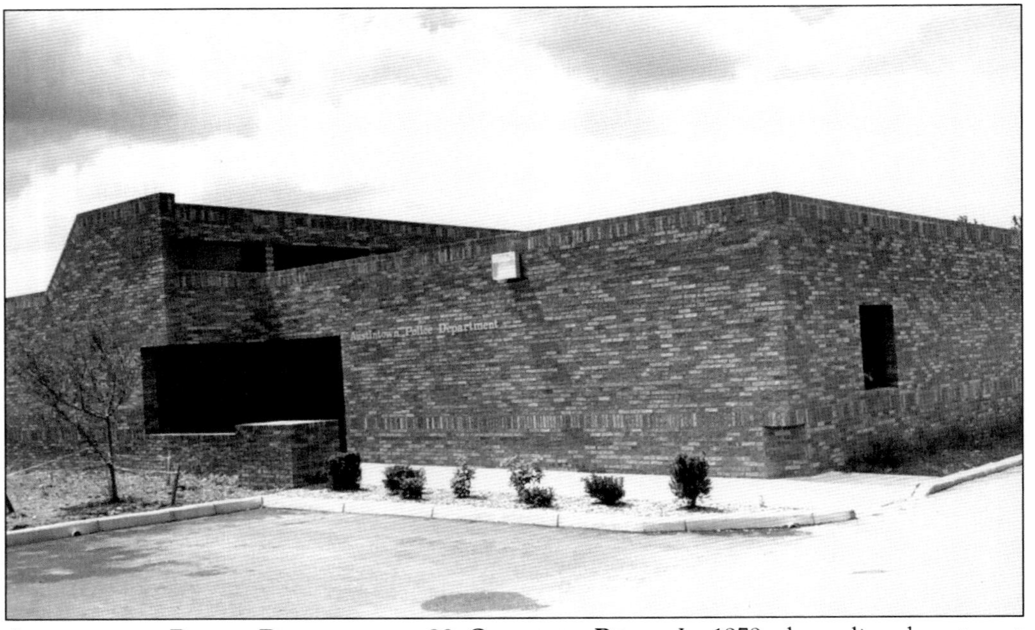

AUSTINTOWN POLICE DEPARTMENT, 92 OHLTOWN ROAD. In 1979, the police department moved to this building from Fire Station No. 1. The building was remodeled in 2000 to provide additional space for the jail and 911 call center. (Courtesy Joyce Pogany.)

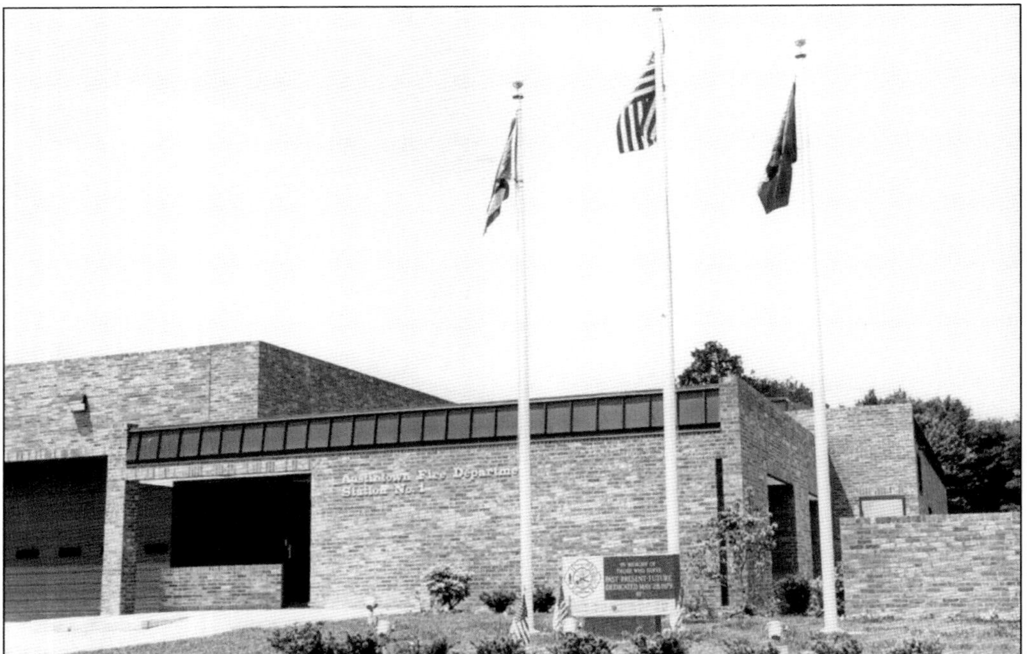

NEW FIRE STATION NO. 1, 384 NORTH CANFIELD-NILES ROAD. The 9,615-square-foot station opened in 1979 and cost $450,000. Station No. 2, 4102 Wickliffe Circle, opened in 1954; station No. 3, 2650 South Raccoon Road, opened in 1959; station No. 4, 1690 South Turner Road, opened in 1986. (Courtesy Joyce Pogany.)

Nine

Building Boom

Throughout much of its history, Austintown was a rural farming community. In 1920, a total of 1,989 people resided in Austintown's 471 homes. In 1930, the population increased to 4,309. In 1950, the population was 10,015. In 1960, the population was 13,152. Five years later, in 1965, the population doubled to 26,482. According to the census, the population in 1970 was 34,949; in 1980, it was 37,664; in 1990, it was 36,740; in 2000, it was 38,001 living in a total of 16,481 housing units.

In 1874, there were just 16 streets with homes. As planned housing developments were created, the population shifted from the major roads to the newly developed areas. Many developments were built between 1950 and 1980 with approximately 3,500 homes built in each decade. These developments include, but are not limited to, Kirk Haven Estates, Kimberly Acres, Brookwood, Trophy Estates, Highland Park, Timberbrook, Wedgewood, Bexley Estates, Green Brier, College Park, Country Green, Capital Estates, Woodland Trace, Falcon Manor, Meander Woods, Easy Street, and Whispering Pines. Since 1990, new developments include, but are not limited to, Lexington Place, Top of the Town, Countryside, Cider Mill Crossing, Heron's Landing, West Hampton, the Preakness, Meander Cove, Fox Chase, Stone Hollow, Spring Meadow, Boulder Creek, Victory Hills, Falcon Ridge, and Chapel Valley. Austintown led the Mahoning Valley in new single-family home construction for most of the 1990s and the first decade of the 21st century.

Austintown, sometimes called the "Crossroads of America," is midway between New York and Chicago on Interstate 80 and midway between Pittsburgh and Cleveland. The construction of Interstate 80 divided Austintown and literally split some roads in half. When constructed in 1966, the Interstate 80, 680, and 11 interchange was the third-largest interchange in the United States.

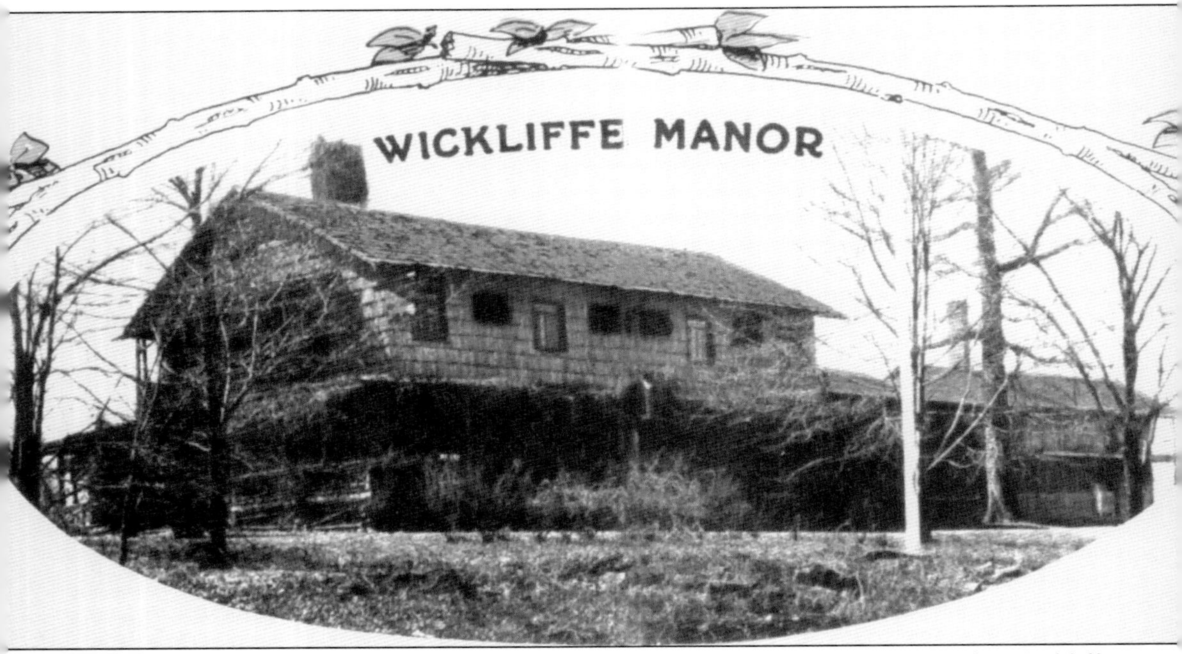

WICKLIFFE MANOR. In 1810, the Wick family purchased 100 acres, near present-day Wickliffe, for $2.75 per acre. Henry Wick built this house, Wickliffe, on a cliff near present-day North Yorkshire Drive. Wickliffe was converted to the Wickliffe Manor, a dinner and dance club, the site of wedding receptions, dances, and the 1939 and 1940 Fitch proms. In 1930, Anna Sabine, manager, was assisted by Maude Perry; Mary McCreary, cook; Helen Popovitch, maid; and John Smith, janitor. Wickliffe Manor was razed in 1941 to make way for apartments. (Courtesy Tom and Carol Stellars.)

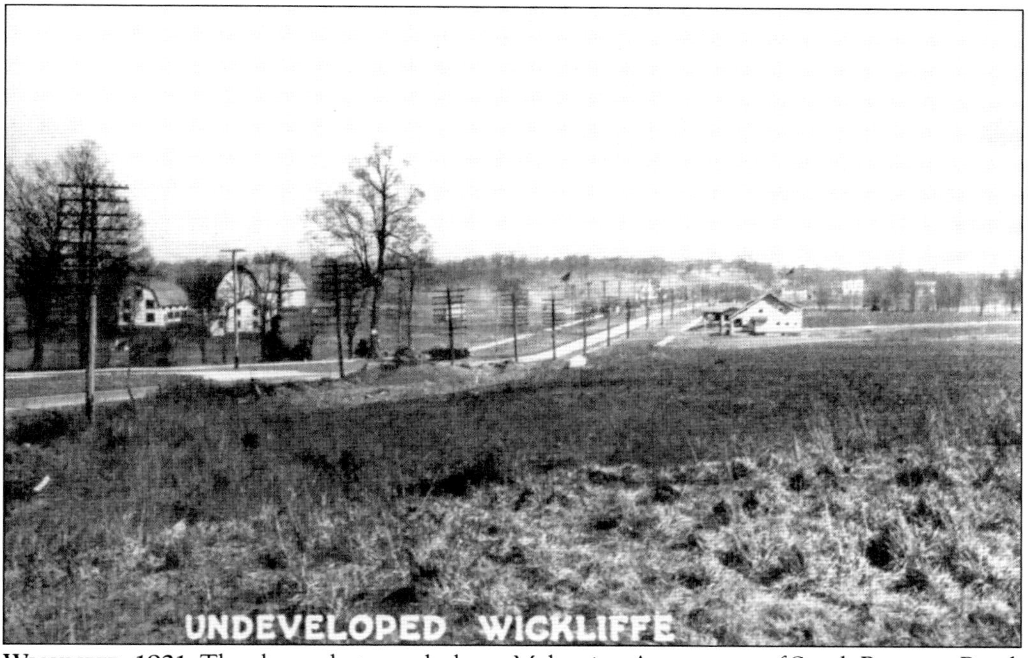

WICKLIFFE, 1921. The above photograph shows Mahoning Avenue east of South Raccoon Road. Lake Wickliffe was on the southwest corner of Raccoon Road and Mahoning Avenue; pictured are the Houk barns. The 800-acre Wickliffe area, on the north and south sides of Mahoning Avenue Extension, was Austintown's first planned development in 1920. The Realty Security Company built sidewalks, sewers, and streets and sold improved lots for $795. Homes for the "higher class of workingmen" sold for $6,000–$8,000. The Realty Security Company set aside land for Wickliffe Elementary School (now Woodside School) in south Wickliffe, Davis Elementary School in north Wickliffe, and Wickliffe Circle. (Courtesy Tom and Carol Stellars.)

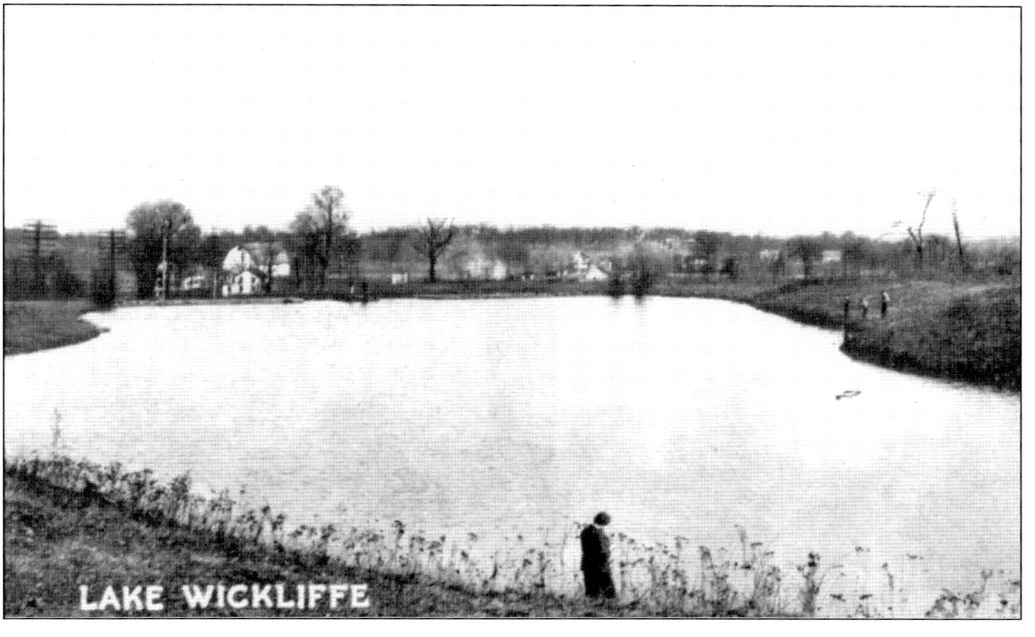

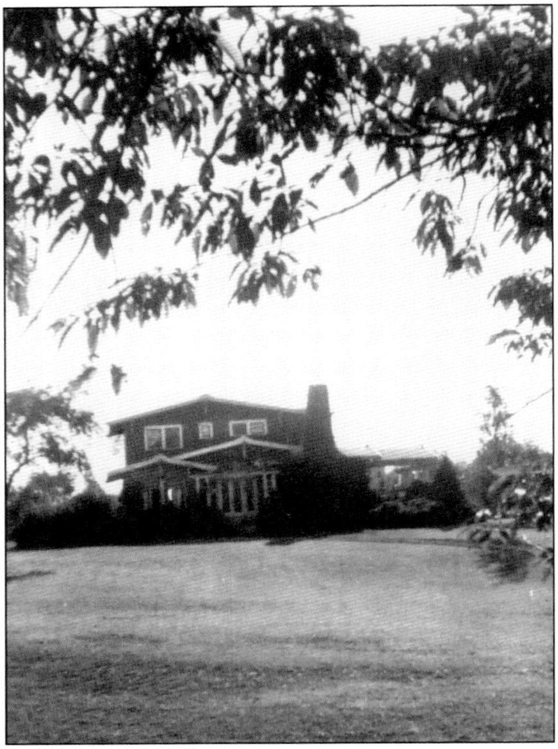

Southwest Corner of Mahoning Avenue and Raccoon Road, 1946. Now part of Art's Westgate Plaza, this house, built in 1880, at one time served as the DuRell Funeral Home. Mildred and Arthur Robert Steiskal Sr. purchased the house in 1939 and filled in Lake Wickliffe in front of the house. In 1950, they built the Westgate Plaza around the house. (Courtesy A. Robert Steiskal Jr.)

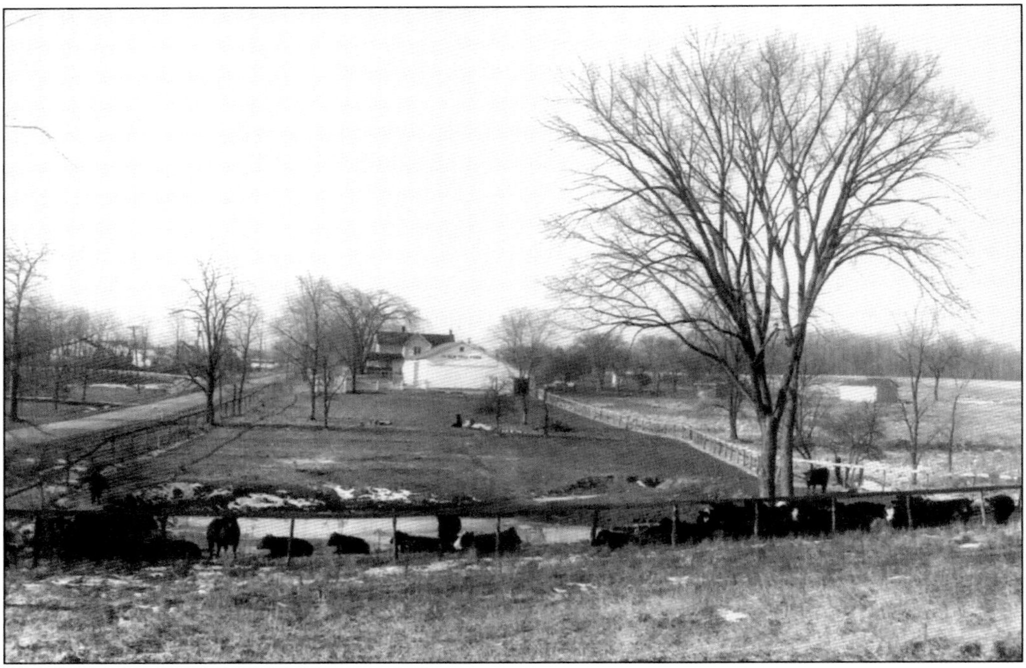

Elm Tree Farm, East Webb Road. Interstate 680 now runs behind this farm previously owned by Bob Lloyd of Lloyd Packing House. Webb Road is named for the Abner Webb family who settled in Austintown in 1814. (Courtesy Bob Lloyd.)

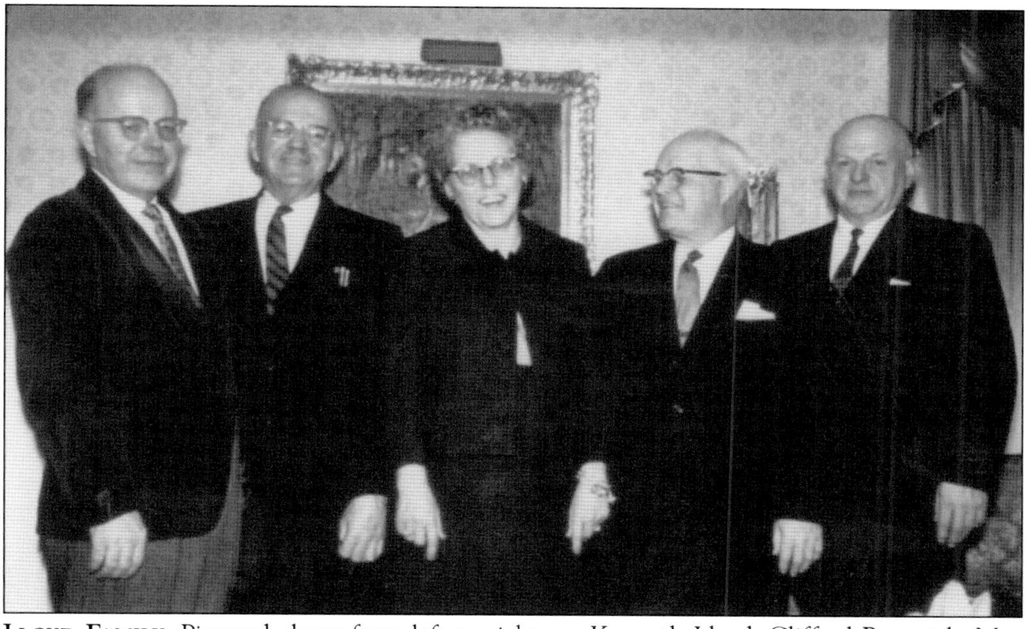

LLOYD FAMILY. Pictured above from left to right are Kenneth Lloyd, Clifford Bostwick, Mae Lloyd Bostwick, Paul Lloyd, and Armour Lloyd. Their father, Richard Lloyd Jr., was born 1866 to Welsh immigrants Richard and Anna Davis Lloyd who lived in Mineral Ridge. He began his butcher business with $14, peddling meat from a wagon. He established the Lloyd Packing House and served on the Austintown Board of Education. Armour, photographed in 1918 with his wife, Marie Brill Lloyd, and children, Bob, age 4, and Dorothy, age 2, eventually owned 800 acres in Austintown stretching from Mahoning Avenue to the Lloyd Packing House, which was between Interstate 80 and Webb Road. Armour and Kenneth Lloyd donated land for Lloyd Elementary School. Bob Lloyd continued the family meatpacking business. (Courtesy Bob Lloyd.)

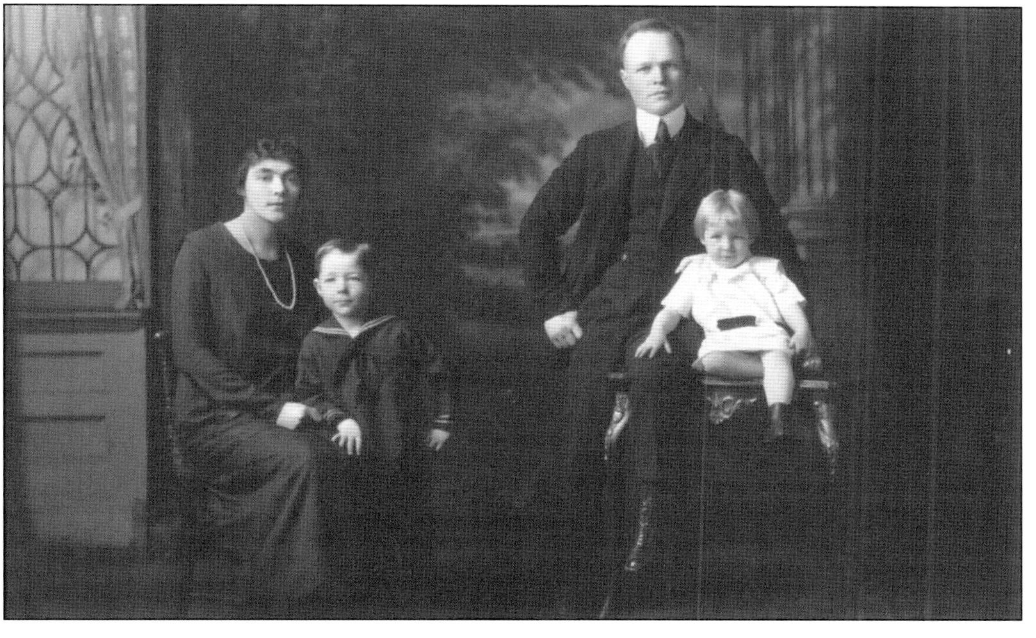

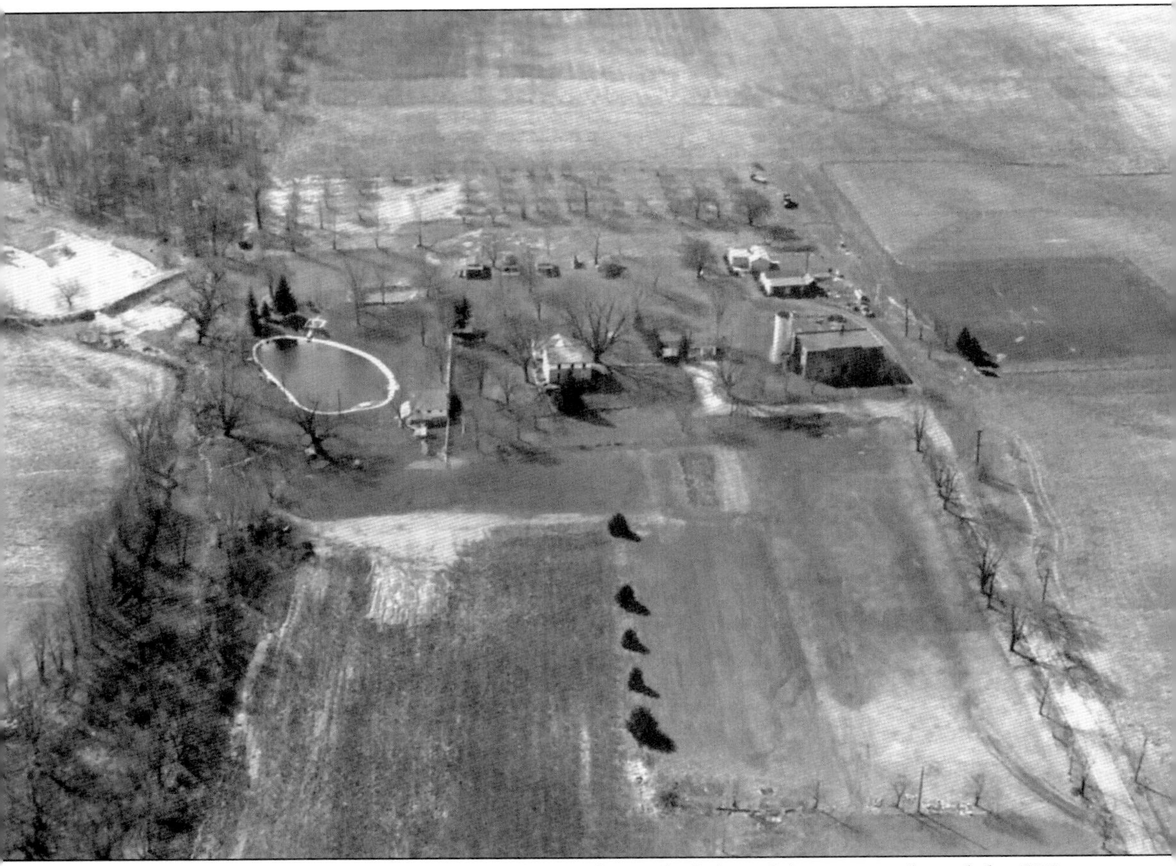

SUNNYBROOK FARM, 1953. In 1939, Walter and Maude Osberg Johnson purchased the 500-acre Sunnybrook farm located off South Raccoon Road. The 250,000-gallon pool on the left, built in 1931, the first concrete pool in the Mahoning Valley, was a site for company picnics and family outings. The tree line on the left is the border between Austintown and Canfield Townships. In the center of the picture is the Johnson home. Between the house and the orchard are summer rental cottages. The Light House, a hall on the property, was rented for weddings, parties, and dances in the late 1930s. In 1962, Don Cook and Nils Johnson Sr. of Cook-Johnson Company built the 420-house Brookwood Estates on this land and donated land for a park in Brookwood Estates. (Courtesy Nils Johnson Sr.)

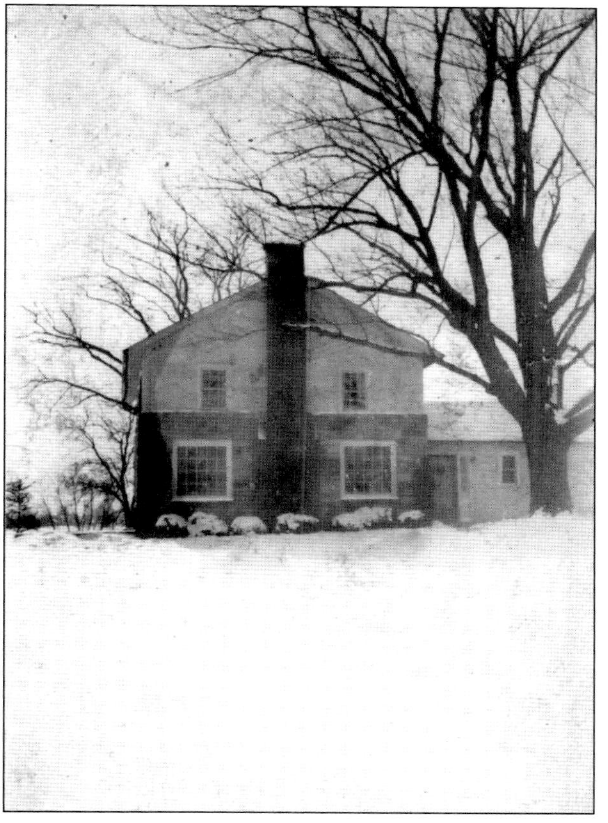

JOHNSON HOME. This house on Sunnybrook farm was originally a two-story log cabin. Walter Johnson and his son Nils cut through the logs to install windows. Stone mason Fred Ciarnello added the stones. The house still stands in Brookwood Estates on Warwick South. Johnson Farm Drive is named after the Johnson family. (Courtesy Nils Johnson Sr.)

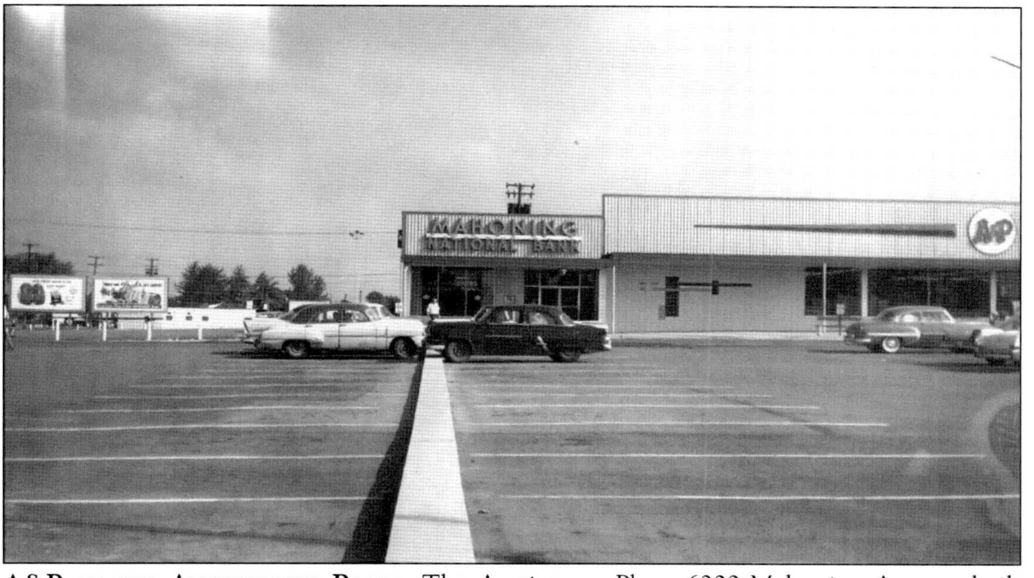

A&P AT THE AUSTINTOWN PLAZA. The Austintown Plaza, 6000 Mahoning Avenue, built by Edward DeBartolo in 1959, was perfectly suited for the suburban residents who flocked to Austintown in the 1950s. Some say the plaza and its stores contributed to the demise of smaller older neighborhood stores. (Courtesy AHS.)

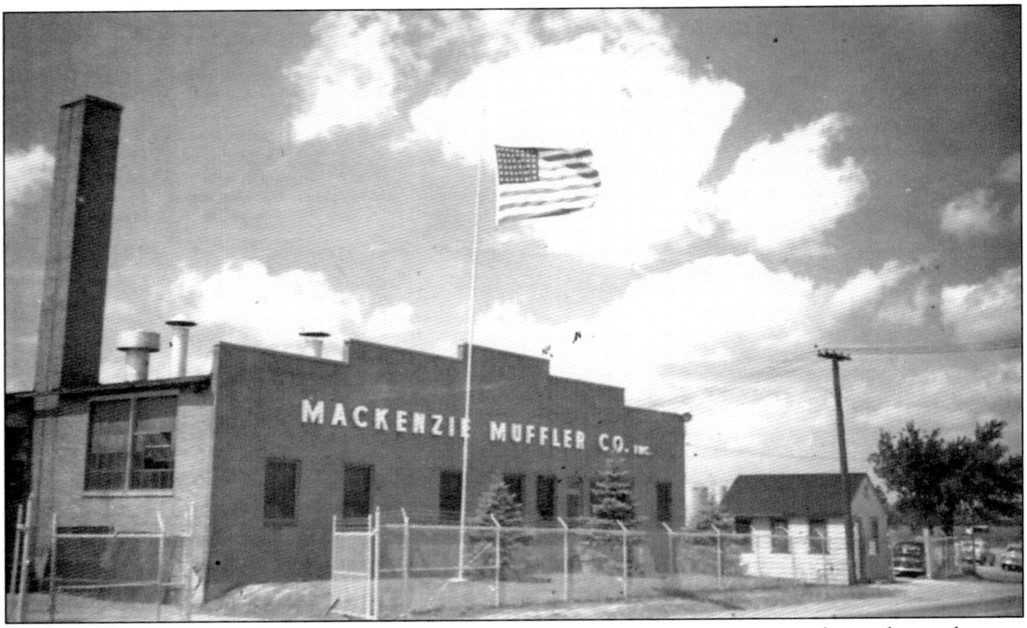

MACKENZIE MUFFLER COMPANY, 1950S. Twenty-one companies were in the industrial zone, established around 1923, on the west side on North Meridian Road between Connecticut Avenue and Henricks Road. Mackenzie Muffler Company made mufflers for the three big automobile companies. During World War II, it made tank parts. (Courtesy AHS.)

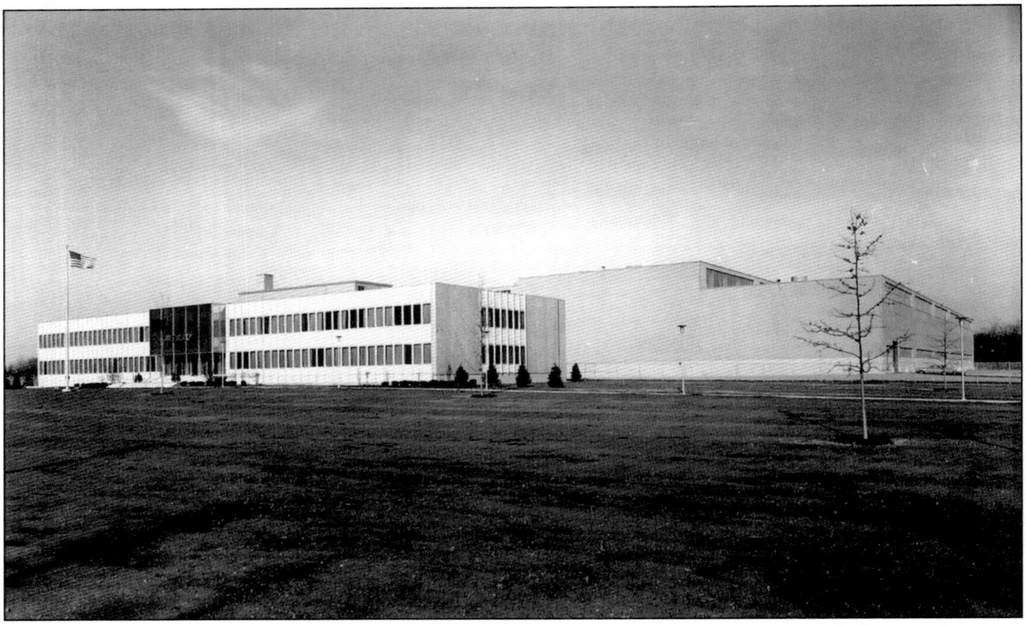

MCKAY MACHINE COMPANY, 1962. Located for many years on Youngstown's Rayen Avenue, McKay Machine Company moved to Henricks Road in 1962. In 1966, McKay Machine merged with Wean. In 1993, Wean United sold its Austintown engineering and manufacturing division to Danieli. Many of the rolling mills manufactured by McKay Machine are still used today. (Courtesy Paul Pogany.)

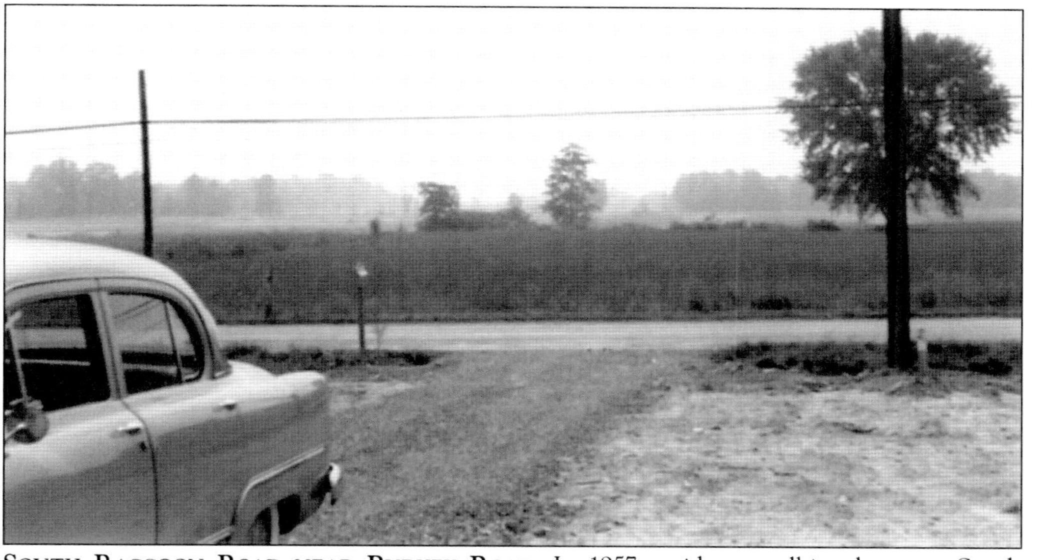

SOUTH RACCOON ROAD NEAR BURKEY ROAD. In 1957, residents walking between South Raccoon and Canfield-Niles Roads found only farmland, not houses or roads. Raccoon Road, the first public road in Austintown, was created in 1802 when Canfield and Austintown residents petitioned a road to be cut from Canfield to Youngstown-Warren Road near the salt springs. (Courtesy Joyce Pogany.)

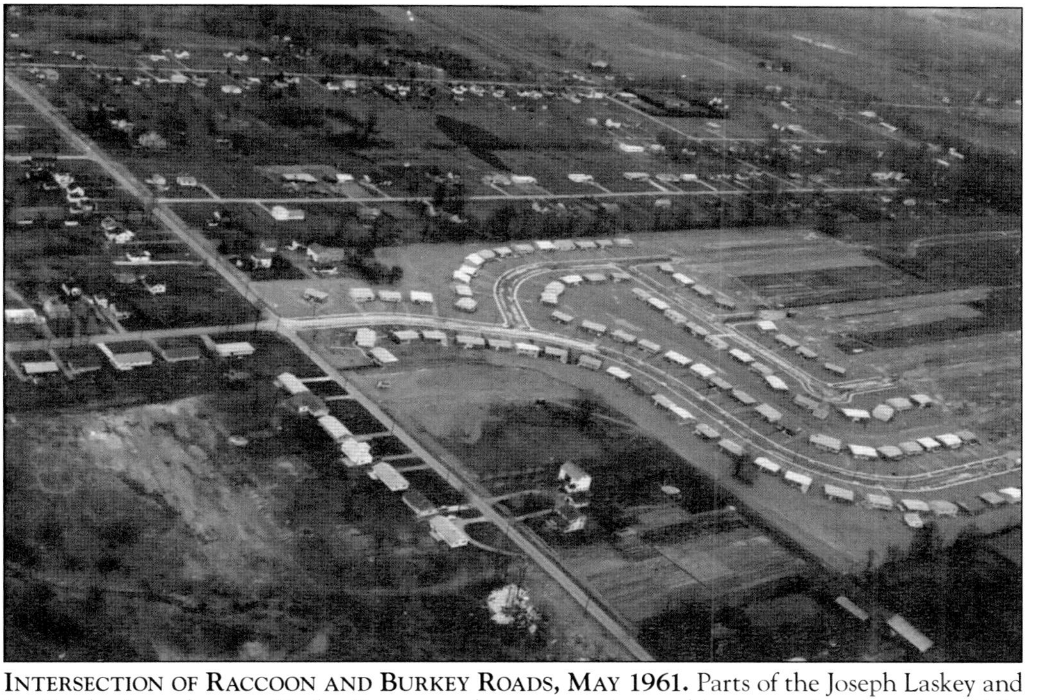

INTERSECTION OF RACCOON AND BURKEY ROADS, MAY 1961. Parts of the Joseph Laskey and Jay Snyder farms became Bexley Estates, under construction in this picture. Land on the middle right became LeChateau apartments. Land at the top became Trophy Estates and Woodland Trace. The barn in the lower center marks the location of the new Austintown Middle School. (Courtesy Joyce Pogany.)

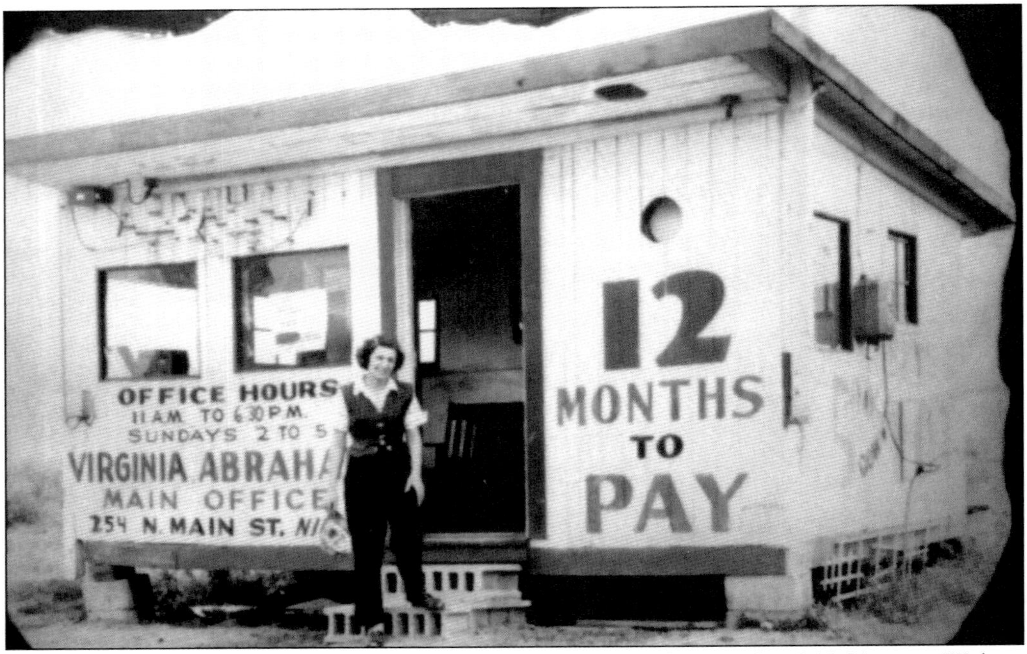

VIRGINIA NEMAN ABRAHAM WALTERS AND REAL ESTATE OFFICE. In 1946, Virginia Walters married John Abraham. Abraham owned 355 acres in Austintown and developed Virginia Drive, naming it after his wife. Dying unexpectedly in 1949, Abraham left unpaid real estate taxes. Walters, a nurse at North Side Hospital with no experience in land development, established this real estate office in Niles to sell the land to pay the taxes. Walters plotted the roads and contracted for installation of electric, water, sewer, and gas lines. She developed Norquest Boulevard; Benton, Rockwell, and Radio Roads; Argonne and Rutland Avenues; Viola Drive; and Baker Street. One of Walters's two daughters still lives on Norquest Boulevard. (Courtesy Charlene Flesch.)

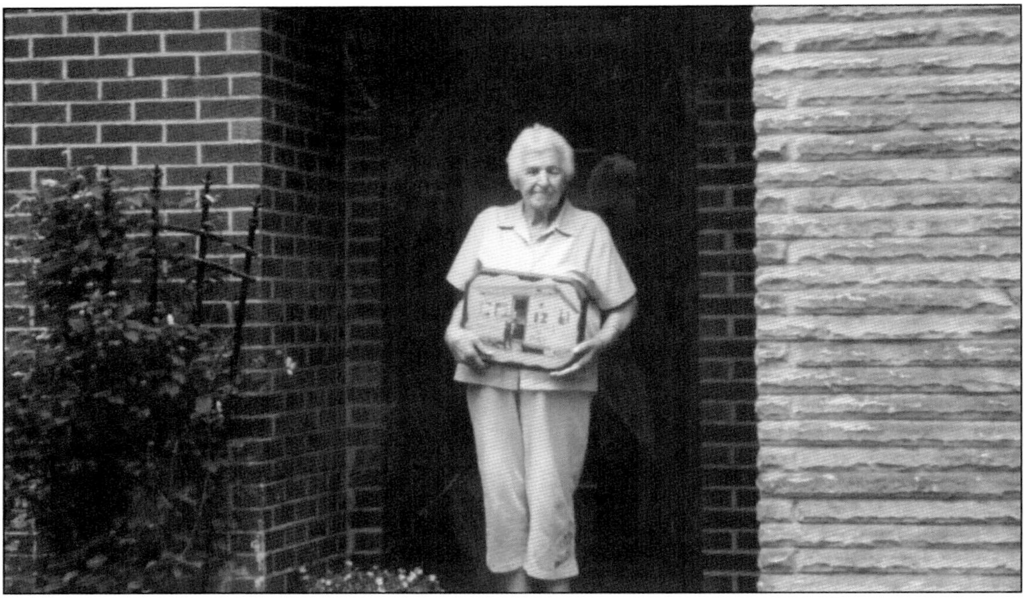

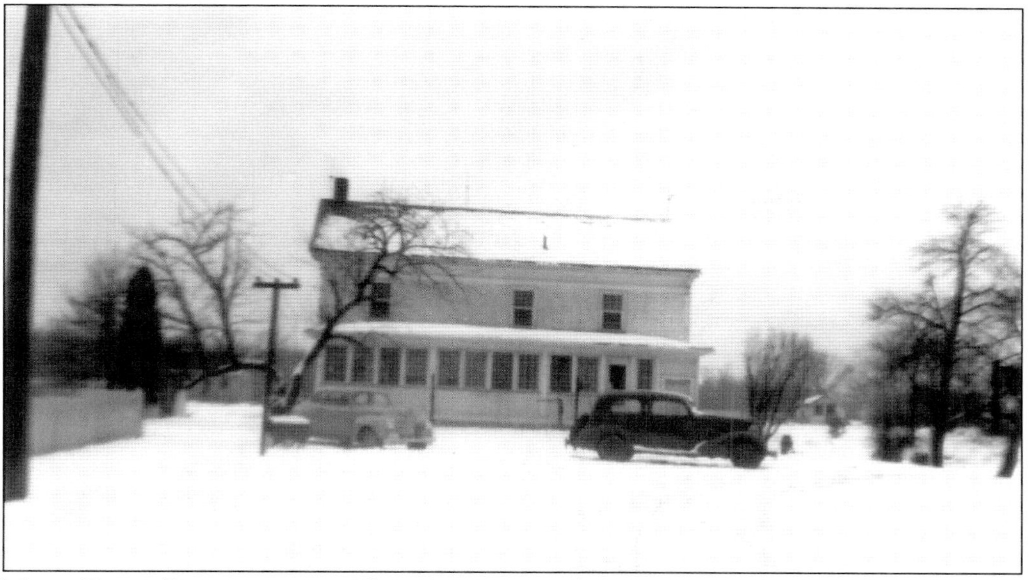

MOGG FARM, JANUARY 1943. The 247-acre Mogg farm extended from Lake Road north to Burkey Road and from South Raccoon Road east to South Meridian Road. Dave "Red" Miles, who managed the farm for the Moggs, lived in this house facing South Raccoon Road, the current location of the bank in the Wedgewood Plaza. To the right of the house, facing south, was the three-story 500-by-100-foot barn and three silos. The barn is the current location of the Wedgewood Lanes. The property also contained a smaller barn. In 1950, the Moggs sold the farm to the United Construction Company (Fred, Charles, George, Tom, and John Paul Shutrump), which developed the Wedgewood area. (Courtesy Jim Bartell.)

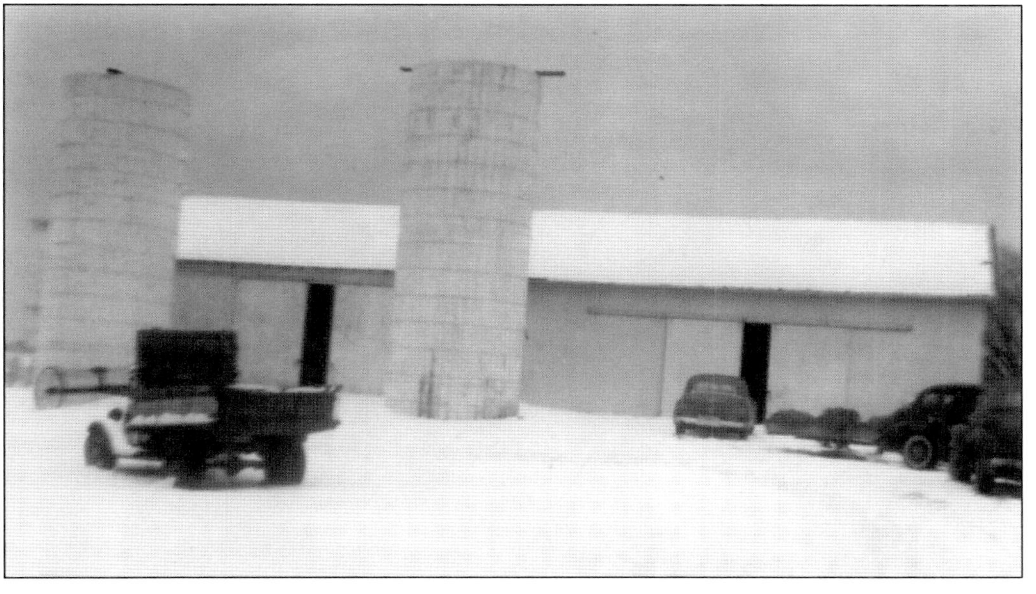

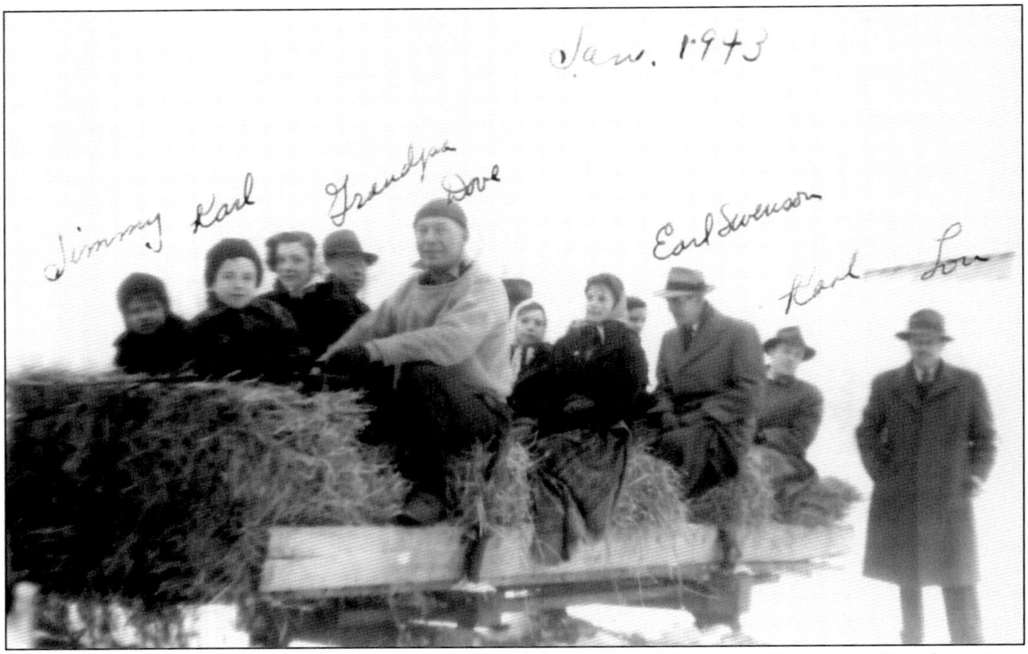

HORSE-DRAWN HAYRIDE, JANUARY 1943, FOR MOGG AND BARTELL FAMILIES. On the Mogg farm from left to right are Jim Bartell, Karl Mogg III, unidentified, Karl Mogg I, Dave "Red" Mills (driving), Delores Bartell, unidentified, Earl Swanson (family friend), Karl Mogg II, and Louis Bartell (standing). (Courtesy Jim Bartell.)

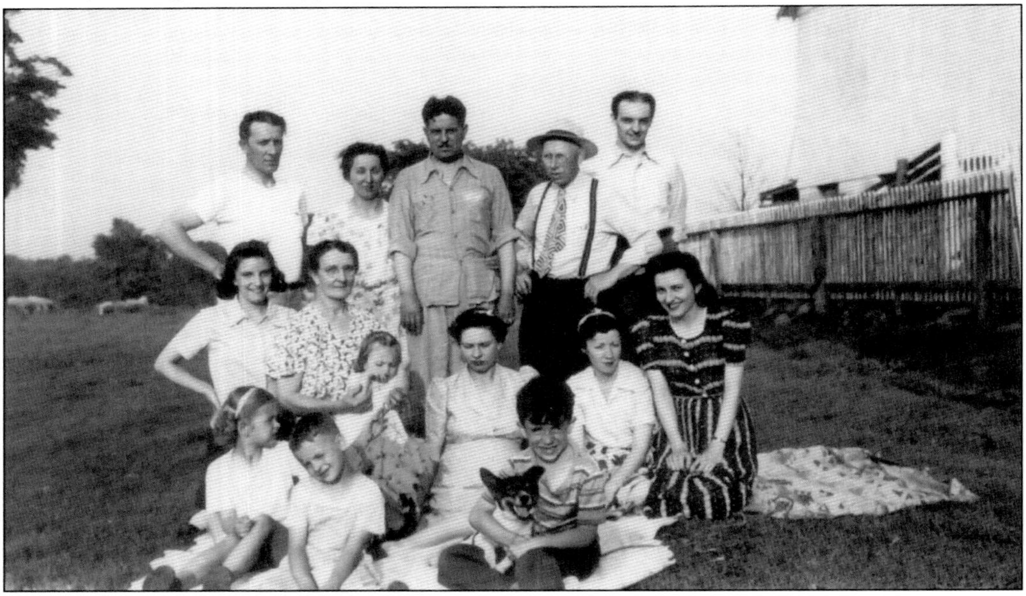

MOGG FAMILY ON THEIR FARM. Members of the Mogg family, seen here from left to right, are (first row) Mary Bees, Jim Bartell, and Karl Mogg III; (second row) Delores Bartell, Mary Spener Mogg holding Barbara Bees, Isabell Mogg Bees, Julia Mogg, and Delores Mogg Alexander; (third row) Karl Mogg II, Theresa Mogg Bartell, Louis Bartell, Karl Mogg I, and Roy Alexander. The barn is to the right of the family. (Courtesy Jim Bartell.)

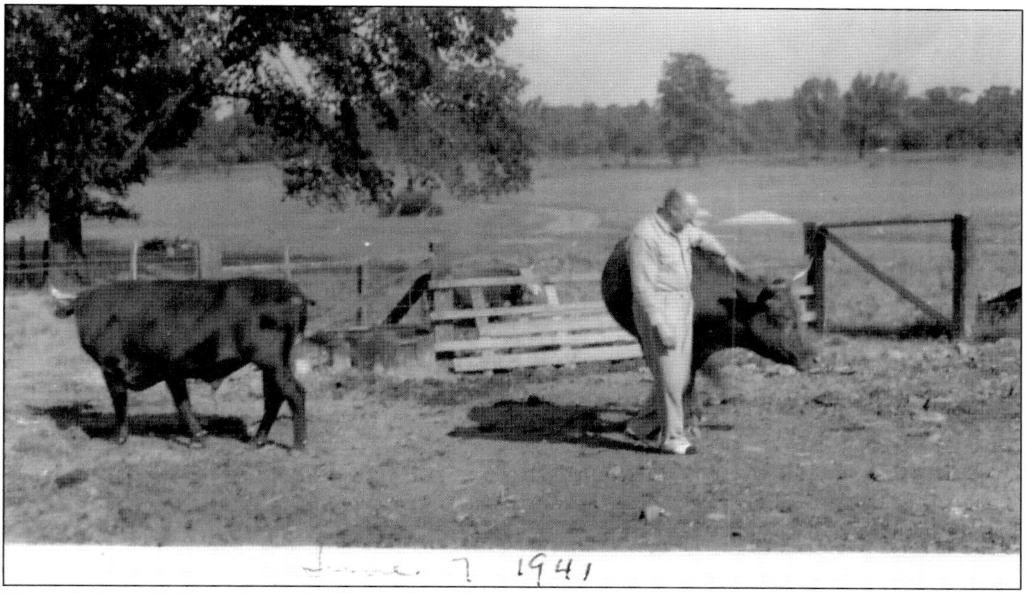

KARL MOGG I, JUNE 7, 1941. Karl Mogg I, with his prize-winning Black Angus bull, owned a meatpacking plant on South Avenue and the Ohio Leatherworks in Girard. Cattle, horses, pigs, and grain were raised on Mogg's farm. In the background, beyond the fence, is the land that will become the Wedgewood Plaza and housing development. (Courtesy Jim Bartell.)

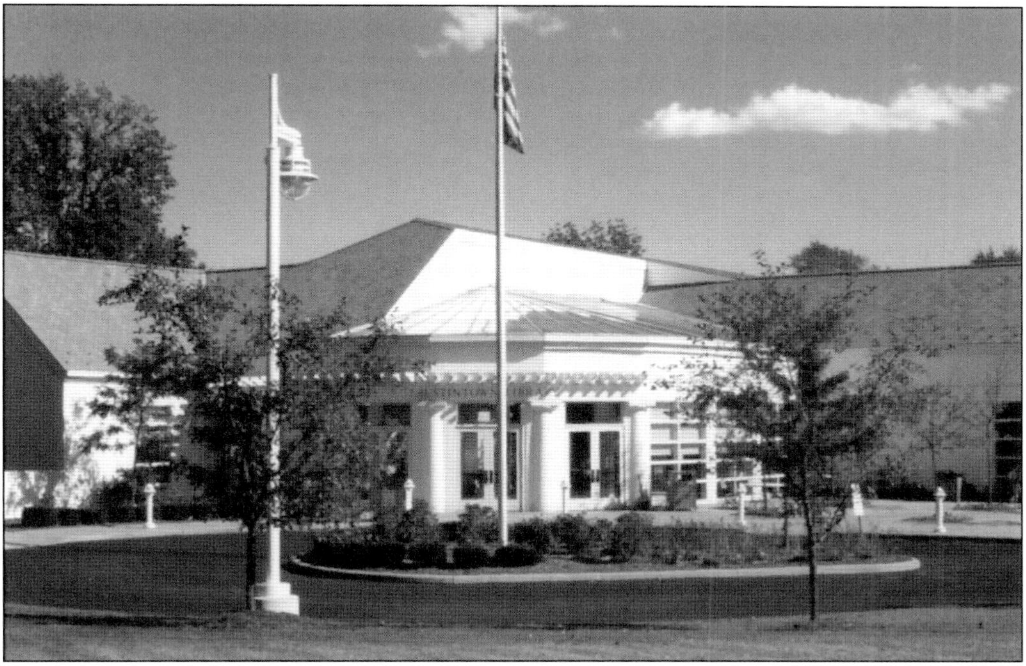

AUSTINTOWN PUBLIC LIBRARY. The 19,940-square-foot library, holding 54,000 volumes, was opened in October 2002 on the corner of South Raccoon Road and Falcon Drive. It replaced the split-level library, holding 12,000 volumes, on Mahoning Avenue, opened in 1965. Prior to 1965, Austintown was served by the bookmobile. (Courtesy Joyce Pogany.)

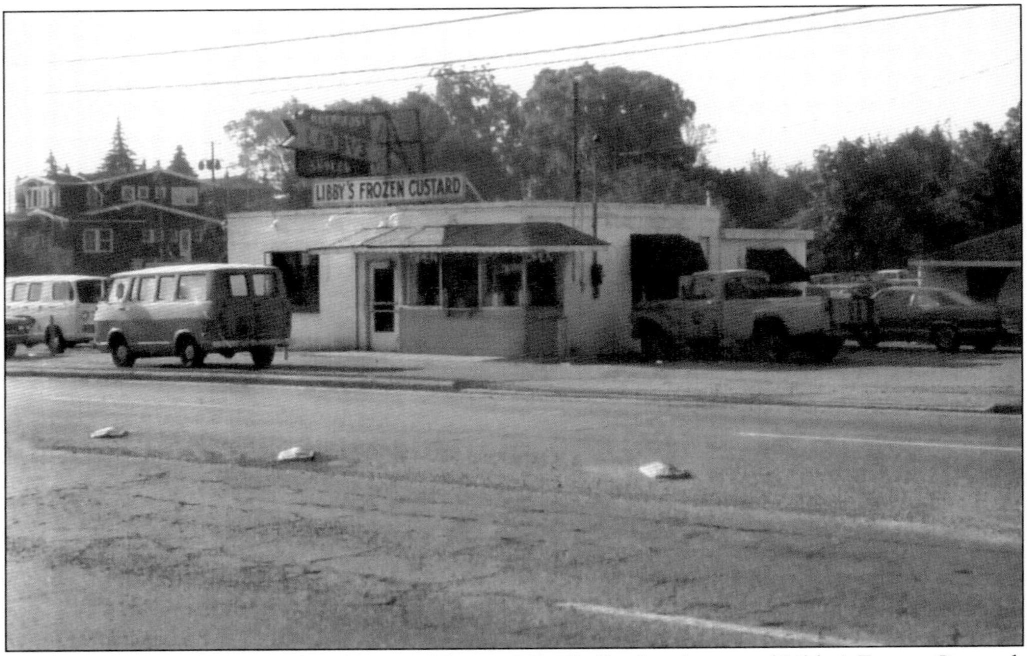

LIBBY'S FROZEN CUSTARD AND RULLIE HOUSE. The Rullie family owned Libby's Frozen Custard, at 4441 Mahoning Avenue, and their home next door. Both were razed during the construction of K-Mart, on Mahoning Avenue near Raccoon Road, which opened in 1962. Mahoning Avenue, in the foreground, was divided by concrete "turtles." The house in the background in the Libby's Frozen Custard photograph is a part of Art's Westgate Plaza. (Courtesy Advanced Marking.)

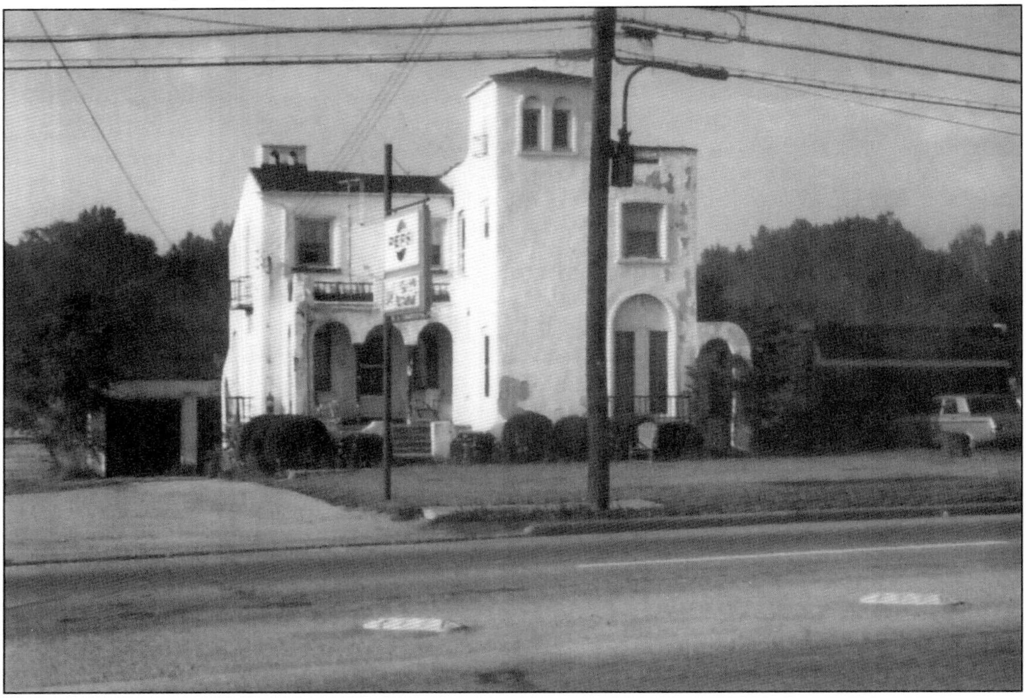

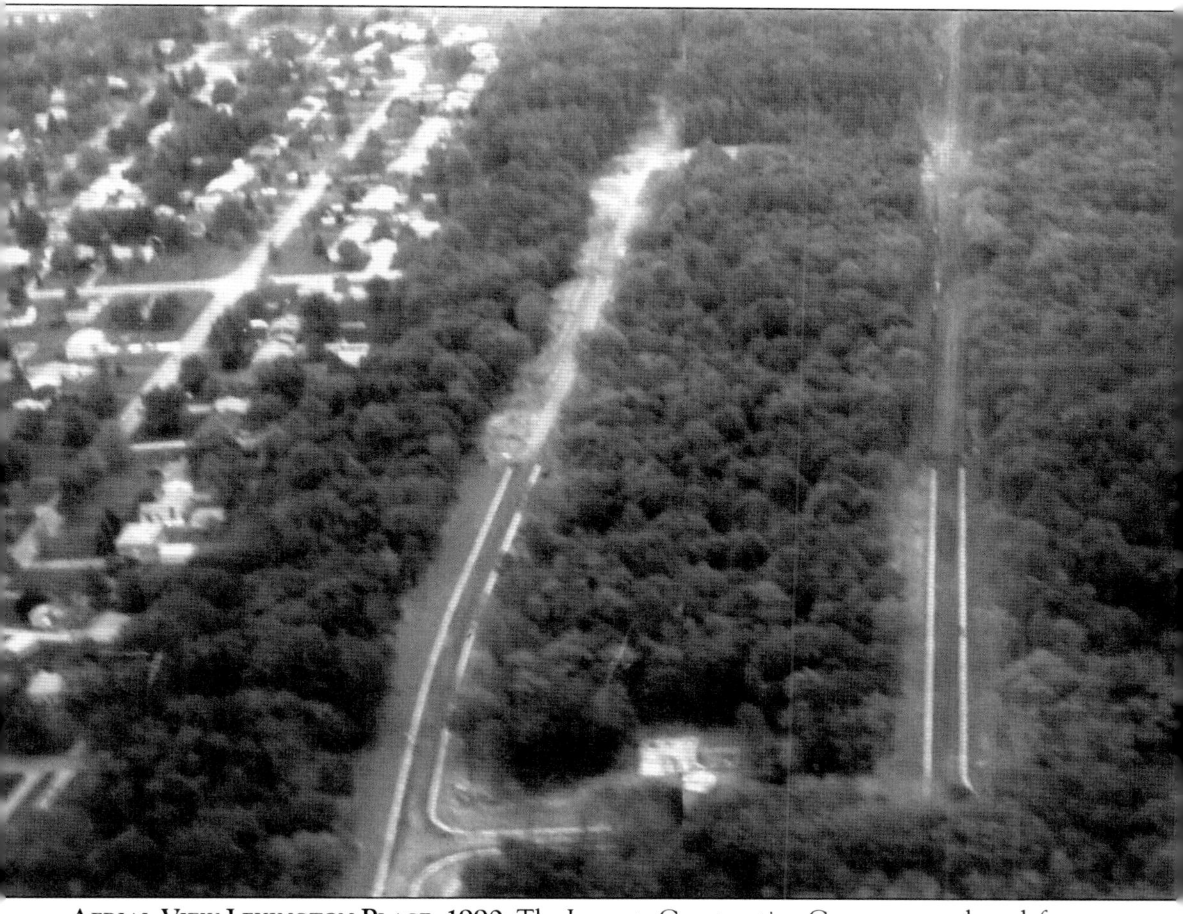

AERIAL VIEW LEXINGTON PLACE, 1990. The Lucente Construction Company purchased, from the Johnson family, 96 acres on the east side of South Canfield-Niles Road north of New Road. Shown is the first house on West Saratoga Avenue in Lexington Place. Undeveloped streets include North Beacon Drive on the left and South Saratoga Avenue on the right. Kimberly Acres is in the upper left. Lexington Place, the first upscale development in Austintown, opened in 1991. The development now includes 98 homes worth a total of $20 million. Lucente also developed Preakness, Villas of Bella Terra, and Pimlico on 92 acres on the north side of New Road in 1996. The Lucente Construction Company employs 75 local residents and purchases materials from local businesses. (Courtesy Bob Lucente.)

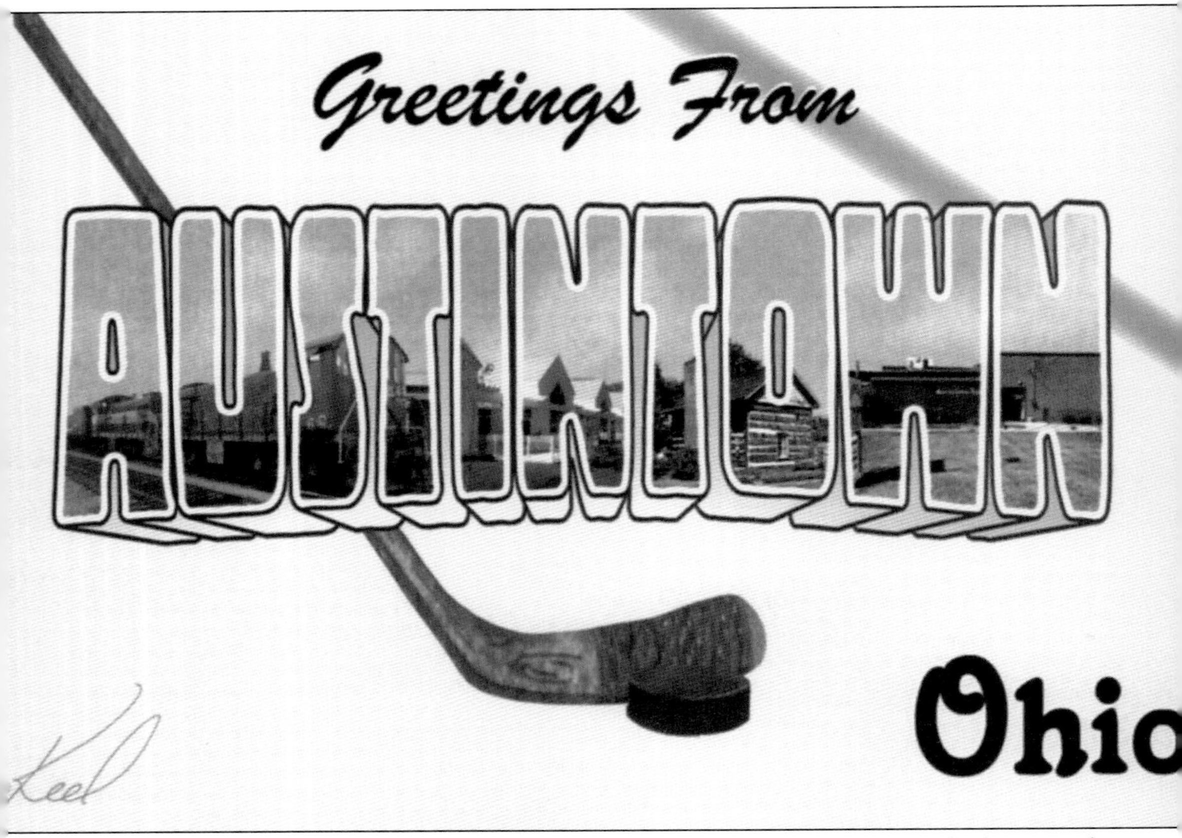

AUSTINTOWN POSTCARD, C. 2005. This postcard shows the old mixing with the new: the train that ran through Austintown on one of the two railroads when coal was king, a tribute to the many Welsh immigrants who mined the coal; the new library; the Austin Log Cabin; Austintown Township Hall; and Austintown Police Department. Although the postcard says "Greetings from Austintown," it summarizes this book. The train steams ahead to Austintown's future. What will a postcard 100 years from now look like? (Courtesy Seek Publishing.)

BIBLIOGRAPHY

Cotton, Aylett R. *Across the Plains to California in 1849: An Autobiography*. University of California Berkeley, 1906.

Everts, L. H. *Atlas of Mahoning County Compiled, Drawn and Published from Personal Examinations and Surveys*. Chicago: 1874.

Erwin, J. J. *The Osborn Family*. Canfield, OH: Mahoning Dispatch Printing, 1923.

Ewing, John Calvin. *History of the Alexander Ewing Branch, Ewing Family: A Survey of the Descendants of Alexander and Ann Woods Ewing in America*. Canfield, OH: Mahoning Dispatch Press, 1931.

Genealogical and Family History of Eastern Ohio. New York: Lewis, 1903.

History of Trumbull and Mahoning Counties: With illustrations and Biographical Sketches. Volumes I and II. Cleveland: H. C. Williams and Brother, 1882.

Howe, Henry. *Historical Collection of Ohio in Two Volumes*. Cincinnati: C. J. Hrehbiehl and Company, 1907.

Holloway, Bert. *The Development of the Niles, Ohio Domestic Water Supply*. Austintown, OH: Mahoning Valley Sanitary District, 1955.

Mahoning Valley Historical Society. *Historical Collections of the Mahoning Valley*. Volumes I and II. Youngstown, OH: Mahoning Valley Historical Society, 1876.

Parkhurst, Jacob. *Sketches of Jacob Parkhurst by Himself*. Unpublished, no date.

Russell family. *History Robert Russell Branch, Russell Family*. Canfield, OH: Mahoning Dispatch Press, 1936.

Sanderson, T. W. *Twentieth Century History of Youngstown and Mahoning County, Ohio and Representative Citizens*. Chicago: Biographical Publishing Company, 1907.

Stewart, J. S. *History of Northeastern Ohio*. Volumes I and II. Indianapolis, IN: Historical Publishing, 1935.

Upton, Harriet Taylor. A *Twentieth Century History of Trumbull County, Ohio: A Narrative Account of its Historical Progress, its People and its Principal Interests.*

White, J. R. *The Archaeology of the Austin Log House Site*. Austintown, OH: Austintown Historical Society, 1976.

Zinz, K. R. *Focus on Austintown: In the Spirit of Our '76 Heritage.*